Yoga inVision 14

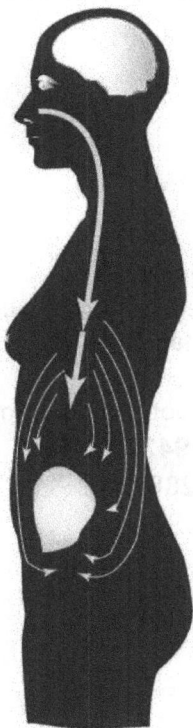

Michael Beloved

Illustrations: Author
Correspondence:
Michael Beloved
19311 SW 30th Street
Miramar FL 33029
USA
Email: axisnexus@gmail.com
                 michaelbelovedbooks@gmail.com

Paperback ISBN: 9781942887348
eBook ISBN: 99781942887355
LCCN: 2020923026

Table of Contents

INTRODUCTION

This is the fourtheenth of the Yoga inVision series. It relates experiences and practices done in 2013. These give beginners ideas of the physical, psychological and spiritual experiences one may have when doing asana postures, pranayama breath-infusion and *pratyahar* sensual energy withdrawal. Beyond that is higher yoga, which Patañjali named the *samyama* procedures. He defined *samyama* as a combination of *dharana* deliberate focus, *dhyana* spontaneous focus and *samadhi* continuous spontaneous focus. During practice, these progress one into the other. If one is expert at *pratyahar* sensual energy withdrawal, one may graduate to *dharana* which is deliberate focus of the attention to a higher concentration force or person. As soon as one masters *dharana* one may slip into *dhyana* which is an effortless focus on a higher concentration force or person. Once you practice *dhyana*, *samadhi* happens as the continuous effortless focus on a higher concentration force or person.

Many persons on a spiritual path feel that they can construct a process as they advance. This idea denotes failure. After all, if the supernatural and spiritual environment, is not already there, no one can create it now. It is either there or it is not. For instance, if one intends to moves to a different country, then of course one will fail if the country intended does not exist. It has to be there prior. Similarly, what you aim for as spiritual life, must be there already, or one will find that the aspiration is incorrect. This is why I speak of a concentration force or person. I could have said concentration person or divine person, or God. I did not because I do not know how anyone's spiritual path will develop.

One may leave an island in the safest boat and still the vessel may sink. One should keep one's mind open and be willing to work with fate. In spiritual development, there is providence too. What one desires to have one may not achieve. What one wishes to see may never appear.

These Yoga inVision journals show how sporadic my course of yoga was. This is after years of practice. It gives some idea of what to expect. Once you get through the lower yoga practice, you will see advancement in a more stable way but it may be incremental, accruing little by little, with bright flashes here and there.

Part 1

Arrogance of Youth

This morning I had the occasion to observe a certain arrogance which is an integral part of a youthful body and which is placed in such a body by nature, irrespective of the intentions of the transcendent self using that form. This arrogance is an ancestral empowerment. It is the possession by the ancestors of the body of a youthful descendant.

The secret of this is that when the ancestor takes possession of a youth or young adult, the possessed individual has no idea of the being controlled. In some primitive societies, these possessions were officially recognized in rituals of passage through ceremonial procedures to acknowledge the advent of adult status and the need for a fulfillment of sexual intercourse. The modern situation discourages such rites of passage. Most youths feel that the increase of sexual interest and lust is theirs only. There is no idea about ancestors using their bodies, influencing their moods and saturating their emotions.

The body may become happy when the ancestors saturate their power in it. The body becomes sexually attractive through its exhibition of sex appeal. The self in the body, as ignorant as it is, assumes that it is the cause of the attractiveness. It cannot sort itself from the imposed ancestral influence.

Worse still is the infatuation with ancestral power which comes with sexual pleasure, where the parties involved cannot in any way know that the energy is the contribution of ancestors.

Subtle Body Importance

Over time there is mastery over the rise of kundalini into the head of the subtle body. It takes time. Some students master it within a few months. Others take a few years or more.

The rise of kundalini through the spine is the beginning of the process of creating a *yogaSiddha* form. There is much more to be done to complete this accomplishment. The best approach is to practice steadily so that there can be a cumulative cleansing action of breath infusion and kundalini's positive response.

Initially the mind will try its best to protect the physical body. This is a good attribute of the mind. What would it be if we did not have such a mind which protected the physical body from harm? Despite this appreciation the yogi must eventually junk this and push the mind into a new version of security which protects 99% to the subtle body and just a tat of the physical system.

Each yogi/yogini must start where he/she is. Step by step in months, years or lives, one should cause the mind to abandon its anxiety about physical world and transfer the interest into the subtle body.

Recently someone got information to me that one of my girlfriends said that I should get my teeth fixed and should dye my hair. I have two missing front teeth, a terrible thing. I have some slanted teeth, an awful thing to see. Most of this occurred in childhood due to family mishaps.

What should be done?

I am not responsible for these uglies but should I take responsibility for this and get dental surgery? As for the grey hairs, that is based on the genetic attitude of the body I got in the family. Should I take steps to disguise those biological defects?

Once I was to go somewhere with a friend. This was some years ago. This person is involved in spiritual groups. He said to me, "I cannot dress like you. What do you think? I have to look presentable." Even though he was a friend, he insulted me. He felt that I was not properly attired.

Perhaps, you read of the story of the five wise and five foolish virgins. It is a tale attributed to Jesus Christ, the very special son of God. In that story there were five wise and five foolish virgins who were hopeful to get married to an aristocrat. The five foolish ones expended their value before the man arrived. Subsequently they were rejected.

Should I invest energy to pretty up this body so that it is appreciated for physical beauty? Or should I neglect it and disappoint somebody?

Should I invest energy in the subtle body, to improve it, so that people who have subtle perception can regard me as appealling?

The truth is that if kundalini is attended in the subtle body, the physical system will be controlled automatically but this is true only for students who are advanced and who developed psychic perception to tag the twitches and twirls of kundalini.

Relationship with the Teacher

For this meditation practice, one should not be an atheist or a person who feels that everyone is equal and that there are no perpetually superior persons and deities. But all the same one should not be a fanatical theist. Both the fanatical theist and the atheist will make little progress in this practice.

Since we learn this practice from others, it goes without saying that our relationship with the masters of this procedure should be one of student to teacher, where the teacher will advance exponentially in reference to the student. The idea that the state of enlightenment is terminal, that the student will be on par with the teacher and will be his equal sometime in the future, is only applicable to a static enlightenment process.

This system is not a dead-end progression. It continues endlessly. There is no question of jostling, confining or coming abreast with the teacher. Such ideas should be discarded.

Wet Dreams

Wet dreams were and continue to be of great interest in the psychological study of human nature, as to its cause, as to its impact on reality. The most disgusting and most frustrating part of wet dreams is the lack of recall. Without the recall one cannot enjoy it, at least not while situated in the physical body with the idea-memory which that body affords.

There is nothing more frustrating than a wet dream without a sharp memory of the event. Perhaps, there is nothing more pleasing than the same with full memory of the incidence.

Having a wet dream and not remembering it, is unsatisfactory. This reminds me of when I first saw a soft porn movie. I was Trinidad as a teenager. There was a movie with Bridget Bardot.

The main scene of the movie which was a sexual act was cut by the government censors but one did not know that until one paid to view the film. There were mostly men in the theatre. When the most revealing scene happened, there was a cut off and a jump of the film to some other scene which had nothing to do with sex. A great uproar was heard in the theater with cries and moans from the men. Then there were obscenities:

Fuck you!
They fucking cut it.
The assholes!
Fuck this!
Burn this place!
Play that again with the full scene!
I want to see that!
O that would be lovely!

It was a scene with Bridget making love in a very uninhibited way. She removed her clothes. Her partner fondled her. They were inflamed with sexual interplay. She removed her bra. Her breasts popped out like two mad bulls at a Spanish arena. The man removed her undies. Then the scenes were cut. The men in the theater went crazy because the camera was focused on her sexual access but the film was edited to deprive the full nudity. At the time one group of viewers went into absolute silence. Some who ate popcorn, stopped moving their mouths. Those who drank beverages froze with the bottles in their hands. Those who came in the doors, stood still like trees.

Nowadays such scenes are common in movies. One can see such displays on the internet but at the time, there was hardly a mini-skirt. Women did not wear sexually revealing clothing in public. That movie was a sensation with a disappointment. That may be compared to how a person feels if he/she does not recall a wet dream.

It brings up an important issue for student yogis which is why the coreSelf requires to have physical sexual experience, or at least physical memory of even subtle sexual experience. If I am essentially a psychic being, why do I have to consummate sexual acts on the physical side?

There is the downgrade to the subtle body. There is the second downgrade to the physical level. Why is that second descent necessary? I have so many girlfriends. Will I have to take separate sequential births in physical bodies to be with these women for physical sexual activity? When will that stop? Why can the satisfaction not be complete at least on the psychic plane?

Why is the wet dream not completed on the subtle side?

Why does it have to be remembered and relished on the physical plane even?

What is a wet dream?

Basically, it is the physical body mimicking the sexual expression of the subtle form, and doing so while the subtle body is displaced from within the physical one. In addition, it is possible to have a wet dream while the subtle body is consciously interspaced in the physical one.

Why does it happen?

Because the subtle body is sometimes segregated from the physical one while that subtle one still has a transmission link to the physical side. If the subtle body has a sexual activity and there is no transmission link, there will be sexual activity on the subtle side but no indication of it in the physical body. A friend of mine once slept with his wife in a bed. There was another woman whom he was crazy about. One night in the astral world he began to make love to that other woman. There was a transmission of information into his physical body, so that his physical limbs began imitating what the subtle body did, except that it began to embrace his wife and wanted to indulge her. He even began calling the name of the other woman whom his wife knew. She became awake, was appalled. The next morning when he woke up she was gone with her belongings. Later that week he got a notice for a divorce.

It happens regularly that the subtle body does not remain segregated sufficiently from the physical one during sexual acts. Hence, there is the likelihood of wet dreams.

Memory of these events is an entirely different issue. To have the memory of the sexual encounters you must have a memory capacity in the subtle body at the time of the event, and there must be a transfer of the information into the physical brain.

Even if there is astral memory, transferring it over into the physical memory system is a special process.

Whenever this happens where you become aware of a wet dream and then you suspect that you have no memory of the details, you should keep the mind very quiet. If you do this it is likely that you will get glimpses of what happened but the memories may be abstract. You must have psychic sensitivity to successfully do this.

This applies to any dream. The lack of recall really means that one is materialistic at heart even though one does have psychic interest. One must endeavor to make subtle perception the priority.

Vision of Reclined Buddha

Meditation this morning was at the Zen Hostel, a place established by Tobe Terrell. He designed a meditation room recently. We made an effort to sanctify the place by doing meditation very respectfully to Buddha.

At the Zen Hostel, usually I sit near a cabinet which has a gong within it. Across from this cabinet is a twin cabinet which houses a damaged Buddha sculpture which is to be replaced when one is constructed by the resident artist, who at the time was Oliver Norden.

Usually after breath infusion, we enter this room for meditation. I ring a chime to get the students to focus internally and to settle their minds into observing the benefits of the breath infusion practice in terms of elevating the level of awareness and having perception of subtle realities within the psyche.

When I ring the chime, I usually see Buddha with disciples in a special astral dimension. They usually move silently and quietly. I ring the chime so as not to disturbed them, with a tone and frequency which compliments their movements.

Buddha for his part usually looks and gives a message through his glance only. This morning he did not sit or stand as usually. He was reclined. There were three disciples near to him. Some others were distant. I rang a special sequence of chime notes that suited the occasion.

During the meditation, there was a flash perception of a Buddha deity in South Korea. The vision of him reclined at that place was such that it was semi-dark like at twilight.

Naad Meditation with Endearing Relationship

Today, I resumed the instruction from Lahiri. That may be neglected again. One must take help from providence except that sometimes providence gives no help or bars one from spiritual practice. Providence is supreme even when it facilitates.

When I resumed the practice, the first thing was a full breath infusion session with no gaps in the sequence of postures combined with breathing and in full attention within the psyche and full application of locks and corresponding gestures, even spontaneous inner and outer actions on the physical and subtle levels.

Then I sat to meditate.

Immediately I was with naad. Follow the instruction from Lahiri, I immediately rolled back the tongue and pushed it into the soft palate which it reaches at the back of the mouth. Then I sensed naad again. It was present all along but this was an emphatic observation of it at the back of the head, about two inches up and to the back of the head. I remained there with the feel of the tongue against the soft palate and the naad sound in the back. There was a flash transit where I was shifted to the center of the head. I was aware of naad light which was like a glow of dimly-lit golden nuggets. This light was all-around but only in a chamber which I was in, in the center of the subtle head. I remained with this naad light but heard naad sound as well. To my right there was naad sound meeting naad light at an edge, where they did not mix and did not clash. They were two distinct transcendental phenomena.

Then there was another transit where I shifted to where the right edge of the right eyebrow is but about one inch back in the head. There was naad light to the left and naad sound to the right curving around to the back.

Both were in a relationship with me but I could not define the relation with naad light. The one with naad sound was like when I have a woman friend where there is no sexual attraction but there is endearing friendship.

What is that like?

When there is a sexual attraction there will be demands while with just the endearing friendship there are no stipulations. One is free to do as one pleases with a little jovial objection periodically and with approval now and again.

Sexual attraction is demanding with dos and do nots, upsets and emotional flare-ups, crying and screaming if anything goes amiss, manifestations of irritation if I become involved with another woman. There will be statements like:

Who is she?

Why were you speaking to her?

Are you leaving me to be with her?

She is a witch?

Watch out?

Are you going to have sex with her?

What a cruel person you are?

The relationship with naad was like the endearing relationship a man has with a woman whom he feels no sexual attraction to. It is free of demands and still it is accomodating.

Lucky Yogi with Two Girlfriends

This morning meditation practice had a new feature, one of having two instead of one girlfriend in naad. There was naad light in the frontal part of the head, the area where usually there are the unwanted thoughts and images occurring. At this place the thoughts and images were conspicuous by their absence.

There was no more tracking of thoughts, not even the need to hunt for methods like breath tracking, mantra saying or anything like that. When thoughts are absent one does not have to prevent them or deal with them in some way. Of course, to achieve this I first did a thorough breath infusion session.

At first when I sat to meditate, it was me and naad sound at the back of the head. Within two minutes I was shifted by a force and was located in the default position of the coreSelf in the middle of the consciousness energies, but with naad sound at the back, very near, and with naad light in the front very near as well. It was like two girlfriends who did not contest, disagree, compete and being nasty about each other's presence. Feeling lucky, I enjoyed that.

Having one girl friend is great but getting another who is agreeable and cooperative as the first one, is even better. Which man would not consider himself as blessed in such dual relationships which were spontaneous?

There were supernatural perceptions in the naad light. I invested the interest energy towards the frontal part of the head, towards the brow chakra. I did not apply the vision energy. The interest energy is a pure ray of interest which comes out of the coreSelf. This is usually sheathed by the vision energy or by some other sensual quest. In this case, it was by itself without sheathing. This is the energy which will, in time, cause visual connection into the *chit akash* sky of consciousness.

Kundalini and Sex Organ Chakra

When the kundalini rises into the head, it heads for the intellect orb. If the kundalini has a high charge of energy, it will put the intellect out of commission when it strikes. This will cause the observing self to lose control of the physical body because its control of that is based its relationship with the intellect which is itself the controller or switchboard from which willful actions are controlled.

Advanced yogis, protect the intellect from being hit by the kundalini. This is done primarily by the locks which include a mind lock and an observational peek into the psyche to see what kundalini does and to pilot its expansion and journey.

The kundalini lifeForce is meant to supply sensual power energy to the entire psyche. However, when it comes into the head with more power than should be distributed in the head or when it comes into the head which has a downgraded weakened intellect, it disables the intellect.

Nature set the stage for that by training us to crave sex expression which is highlighted in our experience by sexual climax. Due to that we are disinclined to restrict kundalini. It is always difficult to curb something which gives pleasure.

In sex experience kundalini loops to the sex organ chakra (not sex chakra on the spine).

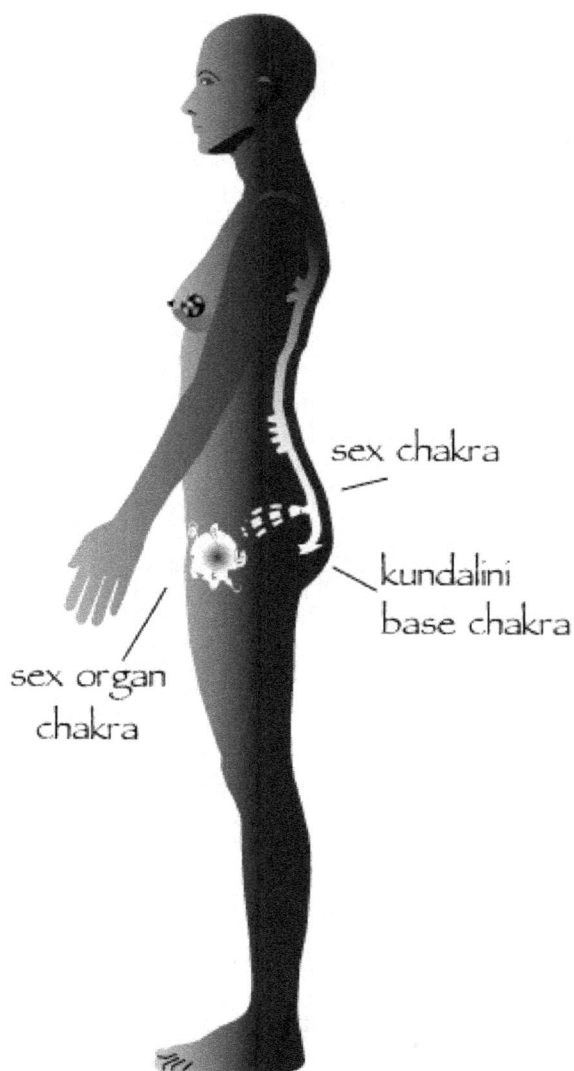

sex chakra

kundalini
base chakra

sex organ
chakra

While this occurs, the intellect is forced by a powerful hypnotically attraction energy to descend to the sex organ chakra to participate willingly or unwillingly in the burst of overpowering energy.

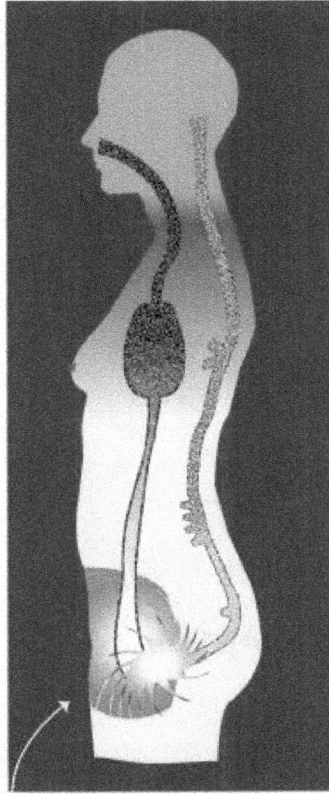

kundalini lifeForce explosion
at sex organ chakra

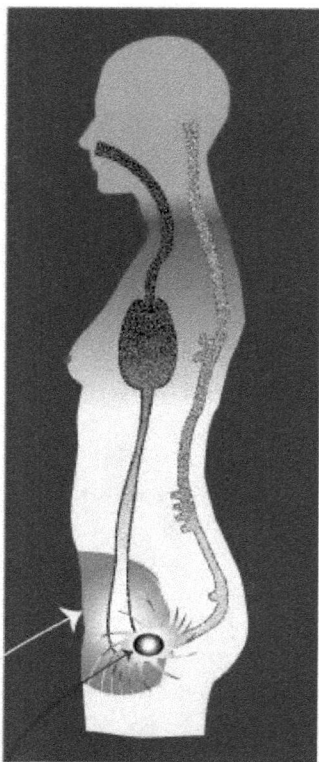

intellect orb relocated to sex energy
and kundalini lifeForce explosion at sex organ chakra

In the case of kundalini rising into the head, it meets the intellect in the head. If it has a sufficiently powerful charge it may put the intellect out of commission.

kundalini lifeforce explosion in subtle head
buddhi intellect orb is affected

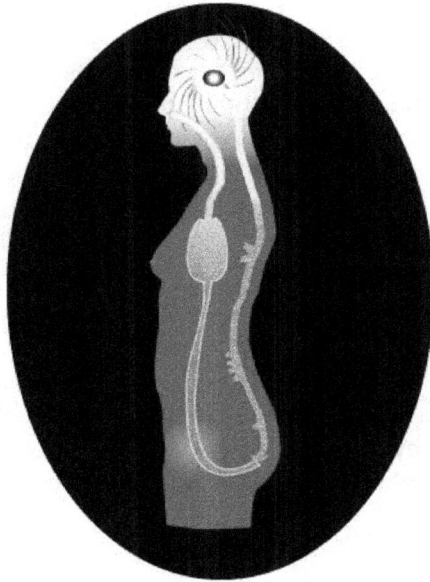

breath-hormone energy arches over
to kundalini lifeforce power central
causing kundalini energy to ascend into the brain
where it explodes into bliss awareness

Khecari Mudra

My opinion on whether one should do *khecari mudra*, is that one should not do it if it means cutting under the tongue (frenum). Before one cuts, one should get an assurance of certainty from the person who advised that.

There are three achievements which relate to this action of cutting the tongue so that it may stretch into the throat. These are:

- Blocking the passage where air is inhaled into or exhaled from the lungs
- Identifying and manipulating the tasting orb in the subtle body
- Identifying and eliminating the nutrition-need orb

Blocking the passage of air by inserting the tongue into the throat is for maintaining longer *samadhis*. This method works only if there is beforehand, a long history of *pranayama* practice by the yogi. Traditionally the *anuloma viloma* alternate breathing was the most popular method to use before entering a prolonged *samadhi*. Ancient yogis used this method but did the *pranayama* for hours before entering the trance state.

Identifying and manipulating the taste orb in the subtle body happens in the mind of the yogi, if the tongue is pushed back to the soft palate. It does not need to be cut. It can be realized without cutting, because the soft palate can be reached even with the natural design under the tongue. The purpose for identifying the taste orb is to locate that sensual apparatus and to investigate its power and functions.

Identifying and eliminating the nutrition-need orb is essential for those yogis who intent to go to *siddhaloka* where they cannot eat in the way that we do in the physical world. The nutrition orb we currently have, is designed for creature existence in the physical world, for the development of physical bodies which survive by parasitic attacks on other species, even vegetation. In higher yoga, the nutrition orb is identified. Steps are taken to eliminate it.

Self in Dimension

During meditation this afternoon, I continued the observation and investigation of the relationships which are possible with naad. The relationship with other persons while in naad would mean that those other persons were in naad or that one reached out of naad either to a lower or higher vibration, to reach other persons.

To be realistic one should give up on trying to reach beyond the *chit akash*, because that is like saying that one will transit to another galaxy even though one cannot reach even the sun which, if one were to travel at the speed of light, could be reached in less than ten minutes.

Looking back into the physical world from the naad sound, one may be happy if one reaches the causal plane or if one reaches the higher astral places which are locations worthy of a yogi who is done with the riff raff existence in the ghettos of these environments, places like the earth, the lower astral regions and the subterranean astral locales.

One can always think about what will happen when one is deprived of the body and one can no longer use its authority on this earth.

What will happen then?

Who can one contact?

Featureless Self

In naad sound, the self is featureless, bare, raw spiritual energy without affiliation, like a new born infant whose parents are unknown to anyone. The infant has no name, number, nor point of reference. It cries when it sees every woman because it cannot recognize anyone as its mother.

The poor thing!

What hope has it got?

But being in the naad is exactly like that, except for the relationship with naad itself, which initially is like the relationship between an abandoned infant and the doctor. The doctor is concerned. That will keep the kid from starving to death. Still, the doctor is not a mother. He cannot absorb the affection for a mother. He cannot cause the attachment that spontaneously occurs for a mother. He has no nourishment from a breast to offer to the child, only a rubber nipple that is an insult to the infant.

This actually happened to me once when I was about seven years of age. I was with an Aunt of mine who was like a mother to me. This person was the sister of my father. We went to a sports event. While we sat in bleachers, my aunt sent me to get shave ice. This is a fruity ice product.

I got to where the vendor was located but when I tried to find my way back, I could not identify where my aunt sat. At that point everyone around me in the field seemed like aliens from Mars. I was scared. I cried thinking that I was lost forever. This lasted for about fifteen minutes with me going here and there and becoming more and more disoriented.

Suddenly I found the way to my aunt. It was miraculous because I felt that some supernatural being lifted and placed me where I could see my aunt directly. I was so happy to get back that I quietly went and sat beside her. I leaned on her arm. She had an arm which was plump. It was the source of the greatest comfort. When I got back to her, she said nothing but her eyes did it all with motherly concern and a sense of "You belong to me. You are my son."

Actually, for all that is declared about God not being a person, one cannot shed the need to belong to somebody. It is integral to personality.

And yet in naad the self is bare, nude, totally devoid of a sense of culture and identity, a something in resonance.

So far, I discovered two senses which operate in naad. These are the hearing sense which is the primary reference and the visual sense which arises only after one becomes attuned to naad with a relationship where naad is like the mother's breast and one is the infant who hungrily sucks it.

Naad Lights

There was a new development this morning during meditation with naad assuming a musical attitude, over the two former developments which were naad as sound and naad as glow light.

When naad has the sound feature at the back of the subtle head, and then has the glow light of itself at the front, the coreSelf gets into a position of taking advantage of each of these evenly, so that there is cognizance of each without contradiction or competition.

Two women with one man is a problem because of the competitive nature of the women and the contradictory nature of having to instruct one in one way and the other in an entirely different manner. However, with naad this does not occur. The coreSelf is not caught in the puzzle of one feature of naad trying to supersede the other. The coreSelf is similar to someone with agreeable wives.

When the student yogi notices this about naad, it is like listening to melodious music which was created by a maestro who could take antagonistic chords and cause them to blend harmoniously.

After a time, suddenly to the left, up ahead about five feet, there were three circular lights which were focused into my left subtle eye directly. I lost contact with these lights within moments. They were definite however. I had other supernatural occurrences, but I was not objective enough to perceive any of them with distinction.

The three circular lights were emanating from a circular configuration which were like tiny one-inch-diameter halogen lights, but these were supernatural objects, not physical stuff.

A Dead Friend Returns

If you ever wondered if you could verify if dead relatives and friends live elsewhere, observe your dreams. Of course, one must first develop the skill of remembering dreams. If one does not recall dreams, one has the assignment to develop recall because it means that one is naturally focused into the physical world in such a hard and fast way, that the mind has little or no attraction to what is subtle, except perhaps when it determines that it is expedient to observe the subtle so as to bring it in line with physical reality.

Verifying that dead people are alive and well on the other side is done through dream encounters. It is that simple. Take dreams about departed relatives and friends seriously. Those experiences are one's entry into their life through entry into a *dream already in progress*.

I had a dream today in which I was with a deceased friend who passed away some time ago after his body acquired the Human Immune Virus. After his demise, he suffered seven long years in an astral place lying side by side with many other victims. He is freed from the condition. His subtle body looks as if it was about 23 years of age. He is sprite and hearty.

He lives in an apartment somewhere on the astral side of Northern Minnesota, just as he did physically when I first met him. His sense of humor and interest has not changed.

He felt that somehow, we should reside together. In the astral place, he has that feeling. He was in an apartment which had two bedrooms, one of which was rented to an old fellow. He thought that somehow, I should reside with them. In the last life, he was a homosexual who did not think that women were suitable for sexual companionship. He is the same person astrally. Nothing changed in his character or methods.

During the dream his idea was that I was to be with a woman. She was to be introduced to the old man who rented the room. He felt that the old man would care for the woman.

He wanted to get rid of the woman so that he would be with me. This was his silent attitude when he was on the physical side. I ignored that because my interest in him was to introduce him to meditation and related spiritual practice.

Some years ago, I convinced him to come to a spiritual community in West Virginia. He stayed long enough to get the first initiation they offered which one got after six months of consistent approved services. Soon after that he came to say that he was to leave the place because the leader of the community pursued him for a love affair. He said he was not comfortable having that relationship in a religious place.

When he said this, I looked at him with interest because in any case I knew that there was something pulling him away from the place. This was a good excuse for him to respond to that pull. He returned to Minneapolis where he had homosexual lovers.

However, I can report that he is alive and well on the astral side which is adjacent to this physical existence. He made no spiritual progress. His attraction to me is the same. His spiritual realization has not advanced. He is the same. It was good to see him.

He is *dead and gone* but *alive and well* on the otherside. He must take rebirth as soon as the mission energy from his immediate past earthly life becomes exhausted.

Kundalini Burst

It is due to sex experience, particularly sexual climax experience, that we focus on raising kundalini for pleasure purposes. The main interest due to the training we were given by physical nature is to produce pleasure from this body. When one is introduced to kundalini yoga the reference to sexual pleasure does not go away. It remains and governs the way one approaches the practice.

The student wants a higher experience, but in reference to what?

What other experience did he have which was more intensely satisfying than sexual climax experience?

There is no quickie method for getting a higher experience when the mind enters the supernatural, seemingly dream state. Over time as one advances, one develops the capacity for a higher experience, for more objective perception. One understands the parameters involved in the rise of kundalini.

The burst of kundalini in the head at the brahmarandra crown chakra (and elsewhere in the subtle head) is the anti-pole to the bursting of kundalini in the sex organ chakra. Just as in sexual climax experience, we are left a loss as to why the energy burst primarily from the genitals, so we are left at a loss as to why the energy burst in the head when kundalini goes up the spine and does not do so in any other part of the psyche with the same intensity.

Why does it not burst evenly in the entire psyche in either case?

Naad the Parent

Naad meditation has a special feature today which is part of the relationship situation. Recently there was no boyfriend-girlfriend relationship with naad. Instead, different types of relationships arose. Today it was the one where naad was the parent. I was the lost child, whom the parent found and recovered to safety.

In naad *dharana* practice, the student searches for naad, finds it and clings as per advice given by the yoga teacher. This is a trying stage, when the student must endeavor, do hours of practice over time and accumulate the merit of making the effort according to blind faith in the words of the teacher.

Day after day the student tries to reach naad, does or does not do so but keeps a sustained effort because the teacher insists on the meditation. After a time, something happens where the student finds that naad is there for the taking. The days of struggle to remain with naad are over. It is smooth sailing like when the wind is behind a yacht, being caught in the sails. Before the smooth sailing there is the rigging of the canvas, the tying of the ropes, the pulling of the boom to bring the sail into the wind pocket.

There is the struggle on and on with little progress made, and some sure frustration. This is the naad deliberate focus *dharana* (dhaa-ruh-naa). After doing this for a time, when the *powers that be* think that one did sufficient endeavor, one reaches the naad spontaneous focus *dhyana* (dhee-aan) stage. The wind is in the sail. It is favorable. It does not huff here and puff, pulling the boat every which way. It cooperates with the captain. Nature decided to service his commands.

When I began this meditation, for some reason, even though there was a good session of breath infusion prior, still I was hauled away by association energy from others. It pulled me to the frontal part of the head, the way a fisherman pulls a large fish across a beach on the journey to the market. The fish is heavy but since it is slimy, it slides easily. It cannot resist because it is out of its element.

The fish for its part has no idea what happened. It can remember that it swam happily. Then it saw a treat. Then it struck at that with its needle-sharp teeth. Then it was over. It found itself being pulled while it felt a sharp pain in its jaw.

It analyzed what happened but soon it was at the bottom of a ship where there were hard materials which it laid on. The sea was never enjoyed again.

But as I was hauled, suddenly I felt that something came over me like a giant form which casts a shadow. It grabbed and pulled me backwards to it. It was naad. It claimed me the way a parent claims a lost child. Naad took me to the back of the head. It was like going home after being lost for a time, after being with mean strangers.

Naad the parent, yes, that is different than naad the lover. With naad the lover, there is some bullying, where naad demands attention and cries out if there is not enough. With naad the parent, it is all cushion. The yogi is like the child. Naad is like the protective mother. The yogi swims in a cosmic ocean of concern. No one can harm him. Nothing can touch him.

Sifting Chit akash

Lahiri inspired a method which may be termed as sifting *chit akash*. This is where the student yogi, after having much experience with *chit akash*, off and on, learns how to detect its presence even when there is a lower level of energy prevailing in the psyche.

Imagine what it would be if one could contact naad even when there are other noises, or if further one could make *chit akash* contact when one is on a level, especially at a time of life when one is not worthy of being in the *chit akash* transcendental level of existence.

Have you ever made contact with naad even though the mind was filled with trashy thoughts and ideas or even when there were noises which lacked spiritual content?

Once one becomes familiar with *chit akash*, one can, during meditation when the mind will not reach that level, sit quietly behind the energy in the frontal part of the subtle head, and pull *chit akash* energy. It is like sifting gold dust from dry clay and gravel.

Interest Energy / *Chit akash*

I was to post this earlier today but the recall of it disappeared into thin air. I looked for the notes. Those vanished as well. I decided that I would be observant if it happened again.

In my history of meditation, if I cannot describe or remember an experience, I usually can develop more clear perception of it in the proceeding meditations. There were some experiences which were one-time events such that they never occurred again. Most of the experiences, I would say about 98%, developed in future meditations with further clarity.

During the afternoon session I again had the experience. I noted carefully what it was and how to cause it. The person who inspired this was Lahiri, who said that the interest energy, when it is isolated and not ushered into the sensual energy of the kundalini lifeForce, will locate the *chit akash*, and will draw the *chit akash* to the yogi during meditation.

This system can be done by a student who is steady in naad, who has proficiency in breath infusion to the extent of causing pratyahar sensual energy withdrawal to occur. The student must have stayed in naad for long periods during several meditations of months or years accordingly.

Then, when in naad and looking forward, if there are no random formations at the frontal part of the subtle head, if there is naad light there and no aspect from the physical existence or from the lower astral realms, the student may look to discover his/her interest energy which is not mixed with the sensual energies of kundalini.

If that interest is found and if it is given attention, it will cause the yogi to be linked into the *chit akash*. The connection with naad light and naad sound remains during this linkage to *chit akash*, at least until there is a complete transfer into it. But such a transfer can only occur after months or years of doing this meditation.

Mobility / Reproduction Retraction

This morning I did a kriya which involved pulling the reproduction and mobility energies in the subtle body. This is part of the preparation for assuming a *yogaSiddha* form.

Mobility through limbs must be scrapped. Reproduction through a biological process has to be scrapped as well. So long as the subtle body has such needs there is no question of the person going to the highest astral regions. These tendencies in the astral body do not go away by wishful thinking. If they are deep rooted, if they stubbornly persist, that is evidence that they will assert themselves, and one will again be condemned to physical life forms.

Getting rid of a physical body has nothing to do with it, because such a body is not the basis of itself. The subtle body is the basis of the physical one. The problems we encounter in physical existence are based on the needs of the subtle form. It is in the subtle body that the changes need be made which will eliminate our needing physical ones.

The mobility feature using limbs and feet specifically, has little or no value in the highest astral regions. The reason is that there one is not hampered by gravity, by a force which one must use in a rising and lowering action for moving.

The reproduction feature has to do with nature's inability to produce durable life forms. Because the physical nature is endless mutable and that is one of its permanent features, which nobody, not even divinities can alter, there is the necessity to reproduce. All life forms carry this reproduction tendency as the second primal need.

The first is to acquire a physical form with which to participate in history.

As soon as the form is procured, the next need is to reproduce as an investment on the next physical form. This is because the acquired one will die soon after it is produced.

A question arises as to why the student, needs to know this.

Is there not a method or a meditation which one can do which achieves this in one effort?

The answer is that yes there is such a method.

It is the grace energy and grace infusion from a deity from the spiritual side of existence.

This answer is worthless unless one can prove that in a specific student's case this is liable to happen.

Opportunity in the Next Life

I was in a conversation with my deceased father two nights ago. He wanted to convince me that he should move ahead with the next physical body on the basis of the high points of his past life performance. His view is that a person should move ahead with the best assets based on what was done in the recent life. He cited some better parts of his life as an example of how he should be allowed to have the next body in physical existence.

Since he wanted me to confirm this and I could not, I told him that it is based on the average performance and not on the high points alone. Those with a higher average will, more than likely, do better in terms of the life opportunity fate affords them in the next life. There are always exceptions to every rule. We can be sure of that. However, unless one is lucky one will have to submit to the norm. We find that some persons are regular recipients of luck. Some others are not. Hence it is best to rate oneself by the law of averages.

In the next life, my birth opportunity will go according to how I best performed overall and not just for specific incidences in which I excelled. An example from my life may illustrate this. During the years of elementary school, I once won a sprint race. Before this incidence, I usually was among those who were last in the sprint. One reason for this was that I was three years younger than most of the boys in the class. This happened because I had a proficient kindergarten teacher. When I first went to elementary school, I was promoted two classes ahead, because I could do everything that was required without being taught. This advantage turned out to be a disadvantage in some ways, as it does with everything else in life, where as soon as one gets an advantage, one is faced with a down side.

Even though I won that one race, I won no other. When it was time to pick runners to represent the school, my name was not in the listing, not even as a substitute runner. The coach totally ignored my one victory because it was the only one.

Not to speak of my father, suppose I take another body. I do not desire one but suppose I am destined for one regardless of desire. What will happen?

How will providence treat me?

Will I be the son of wealthy woman or not?

Will my father in the next life be like my father in this life, a paternal misfit?

Will my new mother abandon me to relatives the way my mother of this life did?

Will my father in the new life be neglectful towards my education where I would not be qualified to be a professional in any field of human occupation?

Will nature think like this?

"Do not give him the opportunity. If he wants to be on top let him endeavor for it. He should not be graced with anything. He is a yogi. He thinks that materialistic living is silly. Do not patronize him?"

Six Months of Practice

Lahiri discussed that consolidation of yoga practice is difficult mainly because of having association with materialistic persons. You can have the best mystic procedure, the very best kriyas. It can come from an exalted yogaGuru. You can study the *Yoga Sutras* and *Bhagavad Gita* to the fullest. Still if you are in materialistic association, there will not be consistent success.

There will be some success, but it will be skip and hop, jerky and somewhat inconsistent.

Whatever I publish may be seen as being motivated. Many people feel that I target them. For instance, someone may be a yogi and may be in materialistic association. Hence after reading this, that person may feel that I take pock shots at his/her face. This happens where people feel that I am after them for one reason or the other. I may or may not be. Still, it is best to read my work as if you are an innocent bystander and not as a person to whom this is directed.

About two months ago, Lahiri gave a procedure. He said that if it was practiced for six months, then for sure it would result in perception of the *chit akash* sky of consciousness. It became evident recently however that at the pace I progress, that cannot happen. The six months may be updated to read six years and even with sixty years.

Why?

Because of materialistic association!

I have some advice.

If you want to scuttle your spiritual life, maintain association with materialistic people.

Naad Sound/Light Technique

Meditation on naad sound resonance may take weeks, years or lives to mature where the student yogi gets the feeling that a relationship develops which is similar to the emotional reliance and nurturing which we receive and provide to other persons in the physical world. Naad sound listening must mature into that for one to reach the advanced stage.

If one gets that far in the process, suddenly one will find oneself located in both naad sound and naad light which has a goldish glow. It does not blare. It does not shine like a ray. One sees it as if one was in a cave or cavern where a glow of light shines to give just enough vision to dimly perceive.

Lift Nutrition / Reproduction Energies

elimination of kundalini-designed nutritional system
nutrition pull-zones
extraction life of nutritional energy
from stomach/intetinal mass

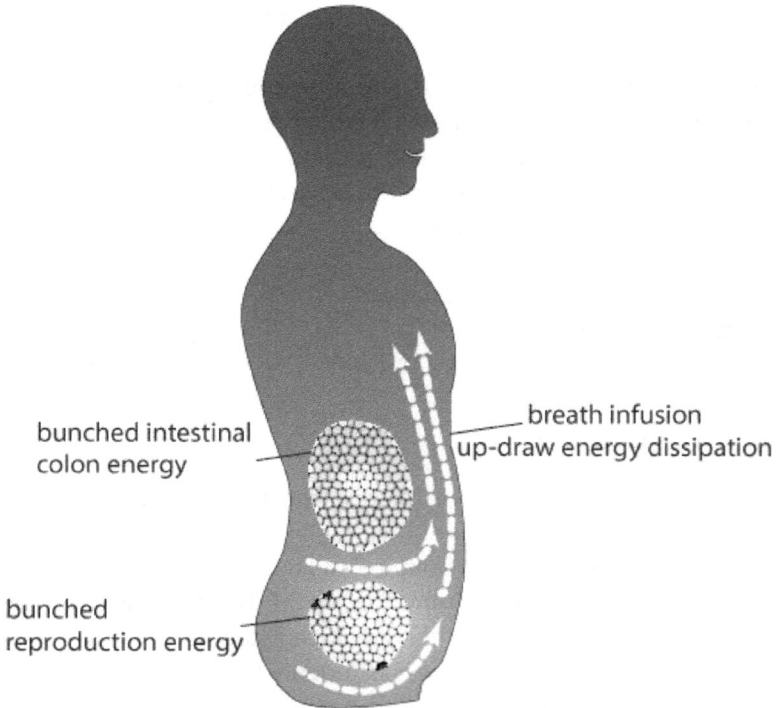

bunched intestinal
colon energy

breath infusion
up-draw energy dissipation

bunched
reproduction energy

The lift of the nutrition and reproduction energies occurs stage by stage when the student yogi relaxed the sex impulse and retracted the passionate desire for that and the addiction thereof.

No one should confuse this with the complete stoppage of sexual activities. Sexual activities in the social format will go on forever so long as the yogi is a resident in any dimension where that must play out. What nature does nature does. That is no concern of the yogi/yogini. Our concern is with what we do and what we desire to exploit.

Once the exploitation desire is shed, nature will still continue with its activities. It will not cease merely because a yogi shed the related desire. Nature will do what nature does, regardless. One needs to understand this or one will never focus on the issue of one's personal exploitation needs which are or were aligned into nature's system.

When I was in my mother's uterus, I was eager for sugar there. When I was brutally expelled from there, I continued the craving. The question is, however, how was I to figure what was my mother's desire in either case.

Since my desire was fused into hers while I was in the uterus, how was I to know which part was my account and which was hers. To make matters worse physical nature sent the billing to both of us in one combined bill so that we did not know who used how much of nature's services. This is all well and good for physical nature but it does not serve the purpose for yoga.

For this process, I should sort my part from her portion. The billing must be separate. Clarity is the hallmark of this process, not confusion and ignorance. If I wanted to pay my mother's bill, that is okay but at least I should know the amount. Paying it does not require confusion and lack of clarity. Knowing which part is hers does not prohibit me from contributing to her portion.

As the infant in her abdomen, I ate more sugar that I desired because she wanted me to eat some of what she ingested into her body for herself. When she felt sick during the pregnancy, her psyche would appeal to me to absorb some ailments. I did that. It was not easy because accepting it meant reducing my yogic attitude. Then the sugar passed through the placenta and did damage to my embryo.

By the time I was expelled, kicked out, evicted, my psyche was addicted to sugar and chocolate. Some people do not know this history. They wonder why I am cautious about eating sugary foods. The reason is that it nearly killed my infant body. That body manifested sores in every part of its skin, due to sugar-cocoa consumption.

It took years to purge the physical body from that habit. I disciplined the diet to get it done but it was part of the cost of getting this body to give this information about yoga technique.

Was it worth it?

Maybe it was stupid to assume this body in the first place?

However, by sharing the truths of rebirth, I will salvage the effort of getting it.

Nature will do what nature will do, undoubtedly. No one will change that. No sympathy or idealism will interfere with that. A yogi should accept that and know what is practical and what is not. Work for freedom from nature, but know that ultimately you will not stop it. What you can do is to stop your inner concern with it.

The nutritional and reproductive energies must be retracted by the yogi.

Will God as Krishna or Shiva do it?

No, neither will.

They do not care for it.

It does not interfere with their divinity.

Will your spiritual teacher reform it?

No, the spiritual teacher does care to see that you complete that but still you must do that yourself. Your hand and your hand alone, is on the psychic lever which is the power to retract it. Begin at the bottom and lift the nutrition and reproductive energies little by little. It will get smaller and smaller as you go.

Kundalini Clearance

Kundalini clearance is special. It is a rare occurrence when doing breath infusion to raise kundalini and clear dense astral energy from the psyche. The clearance occurs after months or years of practice, when the system remains clarified after practice and does not re-pollute as soon as kundalini subsides.

When kundalini clearance occurs, it is like when there is sunshine about 9am in the morning, just before the temperature becomes unbearable. At that time the sun is appreciated for its light. No one curses it for excessive heat. Soon after that time, people look at the sun with a mean eye as if to say to it:

Temper yourself!

Are you silly?

Can you not feel the excessive heat on our heads?

Can you not control your glare?

Serve without causing sunburn.

In a clearance the yogi finds himself/herself in a clear transcendental light in which distinction is hard to come by because everything there in that dimension is made of the same clear transcendental light, such that everything is super transparent. It is a nice place though, so desireable that upon returning to regular consciousness, the yogi smiles with a clean non-avaricious happiness, with a bliss force which has no lusty attitude in it. No passionate energy is present.

But the key feature is that the yogi loses contact with the physical body and still the physical body remains standing and sitting in whatever position it was in. It does not fall to the ground.

Why does it not fall?

We know for sure that if the coreSelf is disconnected from the physical body that form will fall to the ground. That is the law of nature.

Why is this an exception to that law?

The reason is that the kundalini in that configuration can keep the physical body from falling. When the yogi goes into the clear light state and then returns, he/she notices that there is a light shining which is kundalini in its most elevated condition. The yogi/yogini is surprised to find kundalini in that useful condition which it was never in before. The thing has a completely changed attitude which surprises the yogi.

Yogi is Controlled by a Girlfriend

I took a one-hour nap during the day. I found myself as my astral body in an astral dimension which was full of clear light. This clear light is like sunlight but there is no heat to it and no obvious source of illumination like a sun in the sky. This astral place is adjacent to Georgetown, Guyana where I grew up.

I was in an astral building which is a parsonage, where a girl who was a foster daughter of a minister lived. We were in love when I was about nine years of age. Before you color this with an opinion, this relationship means here love without sexual attraction. This is gender attraction only because neither the girl nor myself was sexual mature.

Consider that we were like prisoners who fall in love in a situation where they were the only two people in confinement. When you assume a body, you are, technically speaking, a prisoner of your parents, guardians and local community. You are handicapped. At first you cannot walk. That is solitary confinement. When an infant learns to walk, he/she is limited as to where he/she can go. The adults monitor the movements.

If two people find themselves on a dessert island, they should learn to love each other. That is all there is since there will be no other persons to choose from. In a way, this girl and I were in such a predicament because we were the only two persons attending that church who were of that age. I remember I used to look at this girl and think to myself that she was suitable but strange.

She looked at me with an impression which read,

"He is delicious. I will lick him like I do the ice-cream."

I would then mentally reply like this,

"I am not edible. I am a person. I am not a food."

She would then reply,

"Want to bet? Wait until we are alone. I will show you what I can do with you."

I would then reply,

"I am afraid of you. Girls are different. You are bold to think that in the presence of the adults."

She would then think back,

"I do not care for them. I tend to my needs. Let us be alone to discuss this, you cute one."

That is how it would be. Sometime during my teen years, around fourteen years of age, I left that place and went to Trinidad. Before that however the relationship with this girl ceased because she acquired a boyfriend who was from a wealthy family which was more suitable to her status because I was from a poor situation. Soon after she experienced sexual maturity but my body did not manifest that at the time.

I saw her a few times after she acquired the wealthy boyfriend. Then, her mental message was more like,

"Do not worry. I will still make good my promise. Never mind my rich boyfriend. I still plan to be with you at some other time. For now, I will retire my desire for you."

Looking back and checking on the feelings I had for her when she got that wealthy boyfriend, I see that there was a jealous feeling there but it was inactive. This was like when plants grow near the Arctic Circle. They remain stunted due to permafrost. They exist but they do not thrive due to environment conditions. In the psyche of a yogi, we cannot say that there are no normal feelings. There are but those feelings may not expand and become so expansive as to direct the operation of the psyche. They are either in dormancy or in a stunted no-grow condition.

In this astral encounter, the girl was about twenty-five years of age. This meant that her astral body seemed like a twenty-five years old physical form. She was all smiles, very confident as she was when we were youngsters.

The astral place was full of daylight. There were no asphalt roads. Other astral people were around and about.

She said to me,

"Let us go. You will see my wedding dress. We will be married soon. Our childhood desire will be fulfilled.

She looked me square in the eyes. Her pupils expanded. She said,

"Are you glad that I will be your wife?"

I was shocked but I acted as if everything was suitable. My mind was oblivious on how to respond. I could not honestly say that I was eager. Hoping that she would change the subject, I fidgeted with an embroidered part of her dress. I lowered my eyes like a small dog which had met a giant of its own species and which has to be submissive in order to save its life.

I followed a basic rule of the jungle which is to never challenge a bigger animal. I may be a yogi with opinions but in this circumstance that meant absolutely nothing. I was small in reference to the bigger canine.

"Marry you?" I thought, "Are you nuts? Gender love is one affection. Sexual love is another. What maximum-security prison will I be in? I will be your confined Prince Charming."

Right then as I considered that in a secret part of my mind, she magically moved us to a dress maker's shop. A man was there who sewed a garment. She smiled. I could feel her mind probing, readying itself for licking me as if I was the ice-cream. I said to her, "I must go."

Then I left that astral place.

Will I marry this woman in a future life?

Since this person has a command over my subtle body and caused it to be in that astral place under those specific circumstances which relate to her desire, a desire from over fifty years ago, will I be subjected to her whim sometime in the future?

The enigma is here again. Who owns the body? Except that is about the subtle body, and about its inability to control fate?

Marriage in the Astral World

Some females feel that unless they are married, they cannot or should not have sexual contact with the partner. As far as they are concerned once they are married that is the ultimate approval for sexual acts with a boyfriend. This is so deep-rooted that it is insisted even in the astral domains, locations in which such ideas are irrelevant.

Marriage has no meaning in the astral world. There are no pregnancies there. If one is deceased and carries to the hereafter the materialistic methods, one will try to do everything in the astral world, the way one did in the physical world. One will not realize the difference between this place and the astral regions.

Vajroli/Amaroli Misunderstanding

Lahiri asked me to write about the physical achievement which is known as *vajroli/amaroli* hatha yoga practice. These practices are described in the *Hatha Yoga Pradipika*. Some yogis feel that the accomplishment of this by physical means is the full achievement. However, it is not that simple.

Physical process of yoga, when done to perfection may not include subtle mastery. The opposite also holds true where someone may achieve subtle mastery and not exhibit it physically. Thus, one must be careful in these practices, so as not to fool oneself that one is proficient in all areas because of mastery of a specific physical technique.

Recently I was asked a question about a yogi drinking his urine, as a medical and spiritual practice. Since I do not do that practice, I could not give an authoritative opinion. Whatever a student reads in a yoga book, should be accepted with an open mind but all the same one should leave a little space for reception of proof to the contrary.

Even if a process worked for someone in the past, or even if it worked for you in your past life, there is no guarantee that it will work in this life. The reason is that fate is supreme. If it does not want something to manifest, that procedure will not work even if it worked for a million other yogis.

Arrogance travels with us like a bad brother whom we cannot disown, but all the same we must move with it doing the least harm to ourselves. Thus, we should not be arrogant towards providence. Whatever we do requires many supports. If the props are removed the action is demolished. This means that something may be ineffective if providence pulls away its supports.

In the physical *vajroli* process, a student stands in water and squats in waist deep water. The urinary and perineum muscles are repeatedly contracted and released. After a time, water is pulled through the genital tubing of the male student. The student gets accustomed to this and then tries a liquid with more viscosity. Honey is tried or sugar syrup.

Students who are involved sexually with partners sometimes hear of doing vajroli during sexual intercourse. There were reports of yogis who did this and who did not emit any sexual fluid during intercourse, or did go through a climax experience and did not emit sexual fluids.

Due to these reports some persons got the view that they would do this to enhance and prolong sexual involvement. Especially some male yogis were concerned about this because of an inferiority complex, which males suffer from which is that their sexual system is designed for quick release of sexual fluids and climax experience during sexual intercourse. This system is there for the convenience of physical nature's reproduction plans but the entities are dissatisfied with it, particularly some females do not like it because it does not take into account that they need a longer period of sexual penetration activity to bring them to climax.

They complain about it. Some do not know that this system is nature designed and that the male has little to do with it. Due to these complaints, some males developed an inferiority complex because of the way nature operates this system because nature releases the sexual climax experience as part of the reproduction effort to get male sexual fluid into the female uterus. Nature is not concerned with the pleasure yield of the female in the act.

Some males, after hearing about vajroli, practice it, not for the purpose of yoga, but for the purpose of delaying sexual climax so that their organ remains functional for as long as it would take for the female to experience full sexual satisfaction. However, yoga is yoga and satisfaction of female partner is a different achievement.

The question is:

Why practice this retraction of the sexual fluid if one is not interested in prolonging sexual erection for the satisfaction of a female partner?

Why do it?

What has it got to do with spiritual practice?

The answer is that it has everything to do with spiritual practice because so long as the energy in the subtle body keeps going downward, one will be forever condemned to taking physical bodies and will never become liberated.

There are two motives for doing *vajroli*:

One is to increase sexual prowess for the satisfaction of the female partner and to boost the male self-esteem.

The other is to kill sexual interest for the satisfaction of the yoga guru and the deity.

From the same practice, we will derive different results according to the motive and evolutionary interest.

Physical *vajroli* interest is the one which concerns increased sexual prowess. Subtle body vajroli interest is the one which concerns eliminating sexual interest.

The student should decide what he/she aspires for. *Pranayama* breath infusion can be used to pull up the reproductive mechanism so that it dissolves from the subtle body. This will be a different superior vajroli with interest for making the subtle body loose interest in having physical forms.

There are so many vices of the physical body which the subtle body desires to experience. Sex desire is one such habit. The student should identify these features one by one. He/She should deal with them accordingly.

Subtle Body Kundalini Restricted Release

After mastering the rise of kundalini into the head of the subtle body, and after getting that practice to a proficient level, one should turn about and consider finding every dense area in the subtle body.

It is a bit of a shock for the students when I mention this, because when one comes to kundalini yoga one gets the idea that the achievement is to raise kundalini into the head. Thus, to hear that this achievement is preliminary is discouraging. However, advancement is advancement. If you are serious about this spiritual practice and want to go to the next level which is to develop a *yogaSiddha* subtle body, you must comply with the new requirements which is to identify and eliminate all dense astral energy in the subtle body, not just in the head but in every other part of the psyche.

Kundalini trained the coreSelf to acquire sexual climax experience as the highest pleasure. This training did not begin in the human species. It was there in lower forms. However, in other forms the pursuit was not as efficient and direct because of limitations which nature created in those lower bodies.

When one is introduced to kundalini yoga, one practices with the intent to exploit bliss energy, pleasure force, and in the focused method one was trained in by physical nature. There is a difference though in that instead of the genitals being the focus, the spine and brain become the focus.

However, for the *yogaSiddha* status, this system of focus into a special part of the form has no place. There has to be a new orientation which is for the entire form to be the focus not just the genital, spinal nor cerebral, not just the chakra system.

To cause this development to happen, one must clear all dense areas which means that once the head of the subtle body is thoroughly clarified, there is no need to focus on that any longer.

The idea that when the *sushumna nadi* central passage is cleared the whole system is cleared, is a falsehood. Check your subtle body and see. What happens when the *sushumna* central passage is cleared? It feels as if the entire system is cleared and that feeling is interpreted by the yogi incorrectly.

If when *sushumna nadi* is cleared, you got out of that energy and inspected other parts of the psyche, you could verify this.

Endeavor to reach the other places where dense astral energy accumulates. Infuse air/energy into those areas to completely energize the subtle form.

Kundalini Diffusion Direction

Question:

If a student performs breath infusion during some yoga asanas in an effort to move the kundalini through other parts of the body besides the head will the energy always be felt/noticed? Is it possible that the energy would be distributed through the limbs or other parts unnoticed? If so, how would one know?

Mi~Beloved:

The main objective is to infuse the system with the system itself doing the absorption wherever the system feels it and needs it. That is stage number one, where the student is concerned to supply the fresh air, and he/she is willing to let the system do the distribution but under observation.

This is more about observation and less about control of what happens except to apply the locks to help the system to compress the energy and keep it in a concentrated format.

Students who practiced continuously every morning for under three years, should not be concerned with anything but full infusion and watching to see how kundalini acts. Usually, provided the locks are being applied properly, kundalini will shoot through spine into the brain.

After three years, the student should again study what happens when kundalini comes into the brain, whereby the student can explain in his/her own words what happens. This is because of minute observations not minute control, except for the locks.

On occasion however even a novice will experience kundalini or the infused energy in various parts of the body besides the spine and brain. When this happens, the student will know but the student may not differentiate between infused energy bursting and kundalini bursting or between when the infused energy and the kundalini energize together. This lack of clarity will change with more practice.

There will be intense bliss feelings or intense vision of light in certain parts of the body. That is how the student will know that there were bursts of energy in places other than the spine and brain.

Let me review the basic experience of kundalini. That is sex pleasure. The same kundalini is involved with that. We could apply ourselves to the same inquiry to realize if such pleasure experience occurs in any other place besides the genitals.

Does it ever occur in the lips, breasts, waist, toes, or feet?

It may be that due to the intensity and primary focus in the genitals one is unable to note its burst in other areas but in kundalini practice we must change this prejudice and experience kundalini when it fires in other areas. This would require the shattering of addiction for the high point of pleasure.

Subtle Body Impossible Postures

Some postures practiced by siddhas are impossible to do with a physical body. As one advances in breath infusion and meditation, one may find the subtle body doing postures in dreams which are not possible for the physical system to perform due to its inflexibility.

More advanced students will find that while doing the physical postures with breath infusion, the subtle body, on occasion, will suddenly assume postures which are outlandish and which the physical system could not under any circumstance imitate.

In the places where the siddhayogis reside in the higher astral regions, they use subtle bodies only. They do postures that would astonish a human being.

Sometimes in the higher astral regions, one sees a yogin wrapped in a tight ball where his head is in the center of the ball and his body is wrapped around the head. He may remain like this for thousands of years. These are special samadhi states. These vary from yogi to yogi regarding what they do while their subtle forms are in these configurations.

This is not acrobatics, nor exhibitionism. These yogis are in zones where only other great yogis are in the vicinity. No others see these yogis.

Music and Siddhaloka

For yogis trying to get past the Swarga angelic world, one problem is celestial music. The addiction to music is experienced in an earthly body.

Why is music, mere sound, such an allurement?

Student yogis have the task to transcend the allurement of the heavenly music which makes even the most melodious earthly melodies, not worthy of hearing.

Music in the heavenly world of Indra is so alluring that it is many times more dangerous than even the sexual pleasures which people crave on the earthly planet. It would give a person the jitters and cause a person to completely lose foothold on yoga practice.

Once some years after Bhaktivedanta Swami was deprived of his physical body, I found myself in a supernatural body in a heavenly world which floated in the astral skies. It was a place where he resided. There were astral cows there.

I was there as a visitor-guest. Bhaktivedanta wanted to discuss something and to show how he was regarded in that realm. Suddenly out of nowhere I heard music from the distance like it was from another galaxy. It got closer and closer until it was evident that some angelic women sung to honor him.

They sang and played musical instruments which are never seen on earth. The combination of the sounds from the instruments and the sweet voices of the women were bewitching to hear. I tolerated it and focused on what they sung in Sanskrit which was a glorification of the Swami.

Jai Prabhu, Prabhu, Gorachand.

Prabhu Kanandana, Gorachand

After he was satisfied that I heard it, he dismissed me but the music was so forceful that when I resumed my physical body, it felt as if the music burnt a hole even in the earthly form.

Music should be understood as a form of political and social control. Abolish music from temples and churches and you may find a reduction in attendance that would give credence to the power of musical sound.

More or less if one is to get to the *siddhaloka* places one would have to be free from music allurement just as one has to be free from other pleasures like sexual indulgence. If not, one must face the fact that one will remain in the dimension where the music is heard.

Just as in this world one may go to hear a concert of great musicians and not be allowed to enter their personal residences or be allowed to enter for half hour only, so one may be treated by the astral maestros in a paradise world.

Part 2

Kundalini in Balance

There is interest in balancing the kundalini and the chakra system. Some yogis feel that one should be sure to do so many breaths on one side and so many on the other, and one should visualize everything in equilibrium.

I emphasize that in the system of breath infusion inSelf Yoga™ which I teach, this balance is not the objective. I do not care about it because I discovered that the energy will balance itself in its own way, even if that means that it balances with one quarter to three quarters rather than half and half.

Balance means that in a closed system the energies are balanced any which way, irrespective of if 25% is on one side and 75% is on the other. So long as the total is 100%, it should be considered as being in balance. It is artificial, idealistic and theoretical to think that we can get everything to be 50/50.

Is the sun and moon 50/50?

Is the Atlantic and Pacific Oceans of equal volume?

Is the American continent equally balanced against Europe or Asia?

Is the earth in the center of this solar system?

Is the Milky Way in the center of the universe?

Is the spin of the earth absolutely regular?

How then will one derive 50/50 from a reality which is not uniform?

When teaching breath infusion, we stress that students should be concerned only with getting the energy infused into the system. The system itself will accumulate and then distribute the energy and will cause the kundalini or the infused energy to be compressed and linked to a higher plane. When this happens, the energy will burst from where it is and go to other areas causing the other places to move to a higher plane.

Maintain the practice in any session so that the entire subtle body is filled with energy. Do as if you have a flat tire which was repaired. Pump air into it and it will eventually be evenly inflated. If you infuse the energy into the system, it will do whatever balancing it needs to do even if during the session, the left side has more or less of a charge than the right one.

If in the beginning the right side has a charge or if a certain area has much infused energy as compared to the rest, then if one keeps surcharging the system, one will find that the infused energy spreads elsewhere, until the whole subtle body is surcharged. The yogi should be persistent and steady and not be a person who gives up easily or who does not have the stamina to do a thorough session.

Killing Insects

If an insect was a machine, it would take much ingenuity to create it. Seeing it from that angle, it becomes a marvel. Their bodies are sophisticated machines. Appreciate that. Do not kill them unless it is absolutely necessary.

Just as persons operate the human form, see that there is a person in that insect body, operating it.

If one kills an insect, that person must acquire another body. It takes nature time to create that new form. Nature will note the action. It may charge the killer for the creation of that other body

Would you smash someone's property?

If you did can you pay for its replacement?

Kundalini Sensation

Traditional kundalini yoga is an obsession with getting kundalini up the spine into the brain.

In contrast, sex experience concerns getting kundalini to jump from the spine to the genitals and then to draw down into the genitals the interest of the brain, which comes naturally because of the intensity and compulsory force of sexual pleasure.

When this body was younger, I researched how kundalini operated in sex pleasure. I noticed that the mental interest is drawn to the genitals during sexual experience but in kundalini yoga, the mental interest stays in the brain and the kundalini goes into the brain leaving aside its interest in sexual pleasure.

While in sex pleasure the kundalini arches across a small space from the base chakra at the end of the spine to the sex organ chakra, in the case of kundalini yoga, something else happens where the kundalini travels the length of the spine and then goes up through the lower brain. Sometimes this happens in a jiffy but in some experiences, it goes up slowly and one can observe the transit in more detail.

Even though getting kundalini through the spine into the brain is a sensational event, even more fascinating than sex pleasure, still more alarming than that is getting kundalini in other parts of the psyche, such as getting kundalini or infused energy into every part of the neck except the sushumna central passage where kundalini usually travels. How about getting kundalini into the flesh of the neck?

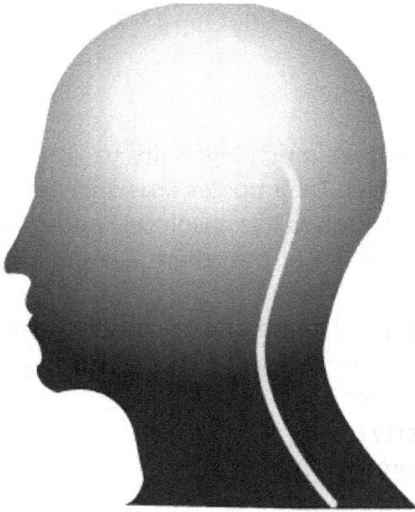

center of spine sushumna nadi   whole neck sushumna nadi

Kundalini Brain-Jump

After doing the breath infusion practice for some time, and getting kundalini to rise into the brain on a daily basis, the legendary sushumna nadi central spinal passage remains open at other times during the waking hours of the physical body. This causes that passage to remain clarified or free from dense astral energy some of the time even during non-yogic activities.

This is fine for the student yogi. Over time the kundalini loses interest in remaining at the bottom of the *sushumna* central passage. At long last, like a serpent which decided to roam the world, it abandons its haunt. This gives a double advantage which is:

The student does not have to strive so hard to arouse kundalini.

The kundalini loses its perpetual love affair with sex desire, sex pleasure obsession. Kundalini forgets sex desire. It no longer has that pleasure structure. This is a big event for the student. He/She can then dedicate the interest energy which was used for sex pleasure to meditative purposes. This accelerates progress.

Kundalini Hang out

A student who did not properly respect the yoga teacher may find that even after the usual memories are reduced, still he cannot consolidate the progress and turn the conserved energy into spiritual advancement. The reason for this is hypocrisy and a lack of deep honesty, combined with a negative attitude towards advanced yogis for real or imagined reasons.

When the yogi consistently keeps the *sushumna* central passage open and the kundalini loses affiliation with sex desires. it loses its attachment to *muladhara* chakra. Gradually over time it changes its hangout to the base of the brain. It shines there like a stub orb.

normal kundalini stem
spine connected to brain

stub kundalini as subtle body brain stem
no connection to spinal passage

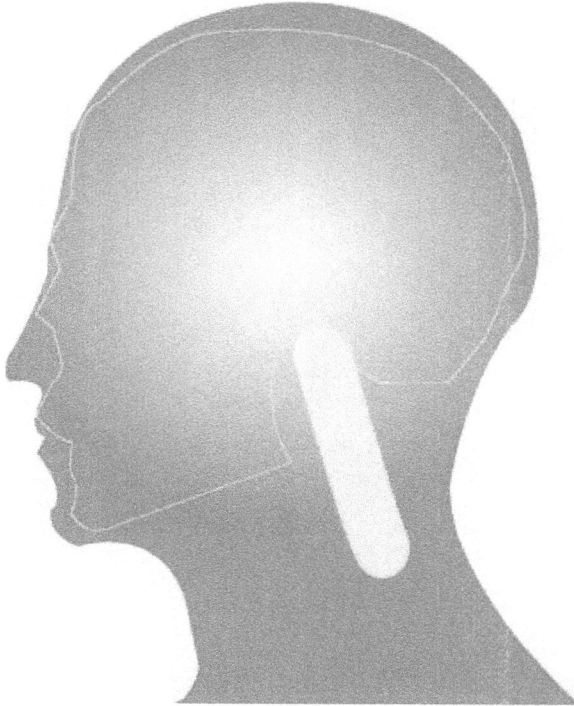

Life without Sex Pleasure

For those who are interested in pushing beyond the limits of what physical nature afforded in the form of a physical body and a subtle form which is prone to developing physical ones, I wish to inform that kundalini yoga is a bit more than the traditional raising of kundalini into the brain.

Due to being conditioned by nature one has the idea that kundalini's rise into the brain is the culmination of yoga practice. Such a view is short sighted and full of the danger of returning to the reptilian kundalini tendencies. If you raised kundalini through the spine consistently for say at least three years, you will know that it wants to return to the *muladhara* base chakra. That is its residence.

What is its favorite pleasure haunt? It certainly is not the brain of the body. It is the sexual organ chakra.

The hormone system in the body is designed to facilitate the sex organ chakra. The reason for this has nothing to do with our need for sexual pleasure. It has everything to do with survival, where the kundalini, which is survival-intelligence at its best, knows that unless it reproduces forms it cannot transmigrate in physical bodies.

Sexual pleasure has nothing to do with it, but that is not easy to admit because we are situated in a position to interpret sex as pleasure.

As soon as I convince someone to switch from sexual pleasure to head consciousness pleasure, that person may be happy but only if I show how to do it consistently from day to day. It is a struggle for that person to abandon sexual indulgence and accept head consciousness pleasure as a fitting replacement even though the kundalini is the same force which is involved in either experience.

When I say that sexual pleasure always has hidden liabilities, some students contend that and say:

"Sex is worth it!"

Other students think that one is helpless when it comes to sexual pleasure. They are pained when it is criticized.

Nutrition and Electricity

From the mix of nutrition and bio-electricity, sexual pleasure is created. If either one is removed, sexual pleasure would not be possible. One may eat as much as one likes. One may get the best nutrients into the body. If there is no electricity in the body at the right place and at the right time, there will be no sexual pleasure.

Conversely if one has the electricity working, and if there is no nutrition, that will generate zero sexual pleasure.

Why discuss this?

If one could retract the electricity and the hormone generation system, the tendency for genital sex would diminish. One would continue existing. One would get pleasure by other means.

Breath Infusion Warranty

To make rapid advancement, to excel in the practice of breath infusion, a student should stringently adhere to at least two practices:
- Keeping the sensual interest in the psyche
- Compressing the accumulated breath energy and rigidly checking how it is distributed through the system

If a student adheres to these principles, what would take four years to master, could be achieved in nine months' time.

The reason is:

The sensual interest will not leak into the external world and into non-yogic thought patterns. If the sensual energy is kept within the confines of the psyche and is not allowed to indulge in non-yogic thoughts patterns, the practice will have a high proficiency in a short time.

The compressed energy will be distributed but it should do so under the observatory and supervisory interest of the coreSelf. When this interest is applied rigidly, the compressed energy becomes even more compressed. That causes it to be distributed in the most concentrated way which results in transpositioning to higher planes of consciousness.

Naad Light Everywhere Else

This is from a meditation about one week prior. Since then, I lost contact with naad. This occurs due to non-yogic association and being involved with materialistic interests of others. It is inevitable that so long as one is in the world, one will be subjected to ups and downs in meditation practice. The ascetic should endeavor with the practice no matter what. He/She should not be deterred by impediments and associations from numerous people who have little or no spiritual bearings.

I was in touch with naad, something that I missed very much. I had a love affair with naad. However now in relation to naad, I feel the way some of my girlfriends feel when I am attentive to someone or something else, like a beached whale with no hope that the high tide will float me to the deep water. Some people say that I have no feelings but little do they know how concealed my deep feelings are. A dried coconut is filled mostly with a liquid. The outer appearance is misleading.

Right now, I grieve for naad, having missed its love for me, and feeling abandoned like a discarded lover. However, I have no alternative but to practice and somehow again link to naad.

The diagram shows that the naad sound was in the back of the head, neck and shoulders while naad light was everywhere else. There was no cognizance of the thighs even.

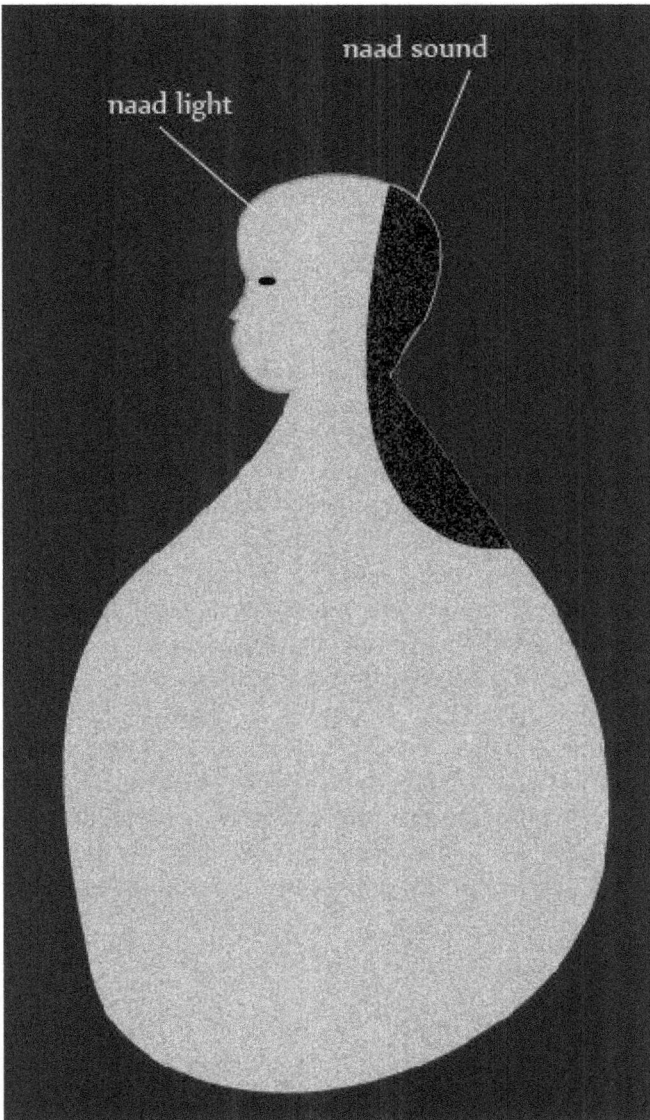

naad sound

naad light

Two Naads Experienced

My relationship with naad, the very confidential one, the one with naad being either the concerned parent or the very precious beloved, was resumed due to intense focus of practice and being released from non-yogic influences which clamped my life.

This morning there was a completely different configuration of naad, where there was a naad like a child naad, within a bigger naad, the parent naad. This was not like where there is naad and then there is one or more nodes within it. This was not like one whirlpool within an ocean. This was more like an ocean within an ocean.

Within a large naad there was a smaller very distant naad which came from within the large naad, like a sea creature rising through the ocean. The vibrational content of each naad was different so that it was easy to differentiate one from the other.

The larger naad claimed me by chugging or grasping me with a jerk movement where I was outside and then inside in one moment. I looked within it as the smaller naad rose from the depths of the larger one.

When naad grasp me and chugged me into the central part of its top, that felt like a parent grasping a child with one lift and moving that child from one place to the other. It was a good feeling, a relief.

After doing breath infusion, when I sat to meditate, there was a stretch force within the subtle body. It was the result of the infusion. It caused the subtle neck to stretch as if it was an elastic material. I could feel it stretching and becoming elongated. My chin had to be checked to stop the stretching action from completely tearing the neck apart. This stopped suddenly. I was transported near to naad. Then what I described above happened.

Sometime after the naad experience, there appeared to be the golden glow light of naad in the front of the subtle head. There was a *chit akash* energy in which I found myself to be. This was a silver-grey energy.

Sometime back during this year, Lahiri gave me a six-month period for reaching *chit akash* permanently. I am yet to figure if that time period will be extended in my case. My hunch now is that it will be due to various setbacks due to materialistic association, pressing demands and yogically-destructive energies.

Muladhara Chakra Relocation

The tradition is that muladhara chakra is at the base of the spinal column. This may be verified by meditation to observe where the basic physio-psychic lifeForce is located.

In advanced kundalini yoga practice, one should move the kundalini from the base chakra repeatedly, until it no longer feels to settle there as its main residence, as its shelter and home.

Students soon get used to the attitude of the kundalini, which is that if it is pried from the base by breath infusion energy, being forced from it, it moves up through the spine into the brain in a huff and a puff. Then it subsides to the base again.

Students sometimes inquire as to why kundalini does not stay in the head.

This is similar to the myth of Sisyphus, where he repeatedly rolled a stone up a hill. As soon he was near the top, his grip loosened, the stone rolled to the bottom. He did this repeatedly. The student of kundalini yoga, is stuck with the repetitive procedure of raising kundalini at least once per day, only to find that it again returns to the base chakra *muladhara* where it settles waiting for the next excitement to occur, preferably sex pleasure.

Kundalini is fond of excitement, of which sex pleasure is a highlight. When it retreats to the *muladhara* chakra, it eagerly and greedily awaits the next sex adventure. For those who lost interest in sex pleasure for one reason or the other, kundalini pursues other types of excitement (*bhogah*). It secretly and attentively waits in the *muladhara* chakra which is like a dark cave, for the next flash of sensation which it will pursue. It may be a sweet food, some juicy gossip, a fiction adventure, a violent act or some other stimulus. It could be music which enthralls.

However, if the student keeps raising kundalini on a daily basis, the time will come either in this life or in some other, where kundalini can no longer remain at the base chakra. It will, over time, shift its base location higher and higher up the spine, until it shifts into the neck and then into the lower back of the subtle head.

When this happens, that new base becomes the habit. The yogi is relieved when the subtle body has the new configuration with kundalini using the lower back of the subtle head for its habitat.

Once kundalini relocates to the back of the head, another development occurs. This is not part of the traditional kundalini yoga practice. The first activity is the lifting of the nutrition/reproduction energy. So long as kundalini is stationed at the base chakra in the spine, it remains impossible to totally lift the nutrition/reproduction energy. This is because kundalini acts as a magnet which pulls the nutrition/reproduction energy downward. But once kundalini is relocated, this magnetic pull is vacant. Instead, the pull comes from above in the subtle head. The student with a little effort can take advantage of this by pulling the nutrition energy as soon as it is accumulated in the chest-abdomen of the physical body.

This causes a noticeable and vital change in the configuration of the subtle body where the kundalini becomes the attractor superseding and replacing the sex organ as the most powerful magnetic force in the subtle body.

This development of pulling the nutritional/reproductive energy, when done to proficiency causes the yogi to become aware of another attractor which is the energy in the thighs. This is the initial sex-charge location in the subtle body. This energy is pulled into the neck and then into the lower back of the head.

While before, the sexual energy was manufactured in the groin area of the subtle body, now such energy is not created there. In fact, it is not produced. What happens is that this energy is not brought to the genitals where it can be processed for sexual expression.

Does the yogi/yogini become sexless as a result?

The answer is no. The yogi retains whatever sexual configuration is natural for him/her. However, the intense interest in genital-provided pleasure is absent in the newly configured subtle form which developed for this yogi/yogini on the basis of the austerities.

See these diagrams:

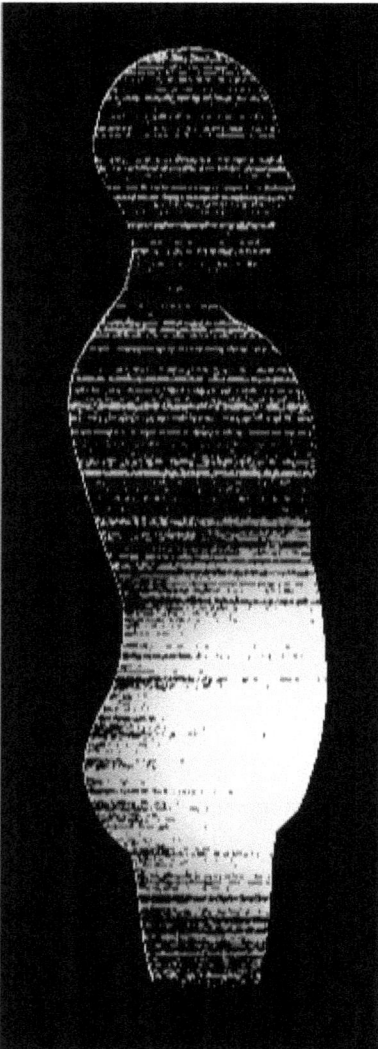

normal human being
with nutrition/reproduction focus
kundalini uses this energy
for sexual pleasure
and other exploitive pursuits

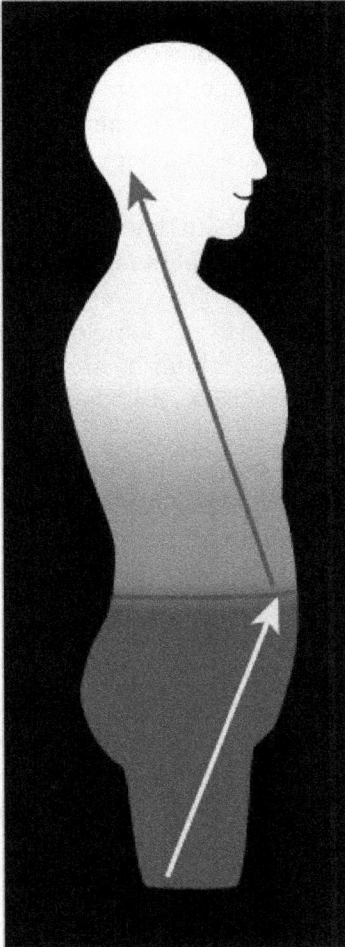

using breath infusion,
lift the nutrition/reproduction energy
from below waist to include thighs
bring these energies above the waist line
then use breath infusion to lift that
to base of brain at back of head

Womb Cavity Lift

Both in the male and female psyche there is a womb cavity, a hollow area which in the physical system would house an embryo. In the male system, this is not as evident as in the female one but the potential for it is there nevertheless. A male ascetic may experience this cavity while doing breath infusion. Do not be surprised if this happens to you. These bodies which we use, even the subtle ones, are adapted in part from the energy of Goddess *Durga*, a patron deity of the world.

She is not the only patron deity but she has the majority share. She is the one with the most emotional energy invested. Subsequently it follows that the psyches, all of them, must be capable of being converted into configurations which parallel hers. Consider what one would be as the collective female potency of the world. That would be a quantum female whom no one could rival or surpass, someone whom no one could resist.

The evidence of the lack of resistance is present before us by our existence in the physical world. It does not matter if I become liberated tomorrow, because even then the history will be that I was once unable to resist. Once in this case is the evidence.

The womb cavity area can be lifted. While doing breath infusion, one can pull in this hollow area, the void cavity, by gripping its membrane edges from the inside and sucking it inward and upward.

With the energy from the breath infusion, this will form a lump of energy which may be like a brick of mineral crystals. If one keeps infusing breath into it, it will compress as it is pulled until it seems as if it turns into a tiny crystal brick which is fused with energy.

Then if there is even more infusion, this will be drawn into the brain and will disappear. This provides freedom from birth and death which is based on forming an embryo in the womb cavity, where one lies on one's side with one's head magnetically aligned to the reproductive chakra of the mother's body. This applies to males and females just the same.

Abdomen Breath Infusion Lift

It is possible to cause the abdomen energy to lift and float instead of going downwards as dictated by the earth's gravity. Nature designed these bodies to make use of gravity for digestion and hormone formation. Nature's system is proven by its master designs of gravity-assisted guts in various species.

This natural system works even for assisting reproduction, where what is eaten is converted into sexual energy hormones which in turn is used for generating new life forms.

To turn away from this, one needs to stop the subtle body from developing embryos. One should cease the downward pull of nutrients which in concentration are manufactured and then stored in the groin area. If this energy was not stored, it could not develop as an impulsive director of the psyche.

Lahiri explained that the abdomen cavity lift, causes the thighs to release their charged energy. This is usually contained in the thighs from the knee up to the trunk of the body. It remains there and acquires a sex polarity charge. But if the abdomen energy is retracted, something else happens where the thigh energy cannot remain in the thigh. Instead, it effuses up and out of the thighs and exhibits no interest in the groin. This is a wonderful practice.

It means that the subtle body of the yogi could assume a higher configuration which would allow him/her to switch away from the normal sense gratifications. He would do so on the basis of form desire and not on the basis of renunciation, denial or avoidance of social rigors.

In the diagram, the normal system is shown with the abdomen energy narrowing and concentrating into hormonal power in the pubic area, while the energy from the thighs fuses with the energy in the sacral bones and the hips. This is the standard configuration which a yogi modifies.

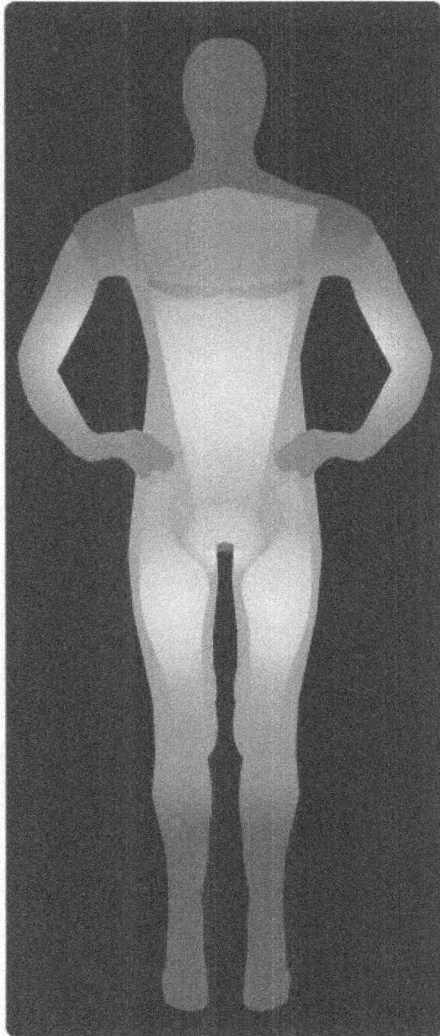

In the next diagram, the configuration is changed, so that the abdomen energy is pulled up and shrunk upwards, while the thigh energy avoids curving inwards and projects through the trunk into the chest.

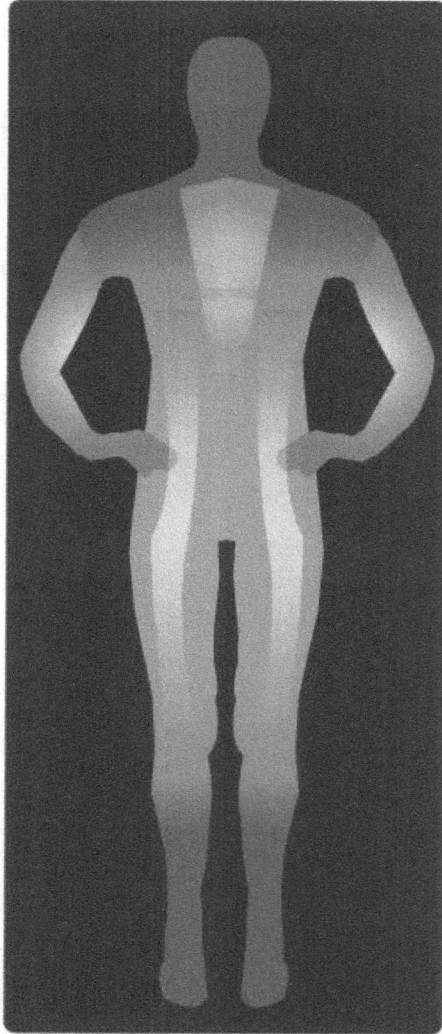

Agnisara Pranayama

In the hatha yoga process *agnisara* abdomen lifts are legendary as something which has to do with muscular lifts of the abdominal pocket.

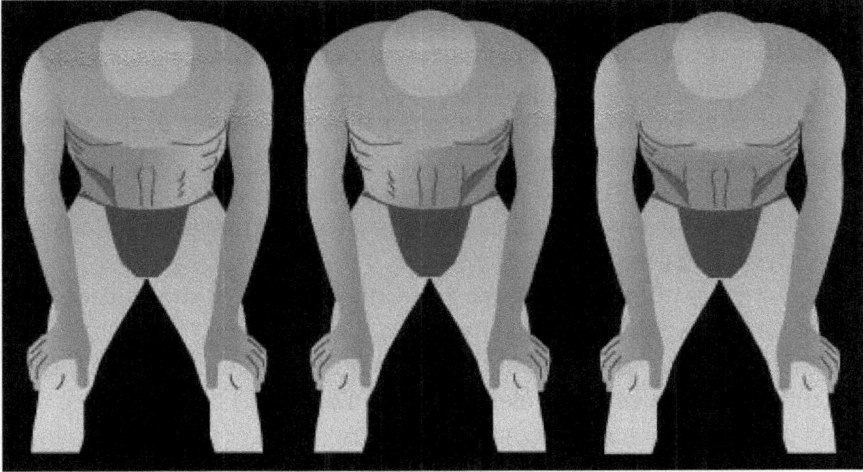

This is a churning motion, mostly regulated by diaphragm movements which results in the intestines being tugged right and left, up and down, in and out, clockwise and anticlockwise, jerked-pulled, and jerked-released. towards and away from the navel.

However, despite the truth about the benefits of abdominal lifts, there is another higher practice. This consists of moving air in various directions through the intestines by doing breath infusion and directing the passage of fresh air, just as one would direct the muscular actions in the churning motion. The fresh air is rigorously pushed and pulled through the system. The physical effects of this are felt as a prompter than usual evacuation.

The real benefit however is the results in the subtle body. A thorough practice for some time, months or years, results in the lifting of the nutritional and reproductive energies so that the subtle body loses its quest for acquiring physical survival opportunities.

Nadi Subtle Tubing Discovery

The perception of the nadi subtle tubes begins in the physical body with the perception of the nerve circuits. This is because the physical circuits are parallel and responding to the psychic ones.

For instance, have you felt a burning or an electrical sensation when going to urinate, especially when you held fluids in the bladder until the bladder seemed to burst? When this happens and one begins the urination, something else happens where there are electric tingling sensations in certain parts of the body, beginning with the bladder check valve. These sensations run to particular parts of the body even into the arms. This is experienced every time that happens.

While non-yogis, as well as some student yogis, ignore these sensations with their tracks or routes, yogis observe them. They catalogued this. It is valuable experience about the composition of the subtle form.

Sometimes when students complain that they never experienced the nadis, I may ask a student,

"Have you ever urinated after you were unable to for some time? Have you noticed the sensations arising? Have you tracked those sensations to see where they are routed in the body?

The urethra tube which leads from the bladder to the outside of the body has a corresponding primal nadi.

Once when for some reason, I could not access a urinal, I was forced to keep the bladder valve from releasing urine. Eventually I got to a pace where I could urinate. There was a burning sensation that I could barely tolerate. I could not expose the organ for urination to do the needful. I squirmed and wiggled to keep the bladder valve from opening, while I fussed with the zipper of the pants. In the meantime, the sensations increased unbearably.

Finally, when I released the bladder valve, there was a sharp highly noticeable sensation of electric current running from the bladder valve to the bottom lip. It was such that the lip stiffened and curled on itself with an intolerable current of electricity running through it.

In another way, it was a source of joy and accomplishment for realizing those nadis which run from the bladder valve up through the front of the body, through the neck and terminating in the bottom lip.

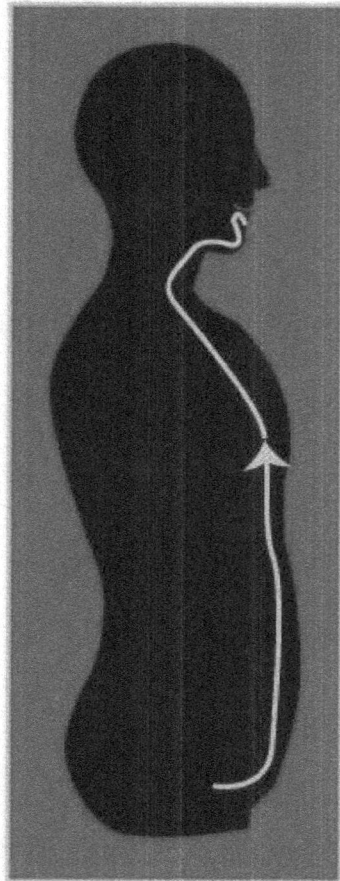

Run on Passionate Energy

The energy content of this universe is the same today as it was when this began so many million years ago. Because it is membraned from everything else that ever existed, nothing can leak from this place. Despite the shifting and warping that takes place as a matter of course, this is a contained system in which everything must remain in balance at all times.

The disturbances are part of that balance. These happen because of the law of interaction which causes one thing to shift here as a result of something else moving there.

It is interesting how after doing yoga practice for many years, people cannot maintain a higher state of awareness. The passionate energy repossesses its territory and ravishes the psyche.

I taught kundalini yoga in this body beginning in 1973 just after I learnt the method from Yogi Bhajan. One thing that keeps coming back to haunt me is the fact that even though some students practice, they still cannot maintain a high level of awareness. Kundalini rises and then sinks. We find that it resumes its normal course and does not adhere to elevated states. People get some higher awareness from the practice. They experience this but like a flash of lightning. I cannot expect a flash to illuminate through the night. It is a momentary sensation.

While for a senior yogi, a flash of lightning will persist through the night, for others it does no such thing. In fact, they may not appreciate it because of its instantaneous display. Their minds are not rapid enough to observe what it reveals in the dense entangling forest of physical existence.

This morning during breath infusion, Lahiri said that there should be a straight-through passage. At the time he peered through my subtle body from the head, through the neck, chest and lower torso. The passage was clear. There was no passionate energy, no bunching of passionate pleasure force. The clarifying mode was present.

What is the access to passion?

How is it that some students are saturated by it?

The universe has diverse energies. One's decision to make use of a certain type of energy, or one's indecision to make use of one type of energy, carries with it the results of that energy's impact on the psyche.

How should one avoid imbibing certain energies?

Whatever one does even if it is done under the auspices of the subconscious or unconscious mind, still the conscious observing self will carry the liability.

Even though physical nature influences someone to act, the same nature transfers the liability to the person who is influenced. Nature itself will not bear the consequences. It does not have the sensitivity for hazards.

Imagine a system like our cosmos. Think of the time in the future when the sun will explode. That will be the biggest nuclear explosion ever experienced around here for billions of years. Think of what is at stake and what will be totally demolished without a trace, without any leniency whatever, without compassion.

Think of the universal displacement which that will effect and very suddenly. But physical nature does not consider this. The assessment is ours to make. It is our experience because we have the sensitivity.

Breath Infusion Advanced

I was asked a question about the switch from *kapalabhati* to *bhastrika*, as to how it is done and as to when.

Students should be determined to stick to *kapalabhati* and should not worry about getting into the full breath method which is *bhastrika*. If one persists with the infusion, day after day, week after week, year after year, in time one will naturally graduate to *bhastrika*. It will happen.

What is the difference between *kapalabhati* and *bhastrika*?

It is this. In *kapalabhati* stress is placed on a forceful exhale. The inhale takes place spontaneously without getting any deliberate attention applied to it. One begins with this where one focuses only on the exhale and makes that as forceful as possible. There is no attention applied to the inhale for the reason of reserving some attentive energy to other matters, such as looking down into the subtle body, mentally compressing the energy which is infused, mentally directing that energy here or there, and maintaining the desired posture in which that particular sequence of breaths is held.

If initially the student does *bhastrika*, the practice will not be as effective because all or most of the attention energy will be invested in just the physical breathing process. That is not the aim of this practice. This process targets the subtle body. A certain amount of psychic tracking should be done.

As one does *kapalabhati* more and more, the forceful exhale will become a reflex. Naturally there will be shift of the attention given to the breathing where one will focus on the inhale to make that occur with emphasis but without disturbing the flow and sequence of the breath's entry or departure from the nostrils.

Sex-Cell Slavery in Yoga

All over the world there are sex slaves of various sorts in various situations. This is the history of humanity, where sexual exploitation is part of the scene. It is said that prostitution is the oldest profession. That may be contested with hunting, which is a more foundational instinct for food procurement. After all, if you have no food, you will not have the strength even to engage in sexually activity.

As it is in social life, so it is in yoga, because sex is a primal interest, but for totally different reasons.

Lahiri appeared during my practice this morning. He continued the lessons about the creation of a *yogaSiddha* body. It is a complex study.

This morning he showed that the sex yield of the various cells of the body, of everything besides the sexual organ / reproduction mechanism, remains stubbornly under confinement and in a non-release state except when given a command for release by the kundalini and only when the kundalini bridges to the sex organ chakra in the pubic area.

There is a special request which the kundalini makes before the non sex organ cells release their concentrated energy. Kundalini refuses to make this request to the cells unless the kundalini is focused into the sex organ chakra during sexual intercourse.

The student yogi has a problem with this natural system and should disrupt it but he/she must also cause it to be released freely without having a sexual impetus as its motive or receptor.

How to do this?

One must enlist the service of an advanced *yogaGuru*. One must know where one is located on the journey to siddha proficiency. Then one must endeavor in the practice for elevation.

Some aspects of this practice one can never figure on one's own. It is futile to think that all by oneself one can discover everything which is transcendental. That is not likely. Be reasonable. Get help from advanced practitioners.

In this practice during breath infusion after the student yogi removed the nutritional zone and caused the thighs to be freed from their impulsive allegiance to the sex organ area, the yogi does breath infusion into the central chest. Since the nutrition zone is no longer there, the energy finds itself in a clear passage in the center of the trunk. When enough of it accumulated there, this energy penetrates to the sides of the trunk, right and left of center. When this accumulates further and the trunk becomes saturated, there is a flash of energy where energy moves from the right and left into the center. This is a pleasure bliss force, the same pleasure force which would burst during a sexual climax experience, when it seems that every part of the body is saturated with bliss feeling which rushes to serve the sex organs.

The big difference is that the energy has no interest in the genitals. It does not go to the sex organ chakra. It is insensitive in this regard as if it does not know that the genitals are capable of a much-desired pleasure. It acts as one would before puberty when one is ignorant of sex indulgence. It has no self directive force which makes it rush to the sex organ climax central. It has no sense of reaching a fulfilment there. It bursts from the cells to reach the center of the trunk. It remains there oscillating back and forth.

When this happens, the yogi pulls the clash of energy in the center. He/She perceives a bunching of bliss bricks, like tiny translucent crystals rapidly moving and flashing bliss energy with insight.

This is a wonderful development because it means that the yogi will qualify for life in the highest astral worlds which are beyond the Swargaloka angelic environments.

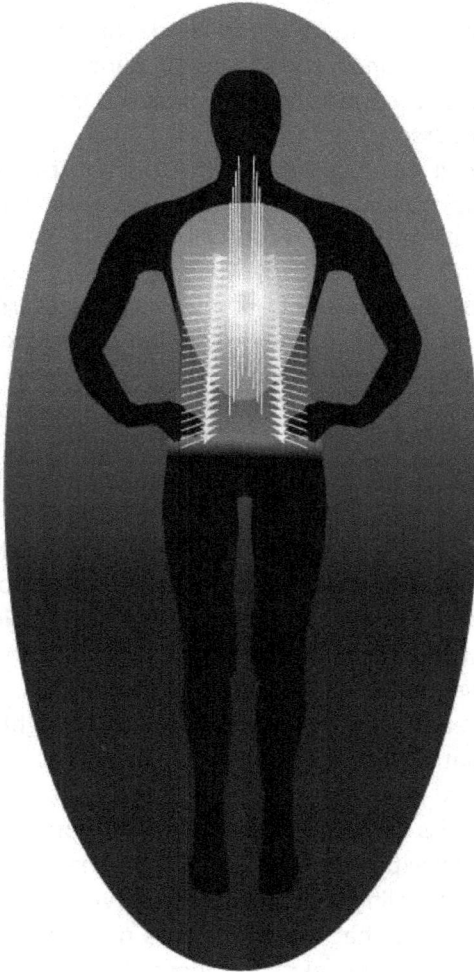

Death for a Yogi

I was asked recently about death for a yogi, regarding if there is something special a yogi does at the time of death.

Is there a mystique to it?

Are there magical moments?

Are there special techniques, which if practiced, would transport the yogi to a desired realm or a special state of consciousness?

Killing the body by depriving it of breath is one solution for those who feel that they should dictate when the body would die. People kill their bodies in the so-called suicide attempts which are more or less an effort to eliminate their stressed conditions. Providence however does not allow the death of a psychology merely by the death of a physical body.

The question stands:

Does one think that one's psychology will be eliminated merely by physical death?

If not, then killing the body with intentions to destroy the psychology would be a futile effort. The disappointment will be to find that the psychological version of the person continues to exist after its physical aspect perishes.

The yoga I teach is not concerned with killing the physical form by depriving it of air. There is such a method but I do not practice it and that disqualifies me from teaching it or giving practical instructions in that regard.

My system has to do with increasing the fresh air content in the body, in all parts of it. The objective is to affect the subtle body, and to allow the physical one to go through whatever changes are required in the process of infusing the subtle form.

At the time of death, the student is required to do whatever he/she can do according to the specific circumstances. Natural death, or even accidental sudden killing of the physical body, is in the hands of fate. A student should not set out to take control of destiny but should learn how to best make use of the flow of providence in which he/she finds the self to be.

Suppose the body is killed suddenly in an automobile accident, or in some other disaster, obviously the student cannot apply breath infusion or any controlled discipline, at least until after being released from the body. After finding the self in the astral form with the kundalini in it, being permanently disconnected from the physical system, the student will have to adjust to whatever condition he/she finds the self to be in. Having lost the foothold in the history of this physical existence, the self must adjust, and will do that in an efficient or inefficient way, depending on what it cultivated in familiarity with the astral situations.

It would hinge on what the student accomplished in previous practice. He/She could rely on whatever psychic proficiency and insight was gained before the mishap.

For those who pass away with painful terminal diseases, that is definitely undesirable especially if those conditions lasted for years before leaving the body. In any case, fate is fate. It enforces itself. A student who must deal with a terminal disease, should grip the philosophy of yoga and adapt the practice to do as much as possible even while suffering from a terminal condition.

Fortunate are those whose aged bodies remains healthy even in old age, even up to the point of death, even if some vital organ malfunctions. These students can practice, until at last the time will come when it is obvious that he/she can no longer function through the physical form.

It is then that the student should be ready to be deprived of the body, just like when a bird finds the door of its cage to be open and it flies into the blue yonder into the freedom life.

When the body is to die naturally, as people say, the student will find that he/she exhausted the impetus to remain in that particular social role. Then time and again there will be experiences where the student feels as if the astral body can permanently disconnect from the physical one and not be reattached to it, as if the coreSelf has the power to keep the subtle body from synchronizing into the physical one. This will be a new power, a new feeling of authority. Taking this seriously, the student should wait for an opportunity when the adhesiveness between the subtle and physical bodies is lessened. Then he/she should be in the astral existence with no urge to adhere to the physical system.

Yogic Lust-free Bliss Force

Here the concern is not with lust as it is conventionally considered, not with sexual lust, not with power lust, but with raw lust force which may be applied to sex, reproduction, political power, social seniority or privilege. It is not with morality or the lack of it, not with modesty or exhibitionist needs, not with any other person but the yogi/yogini himself/herself.

Here we do not work with energy which is polarized in the psyche. This is with energy which is on its way to the polarization glands in the body. This energy was not processed through the hormone glands.

In kundalini yoga, the student begins by learning how to handle and transmute hormone energy. The idea at that stage is that he/she will sublimate the sexual energy which is produced by the sex glands. Once they confine the sex energy and breath-infuse it, it becomes attracted to the kundalini lifeForce. From the groin area, it arcs to the base chakra which is the hideout of kundalini. As when a woman is at leisure in her bathroom and a strange man enters and touches her, she becomes alarmed and may run into her living room, so when the infused sexual hormone energy arcs to the base chakra, the kundalini tries to run from it. To restrict kundalini so that it cannot run here or there but only climb the corridor of the spinal column, the yogi applies certain contractions to close the other entrances and exits.

It may take weeks, months, years or even lives, to master the process of getting kundalini up the spine as it is motivated and chased by the infused breath energy. Eventually when there is proficiency in that practice, the yogi gets a higher instruction from the yogaGurus.

This is when he is told that the nutrition/reproduction system needs to be reconfigured, so that no sexually polarized energy is formed. Once an energy is produced, it becomes necessary to regulate it. But if it is not produced, there is no need to monitor or reform it.

Sexual energy has two composites:
- reproduction potential
- sex-pleasure potential

For reasons of its own, nature connected these. They appear in confusion as one energy. A yogi should sort this to see which portion results in reproduction and which is a pleasure-yield.

Still even after sorting, the problem remains about how it is generated and why it compels the psyche to display its expressions.

Which glands do the charging of the basic energy? Can those charges not be formed in the psyche in the first place?

What would it be like if the reproduction or sex pleasure energy-charging systems were demolished?

Would there be any bliss energy left?

How would that feel?

Could I become accustomed to that, or as addicted to that, as I am to the sex-pleasure force?

When a diabetic is advised to refrain from sugar but to eat foods, which with sufficient time for digestion, will provide the energy which sugar provided but in a non-destructive way, can that patient comply and feel happy about it, just as happy as he was when he gorged sugary foods?

When doing breath infusion, advanced students may lift the energy which is extracted from the gut and take this energy before it is processed into hormonal energy. The ascetic may also lift energy which was formed in the thighs, but before such energy is transported near or into the sexual glands.

When this energy is infused and compressed by rapid breathing, it will be shrunk into a crystalline concentrate. Somewhere in the trunk of the subtle body, this will be felt as a brick of bliss force, like a transparent granite brick which has translucent colors

The yogi should infuse more energy into it. He should do this until it implodes or disintegrates and its energy content becomes scattered in every direction in the psyche. This is a bliss happiness, except that the yogi will notice that it is devoid of reproduction/lust potency and is not as exciting, nor as compelling as the lust potency.

Meditation Results / The Long Wait

One of the most frustrating things about meditation practice is the long wait for results, at least for consistent results. A student may become disheartened. He may abandon the practice, going away to live a socially approved way.

Who is the blame for this?

No one!

Recently I got a kriya technique which is part of the system which some yogis follow when they are students in the physical world aspiring for *yogaSiddha* forms. This is a procedure of naad focus.

First one must be situated in naad sound in the back of the subtle head. Then one must wait in that sound for as long as is necessary for the naad light to appear. This light has a goldish glow. It is a glow only. It does not blare. It does not sparkle. It simply is low effulgence in the form of a glow.

In this light the student should sit and wait.

Question is:

Wait for how long?

Answer is:

Wait for as long as it takes for the *chit akash* sky of consciousness to appear. This means waiting for days, weeks, months, years or lives even.

Lahiri, who gave the procedure, originally said it would take six months for *chit akash* to appear. But for me it will take more than six months because of a failure to follow the procedure to the letter day by day.

However, there should be full confidence that it would appear.

Off and on, a student will experience *chit akash*, even if it is momentarily. Based on that, the student should keep the faith in the experience and wait for the transformation to be made.

Lack of Sleep

Are you troubled by a lack of sleep?

Do you take sleeping pills or herbal remedies for causing sleep?

For the purpose of kriya yoga, sleeping drugs are unsatisfactory. Kundalini yoga is disrupted by such drugs. It is not recommended. Besides the onset of menopause in females, sleep deprivation for whatever reason is counterproductive in kundalini yoga and meditation.

Every student should avoid any stress or anxiety which causes sleeplessness.

Caffeine and other stimulants are counterproductive to the aims of yoga and meditation. These should not be taken. Drugs affect the working of the kundalini lifeForce and disallow the yogi from gaining direct control over the operations in the psyche. As it is nature has the larger proportion of the motivations in the physical world. If one relies on drugs, nature will get an even bigger percentage of control.

Is compulsive thinking getting you down at night, such that it causes anxiety and causes the brain to be reactive, thus keeping one awake on the physical side?

Are you afraid of the power of the mind so that you cannot confront it head on, and smash its dominance when it is time to rest?

Passionate Energy

Today in meditation, I did the *wait in naad light* kriya. This involves first doing breath infusion, but it has to be done without reference to the conventional hormone system in the body. In this system the hormone system which we were endowed with at birth is disrupted so that instead of using hormones after they are manufactured by various glands in the body, the yogi uses the materials which will be used by the glands before the glands transform those materials into hormones.

This is done by the grace of breath infusion where one can pull the nutrients which are absorbed through the gut system directly from the gut itself instead of using them after they are sent from the gut to the hormone manufacturing glands.

The advantage of this method is that the energy charge of the nutrients before they go to the glands is relatively neutral. These will help to produce a neutral and very clean bliss force, which when surcharged with breath infusion, will be accommodating to the idea of reaching the *chit akash* sky of consciousness.

The main impediment for reaching the *chit akash* sky of consciousness is the passionate energy in the psyche. This means the essential passion force, not just its peculiar applications like sex energy.

Some people condemn sex energy because it is a primary highlight of the passionate force. Still, if one destroys the sexual capacity of a body, still one will have to deal with the passionate influence through its other facilities.

As infants before puberty, we did not have sex to deal with and still we were not self-realized and did not reach the sky of consciousness. As elderly adults we lose libido sex drive and interest, but we do not naturally become self-realized?

This means that sex has nothing to do with it in the final analysis even though sex is useful in locating passion, in identifying it, and in it studying how it confiscates the reproductive systems of these life forms.

A lack of sexual indulgence on the physical level does not mean that one accomplished celibacy in the full sense. It may or may not mean that, all depending on the log of conscious and unconscious sexual activities. Reserved, retired or even dormant sexual capacity will effectively undermine any celibate claims.

After sex is sublimated, if the ascetic can do that, then he/she will be confronted with the passionate energy, in one or more of its channels, like in its channel of desire, or lack of fulfillment of desire, or anger because of disappointment and/or frustration, or possessiveness even towards good results in the cultural medium and to so many other avenues which the passionate influence will commandeer.

Sex is the easiest thing to target because it is such a blatant demonstration of passion but what about the *not so obvious* routes which it uses?

So long as the passionate force is not routed, there is no hope for reaching the *chit akash* situation. With so many reputed gurus as the source of mystic procedures, doing this kriya or that kriya, is a waste of time if the passionate force remains in place and can do its covert or overt routings.

Can a student recognize the passionate energy when it is not sexually surcharged?

Can he/she free himself/herself from the idea that sex alone is passion, because otherwise that student cannot make advancement beyond the elementary teachings of yoga?

Once the passionate force is rooted, the breath infusion process makes a jump to a higher level of practice. It is the same practice but the results change for the yogi. The bliss force is clean and pure, seemingly neutral and somewhat tasteless from the old passion taste perspective. It has sensual variance but not when it is rated from the lusty position which has passion at its base.

Naad and *Chit Akash*

Once you are in naad sound and it comforts you, it becomes the parent or caring lover. The next step is to wait in that situation until the naad light dawns. Naad light seeks the yogi. It pronounces itself to him/her. When it comes the yogi will know because it will be there in a blink, where suddenly he finds himself to be in and to see the glow of light in a chamber of silence, in a night glow, a dim golden glow.

Once that happens the yogi will stay there, in a happy mood, like a child who found a toy, which was lost so long ago. He will not be excited. He will not declare to the world that he found it. He is selfish and does not want anyone to know that he has it. It is a secret, very private.

Staying in that naad light, the yogi will remain in that dimly lit chamber with that golden glow, waiting and waiting for who knows what, waiting because the *yogaGuru* said to do so.

Then after waiting in every session of meditation, for weeks, months or years, as the case may be, the *yogaGuru* will direct the student to pull *chit akash* energy. This means to pull it into the naad light chamber.

This is all feeling, nothing visual, no other sense is involved but the one of feeling, of knowing that *chit akash* energy is present even though it is not visible.

On that basis the student pulls that energy. It is satisfying. The yogi is in a cozy chamber where everything is neat and appropriate. He is fed every which way simultaneously to the fullest, continuously to his heart's content.

Passionless-Content Bliss Force

During breath infusion session this morning, I considered how students could experience and appreciate the passionless bliss force. Even if one has the experience, one may not recognize it, no more than a sugar addict could recognize the sweet taste in a boiled potato.

Science tells us that there is sugar in a boiled potato but who can taste it? The sense of taste denies the evidence. It is left to our muscular performance and brain operations to show indirect proof which supports the conclusion of science.

Even then we are left with the taste demands of the psyche which reject indirect evidence. If you cannot taste it, what is the use of the sugar in a potato?

A similar dilemma occurs for yoga students where they desire the bliss energy with the passion content and fail to recognize, much less appreciate, the bliss energy when it is not laced with passion.

To some students the passionless content bliss experience is similar to that bland flat-tasting potato which was boiled, not fried, which had no salt, not even a tat of butter, nothing, served like that, tasteless and disgusting to the eye.

Today I examined this situation, hoping to have a recommendation. I know that some students do not appreciate the passionless content bliss energy during breath infusion practice. This is important because it allows a jump from these lower astral regions to the *chit akash*. It is everything to a *chit akash* yogi, a great secret, kept hidden in his mind, as he travels here and there in this world, noticing how stunted other human beings are.

Pleasure addicts, who are really passion slaves, come to do yoga. When they are advised to leave aside the passion enjoyment in any or all of its phases, they peer into nowhere as if to say,

"What will be left if passion is removed?"

During breath infusion the passionless content energy arose while I was midway through the session. It was like feeling micro pixels of translucent neutral bliss energy of various hues, like ice crystals packed tightly in a container but in specific parts of the trunk of the subtle body only. These are ice crystals with no cooling influence with a slight temperature difference where they can hardly be perceived in reference to the body's temperature.

Because of having abstract perception, I detected this and focused on it.

This was clean bliss energy, totally without the passionate touch, without a bewildering and intoxicating influence, without the compulsive in-demand happiness which passion so freely affords.

On one side of consciousness, I enjoyed this and was nourished by it, but on the other side it yielded nothing and seemed not to exist. I considered how I could convince students to locate this energy, feed on it and get satisfaction from it.

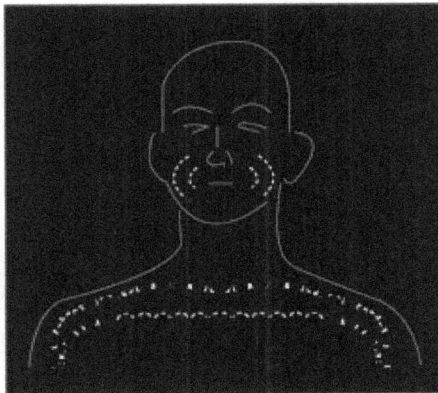

The bliss energy puffed the cheeks. First it rose into the shoulders, filling that area. Then it spread to the cheeks and caused pockets of soft fluffy energy. These inflated and puffed more, reaching a final stage without bursting.

Bloated Bliss Body

One may from time to time experience a bloated subtle body which is higher than the conventional astral form. It is a higher body. The experience of it tells the student so. No external evidence is necessary. The student loses all doubts about the possibility of higher forms and existence in what is other than the physical, existence which is durable in reference to the physical.

When the student either deliberately or accidentally gets the subtle body infused with sufficient subtle energy, there may be a transit into the bliss body which is devoid of the mundane passionate force. This gives a new experience. The student learns of the possibility of a life which has no trauma, a divine situation.

Small Mental Commands

In meditation practice, one may crave the big issues. Students like to hassle a teacher for methods to deal with the big achievement and stubborn negative habits which are difficult to overcome.

There is another vital part of yoga which has to do with identifying the small issues, like mental commands in the mind which pertain to seemingly trivial things but which one should be wary about and should tightly control.

Here is an example:

Today after a session of exercises, when I walked to enter a building to do meditation, the sound of someone's footsteps was heard. Immediately, there was a tiny whiny mental command in the head of the subtle body. It said this:

"Check to see who walks."

I immediately sent a counter-command which said this,

"It is not our business to check the walker. Our concern is to walk to the place for meditation and to keep interest in the resulting state of consciousness after the breath infusion session."

As soon as the reply energy of that was released, the command to observe the walker disappeared. That was a seeming little event but it is vital in this practice, to catch the mind in its inquiry-interest game when that contravenes yoga, even when it is a minor deviation. If the yogi permits tiny commands, how can he/she expect to resist the huge ones? Be practical. Arrest the tiny ones. Shrink and terminate them. Gradually over time, that will give confidence to tackle big issues.

The big achievements are a problem for sure but the little ones have value. If one successfully stifles the little agitations, one can develop self confidence that one can control the mind.

Desires

Desires keep us coming back into the physical world but desires are sneaky. They undermine a yogi's aspirations to stop the cycle of rebirth. This is done in a very simple way which is that a yogi gets to feeling that he/she can become liberated by a simple calculation of willpower against physical existence.

Unfortunately, willpower has little to do with how a living being is conditioned. Therefore, its application cannot reverse something which it did not create. One did not become conditioned in physical existence because one wanted to be in this situation. It came about spontaneously and with sufficient non-willpower where one's willpower is irrelevant. First one must exist here before one can use willpower. Therefore, the idea that one can totally cease the use of willpower is irrational. But this idea does salve a person's self-esteem. It may even remove the depression which comes on when one realizes how helpless one really is.

There are many people who are too eager to grant freedom from physical existence by execution of willpower commands. They fail to take into account the subconscious and the very powerful non-observational energies which run the psyche covertly and make us do things which we would not commit ourselves to if we were free from subconscious influence.

Desire is mostly dormant, hidden from the observing consciousness. Offtimes one becomes aware of a desire after it manifests, when it is full blown, when one cannot stop it because it already happened or because it is so far developed that one cannot stop it from manifesting but must look on like a bystander who is powerless to stop a crime which occurs within his/her reach.

The dangerous desires are the submerged ones which were pushed into the subconscious because of the enforcement of moral values. This enforcement may be applied by the government, the society or even by the person himself or herself.

Self-righteous people speak to others about the value of morality but they do not understand what happens when a desire is suppressed. In the kriya yoga system however, a student must confront the submerged urges.

Is the enforcement of moral values beneficial?

It is because we cannot run a society without some agreement on acceptable social behavior. There will always be exceptions to any rule but all the same, there must be rules. Even the animals have their methods which are enforced in their packs and groups.

Still a yogi should go inside, locate hidden desires and examine them carefully. A yogi cannot lack insight like others who have no way of knowing what is submerged within the nature. A yogi is required to check within the psyche, find the hidden desires and remove them if possible.

If they cannot be removed, at least the yogi should know what they are, and know their power over the psyche and know why they cannot be dissolved.

Desire will cause the yogi to take another body. It is not important if the desire is the yogi's wilful fantasy or if it is imposed by nature or was infiltrated from the psyche of another conditioned entity.

Once the desire is in the nature, it will act. It will set providential forces into motion which will cause it to manifest now or in a million or even a trillion years.

Brick Energy

When during breath infusion if you find that there is a brick like structure full of pranic energy, this is an advanced stage of practice. Keep the mental focus on that lump of energy. Do not shift the mind from it. Keep the posture in which you discovered it. Do the breath infusion while focusing the breath energy into the brick or lump. Keep pushing the energy in until you feel that the breath energy is no longer being absorbed. Then stop the breathing but keep the attention on the brick as you apply the locks tightly, compressing the brick, squeezing the infused breath energy into it.

Then begin breathing rapidly again, infusing energy into it. Do this repeatedly, until it feels that the brick dissolved or that it exploded or imploded. Keep infusing air into it in sessions where you do not let up, you do not release the locks except to do more rapid breathing. Keep pressing in on the brick on all sides, spherically, until it implodes and then moves outwards in all directions to every part of the psyche.

The formation of these energy bricks may or may not be related to kundalini. If they are related you will know it as the brick will try to connect to kundalini in the spine. If it is not related to kundalini, the brick will make no effort to reach kundalini. It will instead be involved in the breath energy with concerns only for the area or zone where it occured.

Glass Bliss

Sometimes while doing breath infusion, when the student is lucky, there will be a bliss-energy stack in the trunk of the subtle body. It will be such that it may or may not include the neck. The head where kundalini may burst on other occasions will not have the kundalini energy spreading through it.

It will seem that the subtle trunk is filled with bliss pixels as if randomly stacked. In some experiences these will seem like long slivers of glass bliss pixels thrown randomly in a stack with the bliss feeling up and down, in and out, with a sparkle happiness texture which causes a silent bliss laugh in the trunk of the psyche.

The yogi may exclaim internally,

What is this?

How is this?

These experiences give the yogi some idea of different textures of existence so that the he/she could become convinced to permanently abandon the trauma-saturated levels in the lower astral places and in the physical dimension.

Samadhi with *Chit akash*

Lahiri gave a *samadhi* draw practice. This is a light in the life of a yogi. Advanced yogis find this to be a natural and easy process. In some reading about the lives of previous yogis from the kriya lineage we heard of this process but when we practiced years ago, we got no results from it.

Looking back, I determined that there was a missing ingredient. This may be compared to a medicine which is manufactured by a nontechnical company which does not have the exact formula and which has no access to chemical process for the active ingredient. Yet they may manufacture a pill and sell that to the public which has no way of telling what is missing in the cheap medication.

In retrospect the missing ingredient is a thorough *pranayama* practice with full removal of the *apana* carbon dioxide from the physical system as well as its counterpart removal from the subtle body (*sukshma sharira*).

It so happens that unless this process of inner energy cleanup is done to the subtle body, the process of meditation, is useless for all practical purposes.

There are various *pranayama* practices for that, but the one used is *bhastrika* breath infusion *pranayama*.

Is there any other process?

Sure, there is. We hear of various types of breath regulation, particular the *anuloma-viloma* process, being done for hours on end by some ancient yogis. They entered *samadhi* and experience the *chit akash*.

Use whichever method one is comfortable with but it must result in reaching the *chit akash*, so that while in the chamber of the individual psyche, one is surrounded with a spiritual texture of energy. One feels that a spiritual bliss force which is devoid of the passionate impetus, oozes into the coreSelf. Once this is achieved, one sits tight in a miniature subtle body and feels the enrichment from the *chit akash*.

There is no looking at the third eye, no looking out of the psyche, no projection, nor imagination, nor visualization, no mantras, nothing, just the bare coreSelf *(atma)* and the sky of consciousness energy silently oozing.

Mantras may be used prior to tapping into the *chit akash* but only if those sounds were given by an advanced yogi who imparted the mantra and the deity involved. The mantra must have the vibration of the contact between the yogaGuru and that deity.

For instance, a mantra may be given which carries the vibration of Shiva, but which Shiva is it? Did the *yogaGuru* actually meet the particular Shiva? Is this mantra a hoax from a guru who says that he is Shiva and that the student is Shiva and that everybody is Shiva and there is no Shiva who is Absolute above the other yogis?

Which person Shiva is the mantra connected to?

Different Teachings / Different Students?

The question arises from time to time, as to why certain students get specific or confidential information.

Is there favoritism in spiritual groups?

Why is it that in the presence of certain students, a teacher divulges more information even in a public setting?

Why does the teacher give special or confidential information only in private to a certain student?

If spiritual life is for one and all, if there is oneness of all ultimately, why the distinction for certain students?

Does God have favorites?

Is God unable to equalize his/her relationship to one and all?

Each student is qualified by a different background from many previous lives. These past life energies are present in the psyche and attract to the student certain conditions of existence which cause the disparity.

The disparity is real because the energies from the past lives serve as the foundation of the present one. To remove the past life foundation, one would have to remove the past lives and that is not possible. One cannot reorder history. Going forward we can make adjustments but only in so far as we are allowed by providence.

When someone's hair turned grey, he dyed it. Then he resumed black hair but only superficially. The fact is that he could not alter the biological process which dictated greyness. Similarly, one cannot alter the past. The effects of that in the present life may be superficially affected but hardly can anyone fundamentally overhaul it.

A yoga teacher may well be a magician but that does not mean that he can reorder the history of a particular student. Those who come with a background of credits from the past lives, may get preferential treatment on that basis and on that basis only. Even if the teacher graces someone, if that person does not have the past life historic foundation, the favor of the teacher will not stick. The preferential treatment of the teacher cannot be the only cause of anyone's advancement. There must be a past life or past existence foundation which is independent of the teacher's favor.

Some students are given remedial training by a teacher. That seems to other students, who are longing for specific attention from the teacher, to be special treatment. These students, who long for attention, may take actions to attract the interest of the teacher so that they can fulfill their need for relation.

This is of course a very harsh regard for the teacher. If they persist, such students may even cause needy students to be deprived of the remedial training they so desperately need.

Other students who are very perceptive may see special energies being transmitted to new students who have no background of spiritual practice in the present life but who nevertheless attract and somehow retain spiritual infusions from the teacher.

These observant students usually fail to see the causal basis for these transmissions. They are annoyed or confused when witnessing the energy exchanges. Such relationships are also known as *shaktipat* transmissions. They are legendary in yoga circles. Students even beg a teacher for these graces.

What is the premise of these relationships?

One way to look at this is to understand that physical existence is the very least of the existential environments, but in physical existence other levels can be accessed either deliberately or causelessly as manifested to specific persons in specific times and places.

A mystic teacher may transmit an energy spontaneously or deliberately, or he/she may have no control over the transmission. There is a story in the life of Jesus Christ, where a woman touched his clothing and energy left his psyche and entered hers. Even Jesus, that special son of God, was surprised that his energy left his form and went into the woman.

A teacher cannot in all instances control what he gives another person either as a teaching or as a grace energy. Much of that is done impulsively or spontaneously. Some of it may be done on behalf of a teacher who is not physically present and who from subtle domains penetrates someone and compels that agent to act.

There were times when teaching yoga, where suddenly I found my body, my voice, everything, acting on behalf of a teacher who was long departed and even one whom I had no formal connection with.

I may favor someone in particular, being compelled to transmit energy or instruction to that person. Even though physically I alone was present with the student, it may be that psychically, others, were in attendance. They were instrumental in the transmission, using my body to issue their energies.

Again, the question of ---*Who owns the body?* --- is relevant.

Part 3

Mean Vicious Cut-Throat Yogi

Lahiri discussed a system of ridding the subtle body of the lower zone which is below the navel. This area of the body is a trouble area for those yogis who want to attain a *yogaSiddha* form. This is because the survival complex of the subtle body is reinforced by its lower trunk, by the three basic chakras which are the base *muladhara* chakra, the sex chakra and the navel region.

The obvious culprit in this is the navel chakra but as it stands, the big thug in the matter is the sex chakra. The hidden gang lord is the muladhara base chakra.

There is no point in trying to kill the hidden gang lord because he is protected by the big thug and by the culprit planner. First tackle the culprit. Report if you put him out of commission.

In this process when the student tries to deal with the navel chakra, it is realized that one does not have the power to deal with it. Besides, it is abstract which means that it cannot be targeted. If I cannot locate something there is no question of controlling or restricting it.

That leaves me with the sex chakra as the target. But this chakra has intelligence. It is not a dumb force. Fighting it, subduing it, will take intelligence and endeavor. It will not be easy. Until that is achieved, there is no question of conquest of either the base or navel chakras.

Lahiri explained that the bottom of the subtle body, from the navel into the thighs, needs be cleared of the hormone energy. Something has to be done to remove this influence. Most of all, the way of the system, which is to use gravity to funnel hormones downwards, must be reversed.

How to do that?

Breath infusion lifting of the energy as soon as it is extracted by the intestinal nutrient-extraction mechanism.

In any war, if one can sabotage the supplies of the enemy, one can cripple his operations. Big cannons are useless if ammunition is not supplied to them. In as much as the big thug, the sex chakra, has high intelligence, if somehow, we can intercept or disrupt its hormone supplies, we could subdue it.

What is the use of a strong muscular body if you cannot feed it?

There are two effective methods for crippling the sex chakra. These are by infusing energy into its hormonal supply and depriving it of hormones in the first place. Novice students only have the hormone infusion process available to them. Depriving it of hormones is complete out of their scope because the kundalini established that system secretly. It is a covert operation which novices lack knowledge of.

Novices have the method of going into the hormone ammunition dump to light an explosive charge. Then they run before the place explodes. Unfortunately, some novices are subdued when they attempt to do this. Or they are caught red-handed by the enemy and punished fittingly. These return to the yogaGuru crying that they tried to disrupt the operations of the dreaded sex chakra and things reversed as a result.

They cry out like this:

What is the matter guru?

Why did this fail?

How was I captured?

Why was I compelled to indulge again?

I should cease yoga and give myself to the enemy.

Advanced students are no longer interested in carrying a charge into the ammunition dump of the sex chakra. They prefer to intercept the supply train of that chakra and confiscate the ammunition which was to be supplied to it. But there is a reason why the novices cannot use this method. It is this:

If the sex chakra is not supplied with hormones, its pleasure-yielding feature will be disabled and that will depress the novice.

Why?

Because the novice is addicted to the passion bliss force which that chakra yields. He/She agreed to forgo this force in genital expression but not altogether. He/She still wants to get the pleasure from this force, except that there is an agreement to get it in the central spine and head of the subtle body rather than in the genitals.

Advanced yogis, having gone mad, are no longer interested in exploiting this passion-bliss force, hence they can boldly stop the hormone transports which travel from the navel to the sex chakra. Intercepting these transports and confiscating them, the advanced yogi no longer has to deal with the impulsive sex chakra.

After doing this for a time, the yogi will hear a loud sound emanating from the base chakra. This happens because eventually this chakra will come to understand that something grievous, something heart-rending, occurred. It will then speak like this from within the psyche:

"Some crazy person intercepted my energy train."

"Where is the mad fool who did that?"

After hearing this, the yogi will retreat into the head of the subtle body to get instructions from the yogaGuru. However, in doing this, the yogi will not forget to keep the uplift of the hormone energy so that not a drop of it goes below the navel.

The base chakra, as the hidden supervisor, can do nothing if it is not supplied with hormone power. That is the key issue.

There is a reason why some ancient yogis starved their physical bodies. It was for the purpose of bringing the base chakra to its knees, completely subduing it, ending its control of the psyche.

Kundalini-less Breath Infusion

Recently a student asked for clarification about how the breath infusion rhythm changes during the practice of *bhastrika* or *kapalabhati pranayama*. This relates to the tone of the breathing, the sound of it as it is heard by a bystander.

In this case, this breathing is being done without respect to the kundalini lifeForce, so that there is infusion into the system but it is not going to strike the kundalini necessarily. This is a more advanced practice which is perfected after kundalini was sufficiently reformed and is pulled into the brain, where its addiction to being near the sex organ chakra, and the waste operation of the colon, is removed.

Pay attention to the word **addiction**. This does not necessarily mean that the sexual activities, or the excretory activities of the body will cease. These activities may go on but the addictive tendency in relation would have ceased.

At first air is infused into the lungs just as it would be done in the case of targeting the kundalini but in this case the air goes where it will go and usually it will form into a pixelated brick shape somewhere in the trunk of the subtle body. This will become saturated with fresh air and with fresh astral energy in the subtle body.

At a certain point while breathing, the yogi/yogini will realize that because they are fully saturated, the cells no longer absorb air. At this point the yogi will begin a new session of breaths either in the same or in another posture. Then he/she will attack the brick either by forcing air around it and into it, or by forcing air from the center of it outward.

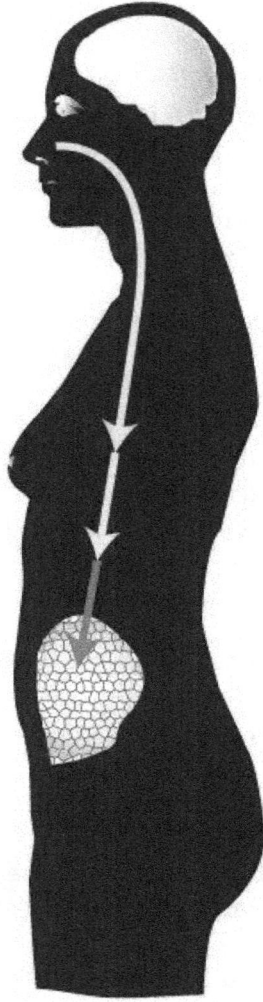

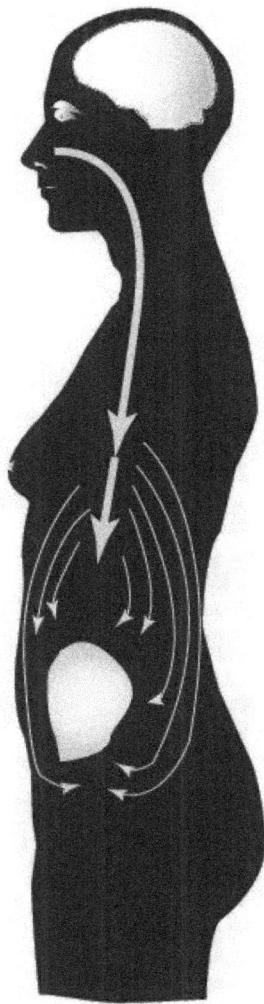

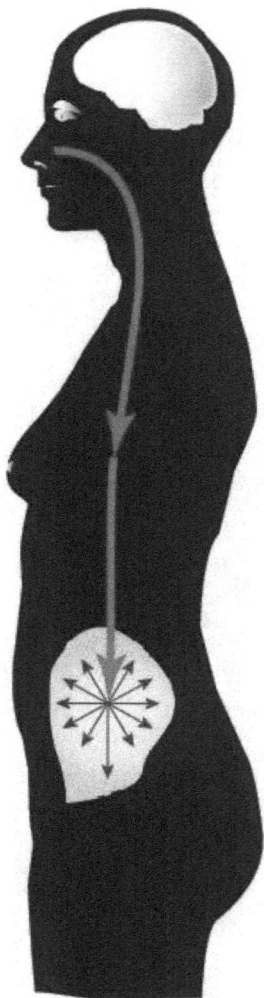

There are two basis outlays when working with kundalini in the practice of breath infusion. These are:

- Rise of kundalini through the spine into the head
- Infusion of energy elsewhere in the psyche with definite energizations in those areas so that the student knows what happened.

Even if the kundalini is not involved, breath infusion may of its own accord cause an energy burst to occur. Be keen on this. When the breath is pushed through the pubic curve and the accumulated energy arcs over to kundalini, it will ascend through the spine if the locks are fittingly applied. Or it may do so even if the locks are not applied.

But consider that the breath energy may not transit in that way. It may accumulate in some other part of the psyche. The point is that there may be no kundalini arousal. Kundalini may not be energized by the infused energy but that energy may energize some other part of the psyche, so that there is an energy burst or an energy compaction.

Kundalini may also avoid the spinal passage and rise through the front of the body in some way, or through the sides or down through the thighs and feet. Be alert for these variations. Abandon stereotyping concepts which will stunt progression.

Practice with a free and open mind. Observe what happens and not what should occur based on theories and dogma.

Desire Dictates

One feature which is dear to the heart is cherished desires. Like for example when I was nine years of age, I had a fondness for a girl who was about the same age. My desire was to be with her always.

Wherefrom such a desire?

At the time I did not care to research this. Now some fifty plus years after, it is hard to review the forces of the situation. Who knows what those forces were and from where they originated?

Within the last week, I was in an astral world which is adjacent to this physical situation. A woman I know met me to discuss the possibility of my travelling with her.

She said,

"It would be nice to travel the way you do, going from place to place, seeing different locations. I wish I could go with you. Do you think that in some life, I will have the opportunity?"

I replied,

"That is an unreasonable desire considering that providence is the supreme facilitator. To ask providence to arrange that is a large order. How do you see that providence would arrange this universe to manifest that desire? How would that affect everything else?

"What planets would be moved into which orbits?

"What would the sun have to do to cause that to happen as you conceive of it?"

She replied,

"I do not know but I dearly wish for it. I find myself telling myself that it will happen."

Then I explained,

"From other experiences which you had in this life, you must know that desires carry a contrary energy within them, such that when they manifest they do so in part only with things which a person dislikes, things which were not part of what the person planned.

"How will you deal with that?

"Traveling is difficult and full of uncertainty. Perhaps living at one place, with sufficient income, is better. Desire dictates what will happen except that usually we have partial insight into what will manifest. Sugar and spice make all things nice but it also destroys the teeth."

Astral Invasion into Meditation

This morning during a good session of meditation, in which I did some techniques introduced by Lahiri, I had a sudden presence in the psyche chamber. My deceased mother's astral body entering into the meditation space.

Suddenly I heard an old song being sung. It is the song known as *Old Man River*.

Even though she did not sing, it was transmitted through space by her. In that astral place one can, based on memory of a sound, transmit it without speaking. When it is transmitted it seems that it is the original sound.

After this my mother smiled and greeted me as her son. She asked about the possibilities of getting another body. She questioned about the grandchildren she acquired through my body. I told her whatever little I knew of them.

She asked about an aunt of mine, who was departed and who also required an embryo. I told her what I knew of that person's whereabouts. Then she left. My meditation resumed.

The mystery of this encounter is how she gained entry into a very advanced level of my psyche during that meditation but that is part of the story about social rights and how people who are desperate and departed, exercise any type of leverage they can when they are disembodied.

Some people who were very kind may reach a point of desperation and then become invasive and demanding for getting the next birth opportunity.

Advancement with Disciples / Yogeshwarananda

Yogeshwarananda visited the practice session today. He commented that I had not reached a deadline. This was in reference to a kriya process which by now I should complete but did not due to pressing concerns from disruptive circumstances.

I asked him if he could assist to advance the progress but he remarked that what slowed it was what needs to be up-ended to make the progress solid.

After this he checked a few parts of my psyche, particularly the naad cave where I go during meditation to do that kriya process. He did not give recommendations. He made no criticism.

He was all smiles. He spoke about what happened at the end of his most recent life, where he left his ashram and books with disciples. He said that lucky for him he was not discovered early on. Early on, he had a good run on the practice as well as no disciples to care for.

There were a few students with me during the meditation session. He said this.

"Who is this one? Who is that one? I guess you can handle this. Disciples are problematic on the spiritual path. There are issues with them. I was lucky. I got out soon after I was discovered. Now on the astral planes, there is, relatively speaking, complete freedom to dodge disciples and potential followers.

"Who needs them?

"Are they sincere?

"Do they think it is a game?

"Can you advance just as quickly when you have disciples?"

I then announced that he was present, saying that others may take help if he permitted.

He was there during my exercise session before the meditation as well. Recently I did not see him for some time, for months, actually. It is auspicious to be with a great yogi. There is no better happiness for a progressive student than to be with an accomplished yogi, who recently pioneered a spiritual process.

Naad Chamber

Meditation this morning was in naad sound and in the naad chamber which develops after one was saturated into naad sound and became subjected to and claimed by naad light, as its little infant to protect.

Imagine a scene where in a jungle in which wild animals prowl, I am left alone to fend for myself. I am two days old. I cannot defend myself. I cannot feed my mouth. I cannot walk away. Whatever little movement I am capable of is just enough to alert the ants in the vicinity that by sheer good luck a soft food source came their way.

The ants discover me. They pinch pieces of my flesh. The only thing in my power is my voice. I cry piteously.

Out of nowhere because of good luck, a forester hears me. He comes to the location of my voice, discovers me, brushes the ants away and picks me up.

At this state of the relationship with naad, it is like that for me, where at first when I heard naad, I had to put myself into it, plunge into it, be attracted to it, stay with it, avoid being torn away from attentiveness to it.

Then I reached a stage where naad claimed me as its child. Then it claimed me as its dependent lover. Then it claimed me outright as its responsibility above and beyond relationships.

Then there was the emergence of naad light which was a golden glow of light in the subtle head. Then there is that golden glow in the chamber, a vast cave where I was kept by naad light and sound as one who is protected from mental and emotional harassment.

Secret Mantras

The cult of secret mantras is current where some mantras are said to be so confidential that one cannot get these sounds except from a satGuru.

Who is a satGuru?

The definition varies from sect to sect. Essentially it means a person who has the power to impart special insights into the mind of another person.

I was present in an initiation ceremony of a girl who was fourteen years of age. The pundit who did the ceremony give her a religious name. He said that he would whisper a mantra into her ear because it was confidential. Only she could hear the mantra.

Recently a caste brahmin from South India, a young man, described how he got a deity mantra where it was said to him alone. He was not to disclose it to anyone, otherwise it would become invalid.

What is this about?

In my experience, one can get a mantra from a disembodied guru. The guru does not have to be physically present. But when one gets a mantra, the authority may give an instruction on how to use it. If the instruction contains stipulation about confidentially, one should abide if for no other reason than to honor the pledge.

A question arises as to what should be done if one gets a confidential mantra and it does not serve the purpose intended after one practiced as stipulated. The answer is that one must decide if to abandon the mantra and get another sound or method which would give the objective.

In receiving mantras from gurus, I found that the best most authentic way to get these is from a guru who practices the specific discipline which one follows and not so much by requesting the mantra from the guru but by allowing the guru to offer the mantra when he is inclined to do so.

In other words, allow yourself to develop as any student would who is in a learning process. Then let the teacher determine if he/she should offer more information.

Recently, a *yogaGuru*, gave me instruction on the astral level. He entered my psyche during meditation. He gave a mantra and a time when that sound should produce a certain result. There was a specific personal energy from the yogaGuru in the mantra. I felt that energy enter my psyche when he gave the mantra.

In addition, some two months before this happened, I found myself trying to say this same mantra during the meditation sessions, even though normally I do not use a mantra in meditation because I do a meditation which is mantra-less and which is supported by naad resonance rather than by a mental or aural sound.

I concluded that this same guru transmitted the mantra to me even before he appeared in my mind. The feature is that the mantra is one of the standard Vedic mantras which anyone can get in a book which lists traditional mantras.

Why then, was it necessary to get this from a teacher?

Why could I not just take it from a book?

The answer is that if I took it from a book, its energy content would be different. Getting it from the teacher is personal and has a specific energy based on the guru's accomplishments.

Should I share this mantra with others?

The answer is that I can share it if the teacher instructs that I should.

If I am given one dose of a medicine, should I share that with others?

Would it work for me and for another person if it was shared?

Naad Screeching Sound

During the past week, my meditation digressed where I found myself back where I was with naad sound. This digression in meditation is bound to happen if one is not in isolation or at least if one is not isolated from associations which are counterproductive to remaining in meditative states.

There is meditation. There is the residual effect of meditation, which one benefits from during regular activity. If the meditation is on a higher plane, the residual effect will be on a higher level too. If the meditation sinks down to a lower plane, that will yield a lower residual effect.

Should a person complain about a lower meditative state which is due to whatever influence prevailed?

The answer is no but one should observe it and know the cause of it, so that if providence permits, one would transit away from that environment.

Everything hinges on taking cues from providence, so that the yogi has no illusions about his autonomy.

Self-government only makes sense within the context of providence and with the allowances which providence permits. Providence is tricky where it may give or afford allowances with liabilities. Who wants to carry liability? At least a sensible yogi is not interested in carrying liabilities which he has to pay for in the future in some disadvantaged situation. Therefore, it is best to work along with providence, getting done whatever it stipulates, regardless of if it is preferred or not.

Arjuna did not prefer to fight a battle but that was the only liability-free course he could take. Once he got the revelation from Krishna, Arjuna took that route even though it had hassles and inconveniences.

Today in meditation, I was with naad sound. It was a good meditation even though it was not as advanced as recently. In this meditation naad sound was shrill. It screeched a loud treble note. In the center of naad there was a laser, corkscrew-like white glowing emanation from where the naad sound emanated. This was not a node or nexus origin point. It was long, about sixteen inches, stretching though my neck and going to where I could not perceive where it ended. It shot through the back of my head and protruded through the top back about three inches and disappeared. It blasted. This was heard for fifteen minutes. I was in a naad chamber when this happened.

No yogaGuru was present. I got this feeling though that Lahiri went away because the progression slowed. There is no need for a teacher when the student crawls through the lessons and cannot complete the assignments.

As fate has it, for me in this life, situationally, I must do self-study. Then I see a teacher periodically. I have no pampering teacher who is with me day after day and who has the time to go over each detail of the course.

Necessity of Questions about Breath Infusion

Email Inquiry:

Why does a student who has a steady practice with steady results, question the practice? Is he/she susceptible to doubts and hesitation at all levels of advancement?

Mi~Beloved:

Questions about practice will continue until one gains confidence in both the path of yoga and the teacher(s). Even if there is full confidence in a teacher, even then there may be questions and doubts.

Realize that much about meditation is vague and ill-defined. This is due to our lack of objectivity in the subtle realm. Our objectivity is based on physical existence. This is why in India there are *murtis* or physical manifestations of deities.

What is the need for a physical deity if one has spiritual senses and can see the deity directly in his/her spiritual environment? It is necessary to have physical representations or installed genuine forms for the deity so long as we are reliant on physical senses.

Until we develop subtle perception we are plagued with questions and doubts. Regardless, we keep practicing, keep making astute observations during practice, keep having a sense of direction about progress being made, and keep the interest in the worlds which are not physical.

In the Satya Yuga, the age of transcendental insight, the advanced people had no physical deity forms. They did not worship God in the way humans do today. The elevated beings used physical and spiritual senses but did not use the physical perception as the primary reference.

There are several levels to contend with in this practice. Here is the basis layout:

- physical level
- base astral level (normal dream level of subtle body)
- astral paradise level (heavenly dream body)
- siddha astral level (yogically-inclined dream body)
- brahmaloka astral level (godly dream body with resistance to physical rebirth)
- causal plane (bodiless state with abstract awareness and full subjectivity and nominal objectivity)
- supernatural switching level (supernatural body which invisible to any perception below this level)
- brahman effulgence level (bodiless spatial state with abstract awareness of being in existence *(sat)* consciousness with no objectivity)
- divine worlds (spiritual body with full features of *sat-chit-ananda* - existing, knowing that one exists - being blissful as a person existence)

End of the Ideas-Images in the Mind

After checking and double checking, reading and referencing, I can finally say that in the month of December of the year 2013, I reached the level of practice where the second sutra of Patanjali is achieved. This is not a visualization, imagination or mantra-support process.

The sutra reads:

yogaḥcittavṛtti nirodhaḥ

The skill of yoga is demonstrated by the conscious non-operation of the vibrational modes of the mento-emotional energy.

Which means that yoga practice begins in earnest when the mental and emotional energies cease their normal activities of correct analysis, erroneous analysis, imagination, sleep and memory.

Method?

For me it was the *pranayama* method which is the 4th stage of yoga, yielding from that practice the result of the 5th stage which is *pratyahar* sensual energy withdrawal of interest from the circumstances of the physical and its related astral levels.

Big secret:

Thorough *pranayama* practice, a complete displacement of the old energies in the psyche on a consistent basis, leaving no part of it untouched or hidden, flushing it with fresh subtle energy through breath infusion practice.

How does it feel?

When I sit to meditate, I do so after doing *pranayama* practice. I make sure that I do a full session of breath infusion using the *kapalabhati* or *bhastrika*, which is an aggressive breathing exercise. It does however rid the system of carbon dioxide if we view this from the physical level. In the subtle body the *apana* energy or negative gases are removed and the fresh air is infused into the psyche. The trick is to remove all carbon dioxide and other negative gases, from every part of the body.

Every part is important. When one fiddles with *pranayama* one does not have a sense of every part. One focuses on the lungs and even on the primary *nadis* and chakras.

This is not that focus. This concerns getting to every part of the psyche especially the *hard to reach*, ignored areas of it. A big issue is to penetrate and remove the sex-pleasure / reproduction complex. This complex must be demolished. If this complex remains as it is, as it was designed by nature, there can be no success with this, because this energy effectively blocks access to *hard-to-reach* areas like the thighs.

When I am in that meditation, it feels like being in a large chamber. I assumed a miniature bodySelf. There are no thoughts, no images, nothing of the sort which usually arises in the mind. For that matter, it is surprising when this happens because one is used to the usual intense thought activity or scarce thought display in the mind. In this state that is absent. It is like when one goes to a theatre during the day when the actors, producers and others are absent. The place is empty. Nothing is there, absolutely nothing. You can dance and fool around to your heart's content. You can jump. You can laugh loudly.

The yogi may giggle some times to himself/herself in that state. How nice it is to be relieved of thoughts! But there is a glow light in that psychic chamber.

To be sure to accredit the yogaGurus, I took help from Harbhajan Singh, Yogeshwarananda of Yoga Niketan Trust, and Lahiri Mahasaya of the kriya lineage. Each assisted on the astral planes. I did learn breath infusion in 1972 from Yogi Bhajan.

Third Eye Mundane Interest

Some students have the idea that everything the third eye does concerns spiritual life but that is just an assumption. The subtle body has both psychic and purely physical interest. It wants to be subtle. It also wants to be physical. It has contradictory interests.

The thing which manages that paradox is the kundalini lifeForce, which is a master of juggling between the purely physical and the lower astral levels which consists of radio wave and light wave energies. The supervisory powers of the lifeForce cannot be denied. It is so expert at this, that the coreSelf gave itself over completely to this kundalini lifeForce, which manages the situations independently.

During a high-level meditation this morning, a friend of my deceased father was in the chamber of consciousness (the psyche) with me. He spoke about things which happened in 1966 in Trinidad, when he was a chief mate aboard a small cruise liner. This was part of a pair of two ships which plied the local tourist run from Trinidad, the most easterly island of the West Indian territories, to Jamaica the most western of the territories.

At the time my father was the one and only, the very first black-skinned human to pilot large vessels in and out of Trinidad harbors. This friend of his, Stanley W. returned from Newfoundland or some such frozen outpost where he completed studies in navigation and then took this prestigious job. My father also rode high on his wagon of prestige of those who were descendants of African slaves who were galley-shipped across the Atlantic to serve as human agricultural machines (tractors on two feet).

During the meditation, Stanley suddenly was in my subtle head. This was a high-class meditation where there were no thoughts and images from the riff raff display of the mind. Stanley showed some views of things we did long ago, when as a boy of about sixteen years of age, I greeted him when the cruise liner docked at Port of Spain.

His complexion was as black as charcoal, except that it had a gloss sheen to it. His teeth were pearly white. He would be on board with his super-white pressed uniform with the epaulets and insignias. I would greet him on board after climbing the tourist ramp. I would go to his cabin. He would offer some premium lager as is the custom with seamen.

During the encounter he showed two women who came to Trinidad from Jamaica in 1966. These were sisters. The elder one was his girlfriend. She was eager to tie the knot but he was hesitant, as is true to our ethnic background which is that we do not marry anyone but we stay close to our mothers no matter what. It is the *trust-a-woman-as-a-mother-but-not-as-a-wife* protection process, for what that is worth.

His girlfriend's sister who accompanied them on the voyage was about 22 years of age. I was about fifteen years of age but the woman examined me as if I was something delicious, something edible. For my part, it was awkward. What was I to do with the affection which she directed to me?

The two of them stayed at my father's house for the time the ship stayed in Port of Spain. They were on the return voyage through the West Indian islands to Jamaica. I heard about the legendary beauty of the black women from Jamaica. These women verified the reputation. Men would look at them and then look away in amazement, not knowing what really happened, as to what struck them, lightning or lust.

In this meditation encounter, Stanley wanted me to consider the situation from so long ago. It was like when you read a novel, leave a marker in it and put it down. You forget it but some forty plus years after, you stumble upon that novel and find the marker. You recall what you read before so that you can continue with the rest of the story.

Stanley wanted us to go back to that time, me and him. We were to be together to work that out with the two women; he with the elder and I with the younger.

If providence recreated that according to his specifications, how would that play out?

He thought that I would have an older body suitable to relate to the twenty-two years old younger one. I would become a seaman too just like him and my father. I was bright and had potential. I studied navigation and could plot ship's routes on charts at fifteen years of age. I would get a good education at a special school. Then I would ply the waves as the skipper on a ship, dressed fittingly with a white uniform as an officer on board and have a pretty Jamaican wife to booth.

What an experience with the third eye!

Anyway, after that experience, I resumed Lahiri's lesson plan which is to attract the *chit akash* into the psyche. And what a better time to do so as when the third eye is active during a meditation session.

Astral Surgery

Yogeshwarananda was busy this morning in the astral regions helping various people who are student yogis. Just before I awakened on the physical side, I saw him moving from one person to the next making adjustments in the energies in their subtle bodies.

This was on a level where the subtle body is radio and light waves only and has no flesh and bones type of configuration. A *yogaGuru* who comes from a higher plane may handle the radio and light wave energies as if they were solid materials, just the way we handle physical objects.

Yogeshwarananda would pull a cord-like set of light or radio wave energies this way and then that way. Or he would pull it completely out of the person's subtle form. Over the years teaching, students approached me for help with psychological problems. Some were of the opinion, that I could alter negative tendencies by magical acts on the astral planes.

However, operating on a person's subtle body is risky. It is also mostly a stop-gap method, meaning that even if it is done, the person's body may resume whatever unwanted tendency it had before, reversing the work of the astral doctor.

We know that recently with the surge of obesity, surgeons developed procedures to remove fat pockets from human bodies and also to cut even large sections of a stomach or digestive track but we find that later, if not sooner, usually these persons resume the obesity. Removing a section of the digestive track does not remove the dietary tendency which is the cause of the habit which is represented in the body as obesity.

Why does Yogeshwarananda do this?

Part of the reason is to relieve himself of his sense of compassion. Another part is that some students do heed the advice for lifestyle changes which would support this.

But there is another reason which is to do it upon request so that some student can see that the idea that he should help them will do nothing unless they make those *hard to implement* habit changes.

Physical Action affects the Subtle Body

Early this morning on the astral side, Yogeshwarananda began a discourse which he wanted me to participate in. First, he spoke about the floods in India, where sometimes there is so much water that there is no place for a human being to maneuver. He said it is as if nature lost its ability to cease the flow of water from clouds.

Then he said that no matter how bad it is, eventually the rains stop. The lands dries and things return to normal. Ant colonies begin again. Human beings who survived get their lives in order.

The lands become so dry that sometimes people again cry for water, for the dreaded rains which ruined their livelihoods just months before.

He said that a similar thing happens in these births, where in one life one effectively curbs a spiritually-destructive habit and then in a future life, that habit resumes with full force and floods the psyche with its energy, forcing the whole being to serve its needs. This reverses the spiritual progress. The ascetic becomes a materialistic person again.

A guru may help to curb the spiritual destructive tendency and reawaken the spiritually supportive behaviors.

Yogeshwarananda said that the spiritual destructive behaviors which flood the psyche and force the ascetic to become a raving sensualist, should be mopped up with the absorbent towel of patient consistent yoga practice over time, so that eventually every bit of the flooded energy is dried, just as when the rains stop, the land gradually but surely dries.

Then the ascetic can consolidate the yoga practice again and move even further than he/she was in the past life.

This experience was a result of two physical actions, namely breath infusion with very rapid and intense breathing, and slapping of the toes on the ground in an all-fours posture. This is a harsh treatment of the toes but one can tolerate the pain.

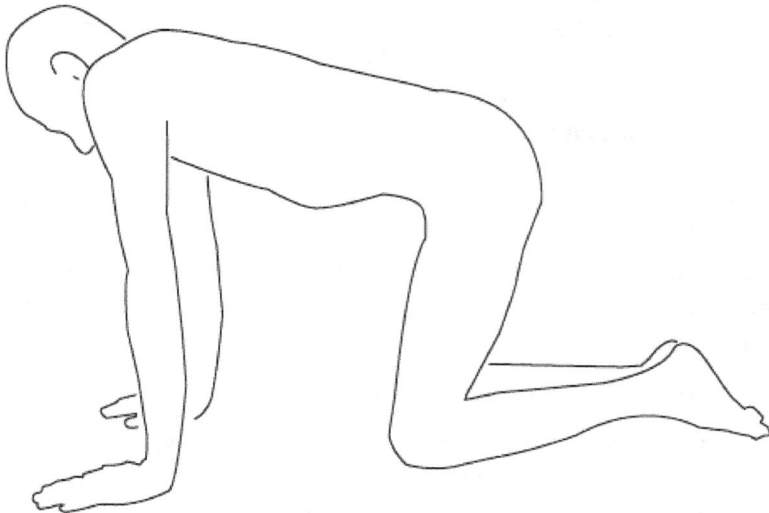

This however is a direct way to target the base chakra because the nerves in the feet are connected into the base part of the spinal column. This process is not reliant of visualization but on physical actions and breath infusion with mental and emotional direction of the energy into the thighs, legs and feet.

Realize that these physical actions do not end on the physical plane but stretch into the subtle level, affecting the subtle body's chakra and *nadi* system. Some curious people feel that I do not stress visualization enough. In fact, I do not stress it at any time because I do not use it. This does not mean that it has no value or that it is not effective. If you have a sensitive psyche, you may use it and get results but if you do not you should use the physical processes to get your objective fulfilled on the subtle level.

After much breath infusion and banging of the toes on the ground as well as some other postures which attack the base chakra by physical actions which affect the tailbone of the spine, I stood up and applied the locks.

After doing that, there was the experience of a firing of the kundalini from the sacral bone down through the thighs, legs and feet. This was a bliss feeling of crystal translucent whitish energy which shot downward like needle-fine springs with a camphor mint expression. These shots of energy were as narrow as a needle or narrower. These are *nadis*.

This current practice is being done as instructed by Lahiri Mahasaya for the complete revamping and flushing of the psyche I currently use, for the purpose of building a *yogaSiddha* body.

Brahma and Buddha

Earlier today, I read some of the Pali cannon information about what happened that caused Buddha to begin teaching what he learnt and discovered during the austerities which cause enlightenment in terms of his objective.

Particularly the text related that a Brahma deity came to see Buddha to discuss his decision not to explain the process. By the deity's influence,

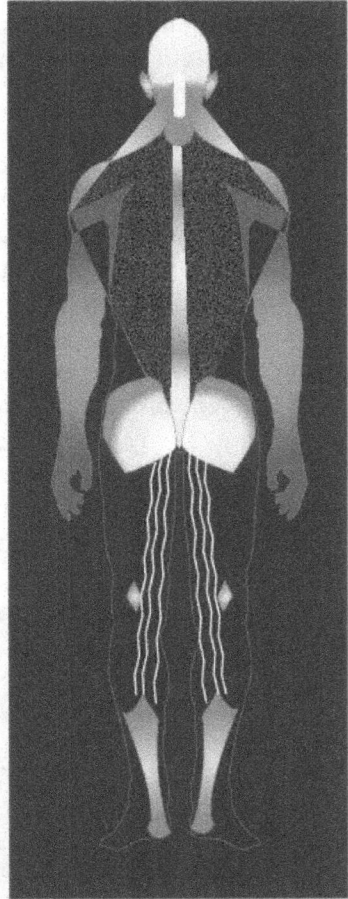

Buddha decided to teach with the insight that most people would not assume the disciplines and considerations which were required.

According to how the scene was described, the Brahma deity offered respect to Buddha as if Buddha was the deity's superior. Before the deity left, he went around Buddha with Buddha on the deity's right which in the Vedic culture is a sign of respect.

Someone who is a Hindu or who is of the Vedic process may feel that this was a distorted description but we learned from the *Srimad Bhagavatam* that a criminal mystic named *Hiranyakashipu* got high praise and respect from a Brahma deity, all because of exceptional and outstanding austerities. *Hiranyakashipu* did austerities which excelled what the Brahma deity achieved. Hiranyakashipu was so exceptional, that the Brahma deity told him that his yoga practice would not be repeated by any other person in the creation because no other person in the universe had the capacity to get that far in the yoga process of suspending the kundalini lifeForce.

Later that day, when I did the afternoon session, I got in connection with a Buddha deity in South Korea. He wanted to speak about the possibility of getting some students liberated by removing them from circumstantial impediments which deter progress.

In the history of Gautama Buddha, there were many examples of persons who wanted to go away from family responsibilities and take to full renunciation where they were not involved in raising children and the related domestic upkeep. It is a long history that when a person becomes involved in family life, he/she does not have time to pursue spiritual progress. The yogi becomes degraded by the end of the lifetime.

How practical is it to get someone removed from the domestic scene?

Can a Buddha do that?

Will providence allow it?

Providence is hard pressed to fulfill various complicated equations of consequential energies which were in motion due to actions in many past lives.

Subtle Body as a Parasite

Lahiri Mahasaya made some remarks about the failure of human beings to get to a deep level in meditation where contact with the *chit akash* happens. Without this contact the meditation is low quality.

The main impediment is the configuration of the subtle body. Its natural state is such that it has no interest in developing connection with the *chit akash*. It wants to stay on this side of the existential divide.

The subtle body may be regarded a parasitic organism which lives on the coreSelf. Even though the core is smaller than the subtle body in terms of the subtle dimensional space the core occupies, and although it supplies energy to the subtle body and takes energy information from it, still from another perspective, the subtle body is the parasite which lives on the core, feeding from it.

In terms of power, the coreSelf is gigantic in reference to the subtle body, but in terms of size in the astral dimensions, the core appears to be smaller, merely because it cannot be represented there in full. The core's influence is extensive, undoubtedly, but it is extradimensional. Its relationship with the subtle body makes it absorbs the liabilities.

Imagine yourself as a great king or queen, a magnanimous kind person, but a fool nevertheless because you are blind, dumb and deaf. For seeing you must rely on a man who has vision. For speaking you must take help from a gifted orator. For hearing you must depend on someone whose hearing is acute.

Take this a step further, where you finally realize that the servants have contrary interests which contradict your own. What will you do? You cannot function without the assistants?

Which is better?

A servant who steals?

Or no servant?

No description of what is seen?

Or perverted prejudiced eye-witness reports?

Lahiri explained that the main obstruction for the advanced stage of yoga practice is the lack of distribution of higher energy to the lower part of the subtle body. This happens because of the design of this area, a design which was created by the kundalini lifeForce as a free service to the coreSelf.

A free service?

Yes! That is what it was when it was first created. The coreSelf being a lord in its own right, was happy to receive this gift from its loyal servant, the kundalini.

There are basically two ways to kill a king or queen. One is the quick method, a stab to the heart, a gunshot wound, something sudden and lethal. A little pain and it is over.

The other method is the slow procedure, where the king or queen is slowly poisoned. This is the most vicious way but it is the kindest method, because it does not cause alarm. What is kinder than to kill someone without causing anxiety?

Food poisoning is one such method, where over time, perhaps in a year or two a poison is administered bit by bit. The king or queen would never realize that life ebbs away. Application of gas into the royal bedchamber is another method which may be used while the monarch sleeps. In such a situation the king or queen will dream away. This will cause a permanent relocation to wonderland, where hopefully the monarch has a parallel reign. There he/she can deal with the astral body of the assassin.

The dead monarch, being alive on the astral side will say,

"You killed me on the physical side. Now I will take your astral head! Arrest him! Bring him to the guillotine!"

How will the core implement the changes in configuration of the subtle body?

Can it change the basic design?

Can it eliminate the hormone accumulation and expression system?

Lahiri spoke of the outright fools and also of the pious dumb-dumbs.

The outright fools are those who have no conscience. They feel that everything should be permitted. They feel that one can do whatever one desires and there should be no adverse consequence. Despite evidence to the contrary, they continue with this feeling about individual absolute autonomy.

The pious dumb-dumbs are those who have a sense of conscience but who think that the social order of human society as we prefer it, is the absolute norm. They fail to recognize the laws of nature which splinter from their value system. They think that they can get a spiritual result from social perfection.

But there is another group of human beings. These are those who realize that changing the design of the subtle body is the way to go. Being a good citizen is a waste of time. Being a social rebel carries unfavorable returns.

Yoga Practice After Death

Meditation this afternoon was done with the right nostril blocked and the left fully open, as the moon-charged energy was prime in the air with the sky overcast and not a ray of sun energy bursting through. The clouds are a blanket of cold air from the northern regions.

When I sat to meditate, naad sound was prominent in the back right top of the head, where it had a peak of energy pushing through, gushing through the top right of the head.

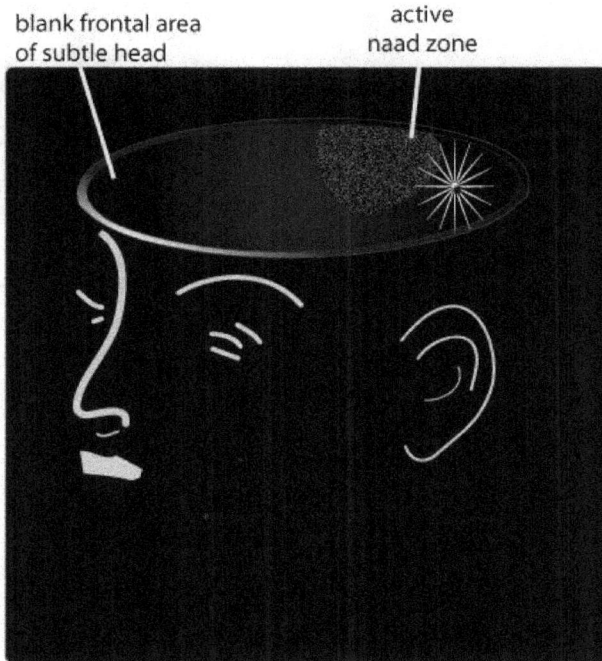

blank frontal area of subtle head

active naad zone

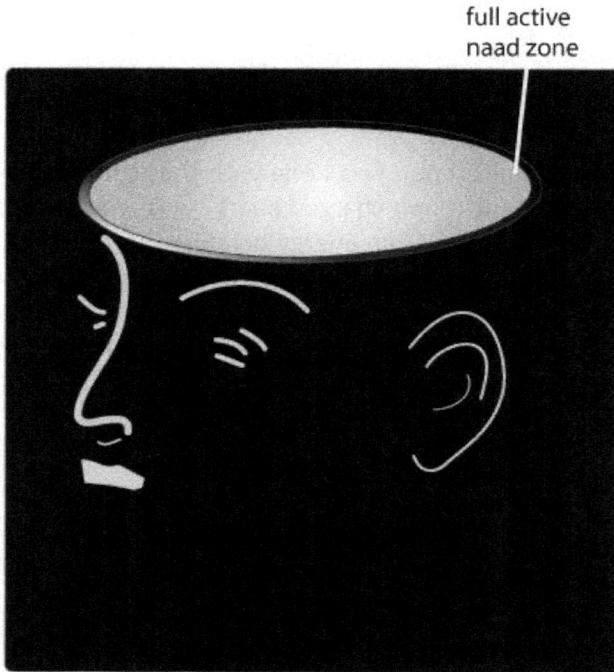

full active
naad zone

Naad was distant. I was present in the subtle head a little on the left side but naad included me in its swath of territory. There was a large chamber full of light but not bright just a glow that was sufficient to see. The perception was visual but there were no eyes. The air of the place could see within itself without visual instruments or orbs. I was a micro-size person inside of the head chamber. From Lahiri there was an instruction-direction energy which manifested in that chamber. It instructed that I go into the thighs of the subtle body and take what he termed to be enlightenment consciousness.

This enlightenment consciousness is the consciousness which was predominant in the head of the subtle body. I did as instructed. I went into the right thigh and then moved in the direction of the trunk of the subtle body and then crossed to the left thigh. In those areas there was no flesh, bones, sinews or muscle, nothing. It was a large space like a huge culvert flooded with light-yellow light. I floated moving from one thigh to the other.

This is part of the process of making a *yogaSiddha* body for use now and after leaving the physical one.

If perchance I do not achieve that, I will continue the instructions for that after leaving the physical form and will complete it in the astral world hereafter. I have enough impetus to guarantee that I can complete this hereafter, even though the preference is to complete it before being deprived of the physical system.

Since only idiots put faith in their ideas concerning how they can make fate submit to their desires, I have an alternative plan just in case circumstances stall me and do not permit completion of the course before leaving the body.

No one should feel sorry for me after my physical body dies. No one should think that I lost anything. All the same no one should tell people that I gained anything either. Whatever I achieve up to that point, I will retain. That should be told.

For me this physical body is not preferred. It caused problems. It continues to be a source of anxiety because it caused me to be aware of the physical world, being subjected to the associations which this place contains. Overall, this was a rough ride through this life. It continues to be a bumpy transit.

However, there is a saying that there is no sense in crying over spilt milk. Better to move on. Accept whatever happened as being the sanction of fate, either at one's expense or just for the heck of fate without one carrying liabilities hereafter.

Recently Lahiri, as a favor to me, gave a place where I can finish the austerities required for a *yogaSiddha* body. This is important because it is best to go to where a great teacher is and take shelter under his influence, than it is to secure an astral domain.

Under the auspices of a great guru, one has the love of a father. That is everything for a sincere student. For a man, the love of a woman is heaven. For a woman, the love a man is beyond her wildest dreams. But the paternal love of a great guru, deity or divine personality is special.

Lord Shiva is paternal to me. I am lucky. Under his divine care, everything could come to order shortly.

Astral Dogs

I had a series of dreams last night with the sons and relatives of a friend. These persons sent me thoughts repeatedly during the past two weeks. They want me to join them. I managed to dodge the encounter. However, last night as fate would have it, my dodging plans failed. I found myself with them during the night. My astral body was compelled to be with them.

One thing which happened in their favor was that the weather changed in the area where I resided. It switched to a cold pattern. Subsequently the windows were closed, which resulted in little air exchange with the outside. This meant less oxygen intake and more possibility of carbon dioxide intake.

That in turn meant that the astral body went to a lower level, where it met whosoever is on that plane to match the relational vibrations of the psyche.

It may be that this cold air and the closed windows was a God-sent from the perspective of my friends even though for me it was hell-imposed. What is good for one person, for a yogi, is bad for a non-yogi. What is great for a non-yogi is all the worse, for the yogi.

Just consider if after working with these austerities and kriya practice over the years, fighting for every step of ground I covered, releasing myself from every tie-up with materialistic human beings who are friends or family, and then in the end, I transited to be with such people and get stuck in an astral place hereafter with them and have to confirm to their destiny, forgetting about the *yogaGurus* and the elevation in the subtle body, and living in that lower astral place which is adjacent to this physical world, and then emerging again sometime after as the son of a relative of my friend's family and being put to use by those people all for their happiness and satisfaction.

Do you think that is what I ought to do so that their desires can be fulfilled, so that I would be kind to them?

On the physical side, these friends have dogs but on the astral side they have even more dogs. Astrally, they live in a place which is relatively clean and had plenty of astral light, even though there was no sun shining. There was sunlight everywhere but no sun as the source of illumination. They maintain this parallel existence along with their physical premises.

Somehow, I always had to help them with their dogs which would attack persons in the astral world to whom they were not related. As a result, my astral body sent mimic energies to my physical form, and persons whom were near my sleeping physical body, reported about this after I awakened.

In the encounter, I gave the dogs several commands to cease chasing other persons. Those commands were mimicked by my physical body which were heard as unfamiliar sounds by persons who were near my body on the physical side.

This happened primarily because the astral level which we were on, was adjacent to this physical existence. It was the first astral place which is nearest to the physical level of vibration.

There are astral dogs just as there are astral human beings. Persons, who have these animals on the physical level, have to deal with the animals on the astral side just the same.

Sex Organ Appetite

During the night, a student of the breath infusion process, asked of the possibility of satisfying the appetite of the sex organs. He asked of the possibility of permanently, once and for all, appeasing the sex organ of his female partner.

He admitted that he was compelled to service his partner sexually and that it was not an acceptable behavior. I listened to his speech for some time. I told him to cease speaking. I asked about what he would do to stop that behavior but he had no reply. The guy was depressed. He said that if he was condemned to such a life with a partner, whose genitals had a voracious appetite, his chances of becoming a great yogin were nil. He had a pitiful look on his face. For my part as a yoga teacher, I decided to leave him to himself for a time because I wrote extensively on the subject in various books and discussed this topic on many occasions. If there are solutions, I printed these already.

A kind person cannot become a celibate yogi under any terms because kindness does not fit into the plan to stop sex desire. Stopping sex desire really means ceasing the primary means of assistance to one's ancestors. That is a cruel act. If you do not have a cruel streak how can you do that?

But a discussion about celibacy, is a failure from the start because it is similar to the discussion a group of pig farmers had about the possibility of a last meal which would curb the eating propensity of their pigs. Such a discussion is good to pass the time, to chitty chat endlessly, with proposals which are fascinating but which would never be of any use practically.

The nature of pigs is to eat. The nature of the sexual organs is to indulge. The concept of stopping their consumption of their respective gratifications is a way of passing time only.

In a conference of pig farmers concerning the possibility of a last fully satisfying meal for their pigs, each farmer had praise worthy proposals but when it was all over, they were faced with the reality which was that they could never stop feeding pigs.

Let us have a meaningful discussion. Let us speak about getting out of the sex business altogether, just as those farmers would have to sell the pigs and quit keeping the animals if they had no intention of feeding.

The question of curbing the appetite of the sex organs is a long-standing query in yoga circles. There were a few successes with this but those paltry results are not a reason for any student to feel that he/she can achieve that.

Ten thousand human beings, who were fit swimmers, left the East Coast of China with the intention of swimming to the West Coast of Canada. One guy somehow or the other achieved it.

What happened to the others?

They never arrived.

Should I write an article about how human beings can successfully swim across the Pacific or should the article state that human being cannot do that.

There were a few successes of yogis who curbed the organs. Recently I had a strange and very unusual experience with Yogeshwarananda. This was about a week ago. We were in the astral world at a place which he resides from time to time. Some other disciples of his were present. Suddenly a woman with whom he has a special relationship came. She sat near him.

We knew that this woman was special because usually women cannot reach him in that astral place This woman came there. She walked to him as if she knew him. Then she lay to her side next to him.

He made an action with his hands. In her body her sexual-reproduction area changed in configuration. It was like he took a large towel and mopped her sexual and reproductive energies. That sexual reproductive area was non-existent from then on. Whatever sexual expression she had towards him ceased. It was no longer present.

In that form her sexual chakras which were in full expression before he waved his hand, shrunk to nothing. He did this in the presence of many advanced students, either liberated entities or near-liberated ones.

That is a case of curbing the appetite of the genitals, but usually it will not happen.

There is no point in discussing it.

Intestinal Naad Sound

I almost forgot this information because when I did the meditation when this was experienced, I could not come out of the samadhi absorption state for fear that I would not resume it. I made a mental note of what happened, but I did not dare to jot notes. The result is that when I came out of the meditation, I recalled none of it. I was at a lost for the information.

Later, about some three hours after, there was a flash memory from the samadhi absorption level, which was like when a star in a distant galaxy flashes for a moment and that streak of light reaches the earth. It crosses trillions of miles to reach the earth. In this case that message crossed dimensions and reached me in this earthly consciousness.

This meditation was in a naad bubble space, a large chamber in which naad sound was heard. A naad glow was there but this was not the usual dim gold glow. This light was grey blue, similar to dim cobalt light. I was there with naad sound in the back left of the place but permeating the whole place with the louder more resonant part of it in the back left. Then everything changed where the chamber extended to the trunk of my subtle body. There was another naad sound which emanated from the mass of intestinal energy.

I could hear this vibration coming from there but it was not as pronounced as the standard naad sound. Suddenly I was in that intestinal mass. It was below a thin layer of energy which was as thin as paper. It was on another plane but from there I heard the standard naad sound.

I then switched to the standard naad sound. From there in the head of the subtle body, I still could perceive the intestinal naad vibration.

Breath Infusion Sun-time / Winter Months

During the winter months, those who live in the northern hemisphere where the sun seems to cant to the south, should do the early morning session as usual. But they should make the afternoon session earlier at a time when they can face the sun and get the sun's rays to directly hit their faces during the breath infusion.

This will allow for absorption of sun-charge energy. During the winter the rays of the sun are not as penetrating and heat-producing as they are during the summer months.

One can do three sessions per day with a midday session as the extra one but at least one should do two sessions, the early morning one and one in the afternoon before sunset and in the fullness of the sun, in an open field or somewhere, where the sun shines on the body during the practice.

Nature's Psychological Operations

During breath infusion practice this morning, I reviewed some information which I got from Lahiri about the momentum of the animal evolutionary drive. On one hand the physical nature assisted the living entity by giving it a place to live and giving it an environment for expression. But on the other hand, the living entity became a physical nature addict. It continued with the operations of physical nature, even after realizing which of those operations are detrimental to it.

Nature manufactured the physical body with a system of digesting and storing nutrients which contravenes our getting control of the hormonal energy of the body. Without that control we cannot possibly change habits.

But nature feels that we should not interfere with her designs. Modern science broke the rule of nature by studying its designs and then creating gadgets based on vital or whimsical needs but that has nothing to do with its psychological operations. In kriya yoga, we tinker with the psychological constructions of nature, to change how she arranged the psyche.

Focus in your psyche by becoming introspective.

Look around.

Is there anything which should be rearranged?

Step number one is to realize that physical nature has a psychological counterpart. It is from that level that it runs these operations, even the very physical and obvious ones.

Can you explain the psychological construction of physical nature, about how it operates and if it can be altered?

Tushita Goddess Visitation

Today during one meditation, I was conveyed to the Tushita heaven by a demigoddess from that place. Even though dimensionally that place is far away, it happened suddenly and instantly without any time taken to get there. When I arrived the supernatural lady showed my old place where I resided. It was empty for thousands of years, it seemed, like I was absent from that place for a long time.

It is not a place where there is dust like on earth but still, I could feel that I must have lived there some thousands of years ago and had to leave for some missions of teaching spiritual advancement.

After this the goddess showed a black space in my record there and said that it needed to be filled and that I had not sent back the reports about what happened. I looked. It was blank as blank as can be. It was like an empty jug which should be filled with water.

I said to the lady,

"I will fill this."

She was not impressed. She merely looked at me with a blank expression. I was conveyed to my body on the earth. There I considered what to do. Usually in these experiences, I feel happy about the visitation but in this case, happiness was absent.

I did however use the link energy from the goddess to begin sending report energies back to that place to fill the blank zone in my record there. The energy began flowing through a portal which she created. I felt relieved. Thousands of years of working in the field of yoga and spirituality, and helping others was giving just an iota of psychological relief, like I had done very little in retrospect.

When the goddess first arrived while I meditated on earth, I asked her this:

"When am I scheduled to get back to the Tushita heaven?"

Her reply was:

"That depends on your personal practice. It has very little to do with your missions. Missions are missions. Missions must be completed. No return is possible if a mission is on. When the missions are done, then you return but even then, it depends on how you maintained the personal practice."

"Secret?

"Maintain the personal practice no matter what. When the missions end, you can instantly return. Completion of the mission to his satisfaction, results in return if the practice was proficiently maintained."

Part 4

Blank Mind

In this kriya yoga meditation it is important that the students get used to and nourish a blank mind. If the student is habituated to having much information, thoughts and images in the mind, this meditation will never be proficient.

Yes, it is true that periodically a student will have calmness in meditation and will have agreeable thoughts but that is not this meditation. At least this does not fulfill Patanjali's requirement for a mind which is devoid of thoughts, imaginations, spontaneous or requested memories and lacking a sleepy, drowsy, lazy, sulky or confused condition.

Those students who meditate and who keep returning to the compulsive mental and emotional operations cannot get a progress which affects the depressed lower states.

One has to learn how to cling to what is higher and abandon what is lower. This does not mean clinging to and enjoying nice meditations, and then habitually and always returning to the old mental and emotional ways of operation.

Teach yourself. Practice with yourself, to be nourished in a blank state of mind where there is no hankering and longing for the usual distracting mental and emotional states.

Sacral Cage Brain Down

This is a practice to bring light to the sacral cage which is in a sense the lower brain or the place from which physical existence is maintained and directed.

The buttock/groin area is built on a skeletal framing which is the sacral cage. In there much indulgence is experienced with kundalini lifeForce having a good time through sex pleasure mainly. There is a practice to bring light and intelligence to this area of the psyche, where the student brings the head consciousness into this area during meditation.

As the kundalini designed it, people do not have access to the sacral cage except to enjoy sex, birth babies and process evacuation. The processing of evacuation is mandatory. Copulating can be waivered from time to time. Basically speaking, the enjoyment also comes from evacuation by the relief it provides for the rectum and terminal part of the colon.

To redesign this sacral cage, a yogi should go into it and shine light there. Kundalini has it, where light is shun in the head only, but the yogi should change this design and shine light in the sacral cage.

intellgence energy
in head of subtle body

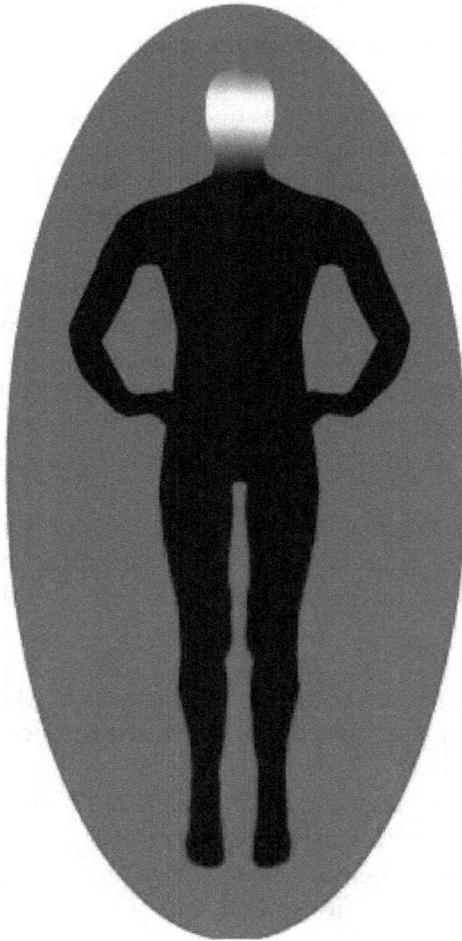

intelligence energy
in sacral cage

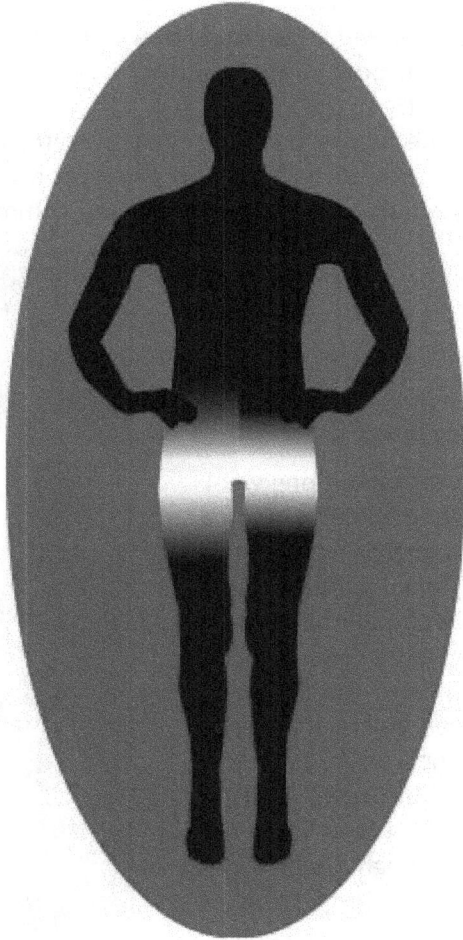

The yogi should also move the pleasure potency of the genitals into the head, thus disrupting kundalini plan to only have acute pleasure in the genital area.

Poverty-Stricken Child

I began this life as a poverty-stricken child but then I thought that the whole world belonged to me and was centered about me. This included the sun, moon, the stars, my parents, the government and everything else.

As I experienced life, I misbehaved, crying for this or that, demanding this and requiring that.

I continue seeing myself as the center of attention. I required global support to maintain this profile.

There is that power which will say, "Now you are dead, you old guff." Then it will say, "Now be born you little scruff."

How will I respond?

As usual with the insane demands that everything surrounding me, should tend to me, scratch my back, itch my palm, pat my shoulder, serve my every need, quickly adjust to my insecurities, and command all to tend to what I require.

That's me the little demander!

I will go down feeling that the world owes me everything.

I will always take myself seriously!

Lymph Nodes Energy Burst

I was to report this about one week ago. Due to traveling, I did not. I made a notation. It was a kundalini experience which was not the spinal kundalini. This was an energy burst during breath infusion practice, where energy shot from the lymph nodes to the right and left of the pubic area where the thighs are connected into the front of the body.

The energy fired through the thigh. It fired through the chest into the shoulders and then through the shoulder into the arms. It had the feeling of camphor and cool mint but it looked like transparent crystal sparkles twinkling away pleasurably.

Locks Efficiency

Some students wonder why they do not get results in some breath infusion practices. There are many reasons for this, like for example:

- inefficient application of the compression locks
- spaced-out practice
- carelessness in assuming postures
- lungs not absorbing the air which comes through the trachea

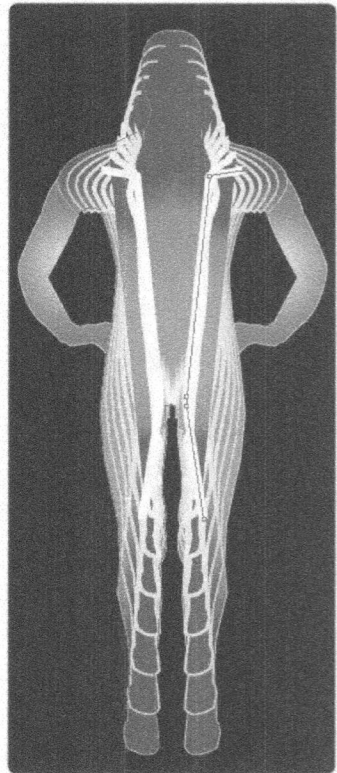

- general resistance of one's psyche to the practice

Any of this may contribute to failure in raising kundalini. The other aspect to look at is the hormone accumulation system.

Is that in order?

Have you sexed out, or worried out, your hormone energy?

Sex is a big consumer of hormone energy, where it uses the hormones the way a large motor sucks electricity from a generator. Sex is like a short in a circuit. But they are other means of energy pilfering like emotional-burn out, anxiety absorption and ill health of body.

Have you checked these aspects? These affect what will happen in a breath infusion practice?

People sometimes wonder, if as a teacher, I am affected by any impediment. The answer is:

Yes, of course!

Still, I practice and forge on. Unlike some students I do not live on ideals. I accept what life throws at me. I forge on. One day was a good day. Then there was a bad day. Practice yielded nothing, but I forged on.

In the end, whatever practice I do will accumulate. That will be my resultant progress. I never feel that every day should be a good day or that I am entitled to all good days. I feel that life is in control. My attitude is one of accepting the whims of fate.

You may read of the compression locks which are applied during breath infusion. These are important. I published a commentary as *Kundalini Hatha Yoga Pradipika*. In that book there is stress on the compression locks, as to their worth for a yogi.

The application of these must be done proficiently to get the full results but unfortunately one cannot learn these overnight. Of course, I can tell you how to do them but so what, you still cannot apply these efficiently even after hearing a detailed description, no more than you can climb into the cockpit of a jet aircraft and fly after seeing a video on how to do it.

One must practice for some years. Then one will gain proficiency over time. There must also be the psychic compressions which occur in the subtle body when the compressions are applied on the physical side. A yogi should master that psychic control. It happens over time. For some in three days, for others in three years, depending on what one is as a coreSelf and what one brings from the past lives of practice.

Ever wonder why some persons advance quickly and bypass others who began the practice earlier?

Ever considered checking on the past life of other students who excel after just a little training?

Cost of Happiness

This morning I had occasion to take stock of my happiness. In many instances, one cannot evaluate something unless one sees someone else in the situation. Then one may, if one wants self-benefit, see how one can put that other person's experience for use in gaining contentment and/or happiness.

A friend who needed money, for some time now, somehow or the other got funds. He was depressed over the lack of money. As soon as he got some, he became happy. During the night he acquired some happiness-producing drug.

Considering this, I decided to take a close look at my behavior in regards to if money causes happiness. First of all, a person may be depressed because of not having money. It is the primary means of exchange of commodities and services in human society.

For the happiness of the children, the father must hold a job which produces money as income. If the father neglects this, the children may become unhappy because of not getting desired sensual fulfillments.

What is the aim of life?

- Is it happiness of oneself?
- Is it happiness of others?
- Is it happiness of oneself and others?
- To what extent should one make others happy?

While in the happy mood which was induced by a drug, my friend found me. He was in delight with a laptop computer. He handed it to me. He said.

"Take this. You can fix it. Buy a cheap keyboard and use it."

Realizing that he was flying high due to happiness-inducing drugs, I replied appropriately:

"Sure, I will take it. Yes, I will get the cheap keyboard."

No friend ruins the happiness of his buddy. After months of depression because of not having funds, at last he found some happiness after he got some money and could purchase happiness the chemical way.

Who is the blame that life is structured in such a way, that one cannot be continually happy unless one is a very advanced personality or just plain stupid enough not to worry for anything?

As great a person as Jesus Christ, Lord that he is, was unhappy on occasion. But Buddha was happy only after he successfully performed yoga austerities. Buddha considered cultural happiness to be delusion. He got the name *Tathagata* (Tut-haa-guh-tuh), which means the person who left cultural life for seclusion.

A human's life may be summarized like this:

I had no money
Subsequently, I was unhappy.

- I got a job.
- I got money.
- I was happy due the services and products I procured.
- When the money was spent. I again became unhappy.

Comparing the Path of Buddha

Today I am at the Zen Hostel in Gainesville, Florida. It is not part of a preset plan but part of the plan of life which is imposed at this time. When I first arrived here, I mentioned to Tobe Terrell that I did not expect to return here within such a short period of time. He replied that he was not surprised.

Since I was here last, the temple room increased in its spiritual vibration. I guessed that there was meditation in that room on a regular basis. During the meditation today, which was after a breath infusion session of exercises, Gautama Buddha was present on the psychic side. He made a few remarks to me. I was in touch with him regularly for about the past month.

Recently a female deity, *Vajrayogini*, from Buddha's palace in the *Tushita* heavens, transported me to that place. She settled some differences with me about how long I was away from that place and also about what would be the future situation, if and when I would return.

I happen to be a member of Buddha's household as a son. In that spiritual relationship there are ups and down, limits and permits. After the goddess spoke to me in private and expressed certain concerns about this and that, I realized that even in the *Tushita* heaven there is a slight, a very slight tinge of dissatisfaction with this or that.

Later, after the goddess related her qualms to me, Lord Buddha called. He inquired of her statements and actions. Then he said,

"Have you noticed that I had no women in the sanga circle of serious followers. There is talk about women in the association but even these goddesses who are far superior to the earthly females, make demands. So, it is my son!

"There is talk about will power and about desire. In the end, it is going to be a toss-up about whose will, and whose desire, will prevail and for how long. It depends on the realm of manifestation. How many disciples do you think you can liberate? How much weight can a sparrow lift? How thick do you think its neck is? It certainly is not as thick as the width of the feathers. It has a skinny neck. The slightest tension will break it.

"They ask for help but how much can you give?

"Always stay close to me. Stand behind me. You will be protected. Stand in the open. You will be wounded."

During the meditation there was a flash vision of what motivated Buddha to do the austerities from which he became enlightened. As I reviewed my interest in enlightenment by any definition, I could not find a similar motive. My objective is different.

At the time of this consideration, Buddha said this into my mind:

Mine was an investigative existential search. That is different to your type of yoga because you operate from a domain search. It is known as gatih in Sanskrit. That means that you search for a suitable domain. You are not focused on fleeing from the undesirable place.

Yours is a search for a suitable external environment. In my case, it was a search for a suitable internal environment, a trauma-free internality.

Relatively speaking the Tushita heaven is such a desirable place but it can be attained from either motivation, either from the domain search or from the existential search. Once the yogi is serious and has the right method and the right teachers to guide him/her, it is possible in either case.

Sleep Away / Why Meditate?

This morning for breath infusion practice, the artist and musician Oliver Norden was physically present. What inspired him to show up at 4am is a mystery. It is however a good thing for a teacher when students attend without being prompted.

For years, I had no ashram. I did establish an ashram in 1974 just before Arthur Beverford returned to the USA from the Philippines. It is a heavy responsibility to run such a situation. Later I was in other ashrams, but as a student, which is much easier than having to supervise an establishment.

When I was in the Hare Krishna ashram, I had responsibilities for boys in the boarding school. I awakened some adults early in the morning. This is a disagreeable service because human beings are innately disinclined to rising early. Their resentment about it is cutting and disruptive. It affects the person who is assigned to make them rise early.

In Yogi Bhajan's ashram, someone came in the early morning about 4am. That person sang a song about rising and shining to give God one's glory. This was interesting because in the background one would also hear a woman singing this song. Her voice was like heaven. It was like being in a hellish place and then hearing the sweet voice of a female and taking relief from that, as if that was really some relief. However, that is the way of the senses to try to enjoy any which way from whatever little pleasure may be extracted in whichever way.

In the Hare Krishna ashram, they had a different approach which was to recite a prayer by one of their deceased teachers, name Bhaktivinoda, where it suggested that one should get up from sleeping on the Maya witch. The song began with the words *jiva jago*, which is Bengali, saying to awaken sleeping soul.

Why did Oliver attend? He is a person who is not habituated to rising at 3.45 in the morning?

To speak truthfully, I really do not care to know. For me the main happiness is that I am not responsible for his rising early. I do not have to exert for it. I can relax. Let someone else do that.

Some students feel that it is the responsibility of the teacher to awaken them. They feel that the teacher should provide an impetus for happiness when rising early. Subsequently, sooner or later, the student becomes sulky and hates the teacher for the early rise.

Sometimes I think to myself,

Why do you awaken people early in the morning?

Why not leave them in slumber?

What is the rush for spiritual practice?

Let them sleep.

Are you sure you want to absorb their inborn resentments?

They will rise. Then later they will resent you. Then later again they will abandon the practice and return to the usual sleeping away?

Who woke Oliver?

Which deity?

Which teacher?

Who feels that he should not sleep at the time when one gets the sweetest most blessed slumber which is between 4.30am and 6am?

Spiritual Value of a Self

Personally, I have no duty except to adhere to my spiritual source. Since such a duty is natural, it makes sense to say that I have no duty. Duty requires exertion. Connection to spiritual source happens regardless of attention or exertion. Therefore, it is not a duty.

For instance:

How is my body living even though I do not think of it? I do not make moment to moment adjustments to keep it breathing? If I say that it is my duty to stay alive, what does that mean? I am not instrumental in keeping my body alive from moment to moment.

Teaching yoga and writing books is part of personal desire but it is more part of the larger mission of the sum total divine source. Since I am a part of that I am part of that endeavor. Take for instance, striding. To stride some muscles and tendons in the feet, legs and thighs are operated. It is a conjoint endeavor. In teaching and writing, I am part of the endeavor.

Suppose I walk, then I say to someone:

I walk.

You can understand that the statement is more complex than the way I expressed it. So many cells, millions of them, must endeavor in some way to cause that walking action.

But suppose there is one particular cell in the big toe where that single cell is at the most convex part of the bottom of that toe. Now this cell has some pride like every other cell, so it begins to speak like this:

"You other cells, hear me once and for all. I feel the need to clear the confusion about who walks. It is I who does it. Please! None of you should make claims in relation to this. It is I alone whom causes the body to walk."

How would that be taken by the other millions of cells. Obviously, they will conclude the arrogant cell as a schizophrenic. In the same way, if I were to say my mission, then it would be to an extent a crazy statement. I am part of a larger, much larger endeavor.

Of course, there is some ego in me. Hence, I must tell myself that what I do has importance. That flattery facilitates the assigned job? I tell myself that I am important and that what I do is essential to the overall mission. Even though I do this, still I know that it is a fix to motivate completion of the assignment. I know that the deities can get the job done through another agent. I never forget that.

Some people disagree with that conclusion, explaining that I have special powers and abilities. Okay! But that is due to ignorance of the fact that in some other world, there may be millions of *Michael Beloved* type people. In contrast, there may be places where a person like me is the lowest class of the existence. On one side of the God face, someone saw me as a speck of color which they liked to see but what about on the other side of the trillions of God-faces. That one spec is not important.

Sometimes in the higher astral world, I meet a person who is my replacement for the next mission. Then I look at him and consider if he could handle the job. But then I say to myself:

"Who cares if he can do it? It is not my concern if he fails or succeeds. I will shift attention to the next assignment. If there is no other assignment, that is all the merrier. For me when I am freed of responsibilities, the fun begins."

In terms of my interest in specific students, this may sound dismal. I may catch some flak for this from students who feel that I should have a personal interest in their lives. However, before the blows begin to fly to my head, please take into consideration that I am not a reality unto myself. I do not stand out as something absolute. I am not God.

I am part of the operative energy of God. As a part, I function irrespective of personal desire. Do I have personal interest in any students?

The reality of it is that since I am not absolute, I must of necessity be both myself and my connection to spiritual source which means in effect that I am merely a utility of spiritual source.

Yogi Laughter

During breath infusion this afternoon, Yogeshwarananda was somewhere near the plane of consciousness my subtle body was synchronized to. I heard some laugher coming from an astral level. When I looked, he was nearby. There was louder laughter. I thought to check on the cause of his humor.

It was due to the fact that many persons on the spiritual path do not understand the value of hatha yoga in reference to gutting out the psyche and replacing its tendency-energies with energies from higher planes.

Many religious people are against the practice of hatha yoga, which they label as gymnastics or unnecessary austerities which distract a person from receiving the grace of God.

There are students who do hatha yoga for health reasons. Some others do it to tone the body for beautification. Some do it with a notion that their moral values are more important and that the austerities may only supplement the range of spiritual practices.

Yogesh said this:

I was lucky to meet Guruji Atmananda. I practiced ardently before that. I did. I did gruesome austerities and honed my willpower so as to bring it under a tight regiment. Still, in retrospect, I was lucky. Suppose that did not happen, where would I be now? I would be recognized as an exceptional yogi but I would not shift to the chit akash.

Mastering austerities would not do everything. Relying on getting help from the valid guru would not do everything either. The student must tighten sincerity and apply the self fittingly to the course.

Awake on another existential plane

The only person who attended breath infusion practice this morning was Tobe Terrell. Later in a discussion with two other men, the subject of the meditation session was discussed, as to how long it lasted and the events experienced during the session.

Tobe said that when he left the meditation hall, my head drooped forward. He left about thirty minutes after it began. I felt compelled to explain this.

This is a development which is the result of years of daily meditation practice as well as breath infusion kundalini yoga practice. There are two occurrences which may happen at this time, the first is that there may be an astral projection, a conscious or unconscious one. Then there may be a dimensional shift in existence whereby one loses affiliation with the physical body.

It is abnormal to leave in a conscious or unconscious astral projection when the body is in a tight lotus posture *(padmasana)*. Usually, the body will induce the person to recline. Then the kundalini will astral project the subtle form. If the physical body is tired, it will release the astral form from just about any posture but if it is not tired as in the case of when this meditation occurred, it will not release the astral body unless that body is reclined in some way, where it will not fall from a sitting posture.

When there may be a dimensional shift in existence, whereby I loose affiliation with the physical body, then I will be conscious in a psyche chamber which is not affiliated with that physical body. Hence, the physical body will be left to its own devices. It will appear from the physical end, that the yogi fell asleep during meditation even though this is not factual because the yogi would be awake on another plane of consciousness.

Yogini Kriya / Scarf Wrap

Recently a Buddha goddess spoke to me about a tunnel-up kriya for female yogis. This is called the scarf wrap kriya, because it is similar to when in ancient times, people carried items in sacks and would tie the mouth of these bags and carry that over one shoulder.

Their belongings would be in that one sack. Near the mouth, it would be tied with a cord.

For some years now I received female kriyas which are specific for use in certain female bodies. Usually, I am given these procedures not for personal use but to share with some other person at a later date. I may not know the person or may not have met the person. Sooner or later that person will be on my path of fate either in the physical existence or in the astral world.

This particular process is for the female to collect and then bundle subtle hormone energy. Once the energy is collected, it will increase in potency. If it is prevented from being expressed through the lower torso of the subtle body, it will radiate upwards through the trunk and neck and then enter the head.

In the astral regions, yoginis who use this technique are easily recognized by those in the know. No light emanates from their lower torso and the only light one sees is the light which gushes through their necks into their heads.

While in comparison some females who should use this process but who do not practice are seen to have a bright light emanating from their lower torsos and no light in their necks and heads.

Here is the procedure.

- Extinguish the radiation of energy which emanates from the lower torso outwards.
- Use a mystic wrap to contain it.
- Tie off the mystic wrap. Go within it. Infuse it with upward-lifting energy.

- Open the tie just a little to test to see if the light will shine upwards.
- If it will not do so, find an advanced yogini for advice.
- If the light shines upwards, re-tie the wrap. Continue the upward-lifting energy procedure.
- Extend the top of the mystic wrap up to the neck, so that none of the energy passes through the trunk of the body, so that it can only go through the neck.

This is useless for males. It is also not applicable to certain females. It is useful to females of a certain body type. It is important to know that I cannot whimsically, or even upon request, explain in detail this procedure. It is specifically given by another male or female teacher because it comes with a package locator which limits its transmission to specific people.

Is this a prejudice?

It sure is!

Why publish this information?

Because the deity requested that it be done, even though the deity had no intentions of giving details to everyone.

When a session of breath infusion begins with heaviness, laziness or a feeling of depression, it is all the better for the yogi because through the breath infusion, all or most of that energy can be removed.

The student should be happy to begin such a session and also be proud of the fact that he/she recognized the negative energy and can reduce or eliminate it.

An example of this is when a yogi awakens in a groggy condition. Soon after beginning the breath infusion, say for about five minutes of practice, the gloom and doom vanishes from the mind.

Yet we find that some students who are in a bad way emotionally and/or mentally, do the practice and soon return to the depressed mood.

Why is this?

In the Vedic literature there is an analogy about this, where they describe an ascetic who is like an elephant. The large mammal goes for a bath in a clear stream but as soon as it emerges it goes to a dust pit, rolls and sprays dust over itself.

Other species do this. Humans who have morbid addictions sometimes get treatments which work for a time but then regardless of the treatment, the addicts again take the drug and resume the helpless condition.

The most beautiful peacock will snatch cockroaches. What has beauty to do with it?

It depends on where the beauty is.

Is it inside the mind or emotions or is it outside in the physical appearance?

Is it in the externally-intended courtesy? Is it deep within below the psychological fascia?

Places Hereafter / Buddha's View

Yesterday I discussed the Buddha's view about locations hereafter. This is from the Pali Canon history of the life of Buddha. In the book *Majjhima Nikaya* which was translated by Namamoli and Bodhi, there is a discourse where Buddha explained to *Sariputta,* his senior disciple, about the destinations a person may attain hereafter.

Buddha list five locales (page 169 of the translation) plus a special one which he termed as nibbana (Sanskrit *nirvana*):

These six were:

- hell
- animal realm
- ghost realm
- human beings
- gods
- *nibbana*

The last one listed is *nibbana* which Buddha described as the person realizing himself with direct knowledge, here and now, enters upon and abides in the deliverance of mind and deliverance by wisdom that are taintless with destruction of taints.

If these places are illusions in the mind, why does he list hell and the realm of the gods, or heaven?

Are these places real or not?

Is Buddha a reliable mystic?

Did he see or experience these places factually, the way a human traveler may experience New York or Mumbai?

Are there astral jails or not?

Is everything besides physical reality just something in a person's mind?

If Buddha was an atheist why did he mention a realm of the gods? Why he did say he was visited by a deity?

There is one hitch in his description which should be known. He did not mention a divine world. The only divine situation mentioned is nibbana which is the state of enlightenment which he claimed to have attained.

His description of these destinations after a person leaves the body is not original. It is adapted from the Vedic description of hereafter destinations with one specific omission which is a divine world where people in divine bodies reside.

How many people know that the word *nirvana (nibbana)* is in the Bhagavad Gita which was recited before the time of Buddha?

Here is a general list of the destinations listed in the Vedic literatures:

- hellish astral regions
- lower-than-human creature existence
- ghost astral beings who strongly desire but who cannot assume a human embryo
- astral beings who are in the course of becoming a human embryo
- heavenly astral worlds which are supervised by supernatural beings who are called gods or devas
- non-environment spiritual energy (energy *nirvana*)
- environment spiritual energy (landscape *nirvana*)

The difference between Buddha's listing and that of the *Puranas*, is the lack of a divine environment where people reside.

There is however in the Buddha's descriptions, a *Tushita* heaven which is a living situation where male and female realized people reside. That place is within the astral heavens, not outside of it, unlike the Vedic divine world of Vishnu or Shiva.

Souls as Functions of Desire

Looking back over my life, I can clearly see that for all I am supposed to be, I am for the most part a function of desire. The questions are:

Is it my desire?

Is it my parent's desire?

Is it my spouse's desire?

Is it my friend's desire?

Is it society's collective desire?

During meditation this morning, early on, I heard and saw some relatives. They were located about one thousand miles away but since I used a supernatural perception, I saw them just as if I was in their vicinity. They were in an astral residence of another relative. They were chitty chatting about getting larger and larger houses, mansion buildings, to live in. An elder in the group, described where she lived years ago when her body was a child. She lived in a one room house which was crouched compared to where she resides currently.

She was happy that many relatives lived in much larger residences. To her the desire for better accommodations was fulfilled inch by inch as the family became more educated, got higher wages and enjoyed greater privileges.

Is that who we are?

Small Achievement in Yoga

Yoga is usually highlighted by the big achievements, like when one experiences the first transcendence absorption *(samadhi)* or like how one may experience the rise of kundalini through the central spinal passage into the head. One may have an experience of being transported to a divine world which is imperishable, and for the duration one may experience the self as someone divine.

However, yoga also has the small achievements which in the short range are incremental and hardly noticeable but which over time, adds gains. Failure to notice opportunities for small achievements is a setback for a yogi, because it means that there will be a telltale inattentiveness which will prove to be costly.

This morning, venturing from the place of meditation to another building, I fiddled with some keys, one of which would open that other building. As I did so in semi-darkness, I groped for a way to identity the correct key. I remembered that there was grey tape on that specific key.

Right then I saw the grey tape in the semi-darkness but my mind was not satisfied that this was the key. It wanted to see more of the key; it wanted to look and feel the key, to be certain that it was the correct one.

This dissatisfaction of the mind is one of the banes of a yogi, in that if he/she does not stop the mind from procuring more information about an object, that will cause stagnation in practice.

What to do about it?

As soon as the mind tries to procure more information than is necessary, one should cease the sensual hunt for more contact with the said object.

If a key was identified positively by a grey tape, there is no need for the mind to inquire further. It should not direct the eyes to see more of the key. It should not direct the sense of touch to handle the key. Its concern for the key should be promptly terminated. The yogi should not allow the mind to indulge with the key any longer.

Failure to make that small restriction would result in a compulsive habit of procuring more information than necessary from nearly every object the mind encounters. That would consume much of the yogi's time, seeking sense objects which are not worthy of attention. It would cause the yogi to be secretly, privately within his/her mind, indulge in sensual contacts which are unworthy of yoga practice and which make the yogi into a failure for detachment from worthless sense objects.

Deity Worship

Worshipping deities is a large responsibility. If one installs a deity one will be committed to be there on a daily basis to have daily ceremonies.

It is regular that someone gets excited and commits to perform ceremonial worship of a deity but usually the enthusiasm reduces. Then the founder of the temple is left with the duties and cannot manage the responsibilities. Disciples and devotees may become disgruntled with a person who began an ashram. The relationships turn sour. The founder must render all services and raise funds himself.

Who will cook for the deity?

Who will say the mantras?

Who will finance the expenses?

If one has a specific deity in mind, is one certain that the deity inspired one? It is one thing to select a deity. It is entirely different to be selected by a deity.

Narad was once cursed by Daksha, like this,

"Since you interfere in the social affairs of others and you do not appreciate the materialistic lifestyle, since you feel that young men should not waste their time getting married and raising children, how can it be that you may remain in a residence when residence itself is caused by the presence of a wife? In that case, my condemnation is that you should not live in a shelter for any length of time. Wander from here to there. Never enjoy the comforts of a home."

I cited this, because if someone requires my support, it will not be reliable because of a similar curse.

Ordinary people say something that makes sense, which is that one cannot have a cake if one eats it. It is either that I keep the cake uneaten or I eat it and it is no longer there. A person like me, who has no appreciation for home on earth, cannot be blessed to remain in any place for long. Look at my life I moved from pillar to post like a wandering nomad. You can imagine that even with four children and their two mothers, I wandered.

One grandfather cursed like this:

"You are different. We do not know why you are weird. In any case, since you are like a rolling stone, you will never gather moss."

Considering this and seeing the power of the earth-bound entities, I came to the conclusion that I would never have a home in this world. As soon as I settle down somewhere, providence pronounces this, "Get up! Get up! Do not sleep here. No loitering. Take comfort elsewhere."

Kundalini / Tushita Heaven

This morning I was shown a method of using the kundalini yoga process for reaching the *Tushita* heaven. This was shown by Buddha, a murti sculptured form which was at the Zen Hostel in Gainesville, Florida. Even though this form was damaged, it is still used as an energy-transport conveyance by Buddha.

Psychically-sensitive yogis may use a sculptured form to reach Buddha for instructions.

He explained that there were several ways of reaching the *Tushita* heavens after leaving the physical body but a yogi should not be anxious about killing the body or discarding it, unless it is terminally ill or has some serious incapacity. If the body is in a coma, people on the physical side should not prolong the state of the body, but should instead do whatever is required to terminate the body so that the spirit who used the body can be transited to the hereafter and attain whatever destination he/she qualifies for.

A question arose as to where the Tushita heaven is located in reference to the Vedic layout of the hereafter.

Is it in the *Swarga* heavenly worlds?

Is it in the *Satyaloka* region which is the residential environment of the Brahma deity who visited Buddha?

Is it beyond the *Satyaloka* regions in *Vishnuloka* or *Shivaloka*?

Buddha said that it was part of the *Satyaloka* regions. In reference to the earthly existence, one who lives in the *Tushita* heavens exists like a god.

A kundalini yogi can reach that place if the sushumna central spinal passage is cleared near the top of it in the neck. That part of the passage must be completely cleared and then the yogi can reach the Tushita heavens even while using a physical body.

It is best if the yogi can transit there beforehand, because then the transit will be definite when there is final departure from the physical system.

Monitor of Death

The Vedic system extols the North and East more than the other directions, with the West being used as well and with the South only being used during death ceremonies and the *pinda* rites for departed souls.

Going north is regarded as a progression to higher worlds, while going south is regarded as a digression to the hellish regions.

The Vedic system gives the north pole as an upward direction and the south as a downward direction. This is consistent with the way the solar system is designed with the sun as the hub with the planets spread horizontally, with an up and down in reference to the galaxy we live in.

In Vedic ceremonies, the sacrificial performer is never to face the south unless it is a death ceremony or one related to departed ancestors who are in a bad way and who need rebirth. The monitor of death resides in the South and approaches to arrest the subtle bodies of socially-condemned persons to take them to the south to the hellish astral regions.

Competent yogis however are not afraid of this deity. They are friendly to him. Incompetent yogis pretend not to be fearful of death but are in fact, squeamish about the deity.

When the god of death comes, the competent yogi usually says to him, "You do not have to evict me. I will leave voluntarily."

But the incompetent yogis usually ask for more time, "Give me a few more years to perfect the practice. Take someone else. Let me practice. Take a bad guy. Come back at some other time."

Chit Akash Light

This morning, the breath infusion session was great, with small rises of bursting infused energy and some direct kundalini shooting. Small rises of bursting infused energy and small firing of kundalini are very important but initially a student has little or no perception of this.

Those who practiced for a time, should get themselves weaned from the big events and focus more on the small incremental progresses. This is where the real progress is made because the micro-sensitivity is developed and one can begin perceiving very subtle phenomena and move away from being a happiness glutton.

When I sat to meditate, I checked the neck click switch. Three days ago, I was to write about this but I failed to file the report because I was involved in social affairs which consumed much time. First, there is a stipulation in the *Yoga Sutras*, about sleep being a vritti, a regular mental modification which needs to be eliminated before meditation can begin.

The coreSelf has to be outside of the influence of the sleep energy of the kundalini when advance meditation is to take place. If one is not outside of this energy, it is a no-go signal that the meditation will be of low quality.

What does it mean to be outside the influence of the sleep energy? After all the sleep energy potential is always there, latent at least, lurking in the background, like a python waiting to strike the yogi and bring him down either to the dream level of the astral existence or to put his objectivity out of commission temporarily.

I do a procedure which I was supposed to complete in six months but which I failed to master due to pressure of time and place. Still, I do it at a slow pace like a retarded student taking an academic course. A course which took the average student three months, took that retarded kid three years to complete.

Lahiri said six months. Then he went away. He will come back when the six months are over, even if it takes six million years. Whatever time it will take me, that time to him will be six months, but I must complete the course.

At this stage of the practice in reaching *chit akash*, there is a stage during the meditation when there is a click sound the neck. Then there is a jump of energy. The coreSelf finds itself to be in a new state of awareness like something happened, like it is awake and then it finds that it is in a new awakeness that is different, that is free of drowsy energy.

At first when this happened, I heard it in the neck. After two more sessions of meditation and observation, I realize that something like a partition screen was removed, causing energy to pass freely from the trunk of the subtle body through the neck into the head of the form. This created the bubble body which is something I was first introduced to by Siddha Swami Nityananda.

Nityananda was a cheating yogi, because he did not want people to know how advanced he really was. He would act as if he was not a yogi of worth but he was advanced.

Why did he do that?

Would someone who love others, hide money and not share it with the needy?

To make matters worse, Swami would eat whatever was prepared for him and in whatever quantity. Some women who were related to him, and some who recognized that there was something special, fed him large quantities of food. He would eat until his belly swelled. Why did he accommodate them in this way?

After I realize that click was in the neck and that it caused the sleep potential to vanish, I decided to descend through the neck and operate the switch instead of waiting for it to operate involuntarily. I used to wait about twenty to thirty minutes in a certain meditative state, before I heard the switch.

I went into the neck and found the membrane and tried to clear it, to cause it to allow the energy to pass freely from the trunk into the head. At first when I did this, I noticed a slight change in the head but it was not enough to be the same as the natural click I heard before. I would have to wait about ten minutes before there was complete removal of the activated or inactivated sleep mode energy.

One sure way of knowing that this actually occurred was to check on the naad sound. In this practice, naad sound is usually found not at the left or right but at the center of the head and in the back straight up. I found it there each time without fail, but after the click sound and the energy would flow through the neck, there was a blend of music in naad. Before that naad was there with one tone. As soon as there was that click and the energy flowed freely from the trunk into the head, the sound was a blend of notes. It was a sweet taste to the hearing sense.

This morning when the click occurred, it was like sunlight in the psyche. There was a source of this light to the top but I could not see the source, I only perceive the light produced. The light stayed with me and filled up the psychic chamber I was in. It did not hurry away as most mystic lights do.

Sleep Research

I currently study the sleep removal requirement which was given by Patanjali where he listed sleep as one of the *cittavritti* ordinary operations of the mento-emotional energy. As a teacher of kriya yoga, I should know these details so that when teaching I do not cheat the students or pretend that I know what I am ignorant of.

Lahiri left some months ago with an instruction, saying that I was to complete a certain practice in six months. Assuming that he is correct, I realize now that six months for him may be six years, or six lives even, for me. That six months must be according to some time reckoning in another dimension.

Part of the study is the sleep *vritti* removal. The other *vrittis* are small aspects and very obvious ones when considered in reference to sleep. Sleep strikes from behind when one least expects. It is like being blindfolded, tied and put into a pitch-dark cave without seeing the kidnapper.

The other *vritti* operational modes are

- valid analysis
- invalid analysis
- imagination
- memory.

If one is alert and has the interest to keenly observe what happens in the mind-psyche, with the help of the *buddhi* intellect orb, one can perceive these operations

But the sleep *vritti* is not so easy to tackle. How can one fight someone who sneaks behind, strikes one in the head with a mallet, binds one and puts one in a dark cave? One never saw the person. One may never ever see him.

Both valid and invalid analyses are in the territory of the *buddhi* intellect orb in the head of the subtle body. These mental functions are plain for all to see. For details a student should study the mental activity in meditation.

For imagination, the student can study that by observing how the intellect creates fanciful ideas using sound and color for the most part. For memory, the intellect is helpful in revealing what is hidden in the compressed information from the subconscious mind. But sleep is a different aspect which is totally controlled by the kundalini lifeForce.

What I observed is that sleep is conquered when the neck region of the yogi is cleared of heavy subtle energy. This region of the body is a bottleneck which keeps energy from passing freely between the subtle trunk and head.

This restriction of movement of energy between the head and trunk is directly related to our inability to control sleep. If I do a thorough session of breath infusion, and somehow manage to extract at least about 80% of the dulling energy in the body, then during the meditation which immediately follows, there will be an awakening. There will be more awareness and less sleep energy in the psyche.

The single and very direct cause of this jolt in awareness is the breath infusion practice. That alone is the cause of this, because of the removal of dulling energy from the psyche

In the meditation this morning there were two bursts of increased awakeness which were in effect two burst of decreased sleep energy. The first was like when there is a bit of daylight at dawn. The second was like about half hour after that first hint of light spreads, and more light is manifested to everyone.

Possibility of Going to Satyaloka

Last night in the astral world I was questioned by four men. They wanted information about transit to the highest astral regions in the super-subtle existence. The basic question was about qualifying to relocate there after being deprived of the physical form.

That achievement hinges both on the qualifications required and an invitation to transit there. It is not just a matter of qualifying, because someone may qualify and still not gain entry. A yogi who tries to force his way into such a place, is called a *kuyogi*, which means a criminal mystic. Those places are deity-controlled zones where one is not expected except by invitation. Still even if one is invited, if one does not quality, the invitation cannot be serviced until the invitee is worthy.

For one reason or the other, a deity may summon a person to a higher realm. It may even be that the deity infuses the subtle body of the person. That would transform the person, causing him/her to transit temporarily or permanently to the deity's place. This relies on the deity according to his/her power to adjust the person's psyche.

One of the four persons asked specifically about the possibility of going to the place which is called *Brahmaloka*. This place is also called *Satyaloka*, which means the realm of the highest-quality environment which could be experienced within the scope of psychic nature.

This place is so fabulous compared to our situation, that it inconceivable to the imagination. It is hard to believe that anyone would leave such a place and descend to live the life we have as high-class mammals.

After having the discussion with those four guys in the astral last night, a Buddha deity informed me of a few things.

To get to Satyaloka, one must be completely celibate in the sense of having lost sexual orientation to vulgar sexual participation. The tendency for sex penetration or reception cannot be latent or dormant. It must not be present in the form one uses to access the *Satyaloka* place.

Those who feel that celibacy means following moral principles or abstaining from sexual indulgence, are mistaken because for instance a person from the earth who is attached to family life in terms of having progeny, also cannot reach the *Satyaloka* place. This includes persons who are religiously inclined and who follow marriage vows and other moral stipulations.

The subtle body must not have the sexual pleasure inclination nor the tendency to function as a parent. Even though some of the forms there are child forms, there are no children who require parental care. The child forms do not appear there on the basis of sexual intercourse, marriage or family life as we have on earth.

One of the guys asked if I would qualify for *Satyaloka*. He expressed doubts on the basis of my having lived with women over the years and as to the fact that I am still in association with women and may be in the foreseeable future. He thought that any type of attraction to women for any reason would disqualify someone.

This is a serious consideration for one and all. However, it is not important to know what will happen to me and as to my potential for transiting to such places. I am irregular. One does not know what use the deity may have for me which may cause my subtle body to alter considerably either to go to such places or to be displaced from there.

The key point to understand is that if a sensible yogi desires to go to *Satyaloka*, he should know what to take and what not to take. An informed traveler will not approach the flight gate of a commercial aircraft with a weapon. He knows that weapons are not allowed. He will discard the gun before approaching the airport. A yogi has to know the qualification for each place and then work to suit in approaching such zones

Deities in the Original Buddhism

So far in going through one of the Pali canons I found no evidence to support the claim that Buddha said that everyone was his equal and could attain Buddhahood on their own the way he did. I found no evidence that Buddhism is an atheistic religion or that the Buddha did not attest to deities or gods.

Repeatedly in the *Majjhima Nikaya* there is mention about heavenly worlds and about disciples and lay disciples going to such places, about the

Buddha having come from such a place and about his mother going there after her demise which occurred a week after his birth.

I read a story about different categories of gods, four to be exact as told by *Ananda* one of Buddha's disciples.

The list which is on page 1004 is:

- deities of limited radiance
- deities of immeasurable radiance
- deities of defiled radiance
- deities of pure radiance

It is important to check with the original sources and to know what was developed or presented later by other Buddhist authorities but which was either not said by Buddha nor stressed by him. Others may arrive at valid realizations and processes but we should be clear not to tag their accomplishments as the declarations of Buddha.

Attention Misuse

In kriya yoga, full attention internally to whatever process one practices is essential for full success. There will always be some partial success if I do a process haphazardly, and that may be enough for me, depending on how much I desire to leave aside the benefits of the physical world.

Someone wants to leave aside all benefits and does so sincerely. Some other person says that he/she wants to go away from it but really does not mean this. It is not what I desire but what my nature craves. That, whatever it is, will prevail. Willpower has authority when it is funded by the essential nature, not otherwise.

Most of us are extroverts. We are interested in using the psyche as a unit for procuring real or imagined fulfillments. But this system of procurements is not yoga.

Some of us do meditation to internalize but only for the purpose of getting ourselves in order so as to be extrovert. There are covert extroverts who appear on first glance to be introverts because they are not eager to socialize. They have a tendency to toe the moral line. But even these covert extroverts fail at practice. It is because they are disguised extroverts.

A simple action, like using a blindfold when doing breath infusion and meditation, would help to increase one's introvert tendencies. Bit by bit practicing to keep the visual interest within the psyche, would help to reprogram the methods of expression and interaction of the psyche.

There are many hidden parts of the psyche which need to be discovered. These can be found through doing breath infusion and the meditation. But even discovery of these hidden parts is not sufficient if one does not attend it and abandon running here and there after meditation to chase other realities.

Each person has just enough attention to fill the psyche with interest energy so that not even a split-second of concern can be afforded to external interests.

Neglecting the Ancestors

During this past week, I spoke to two young men about the possibility of their helping their ancestors to take rebirth. The trend now is to transfer this responsibility to some other person. The young men who are viable think that somebody can do that and they can proceed with what they term to be their spiritual objectives.

Why is this?

Why is there a reluctance to beget progeny, to support and invest in the human continuation pool?

Why after getting a body, one is reluctant to contribute to anyone else who may need an embryo?

Early Rise Negativity

One of the most difficult things to establish in oneself and in others is the early rise program which was in vogue in most yoga ashrams in ancient times. This became legendary under the term of *brahma muhurta*.

Muhurta means hour and *brahma* means a special time of day about one and one-half hours before sunrise, say about 4.30am near the equator, when it is most facilitating to reach the brahma level of existence, the exclusive spiritual zone.

Near the equator, roosters crow around 4.30am, but this happened before the advent and prevalence of electricity. Since we have lights blaring through the night, even roosters become confused and have no idea when to begin the day's crowing session.

Once I lived near the equator, where a rooster crowed from about 4.30am every morning without fail. The bird would keep crowing every ten or so minutes until it saw human beings moving about.

I lived at another location where the roosters would crown across the village to each other's beginning at about 4.30am until about 5.30am when the crack of dawn first appeared. One rooster who felt that he was the king of the birds, would crow at first and then he would listen, then another one would crow, then that bird-king would crow to signal approval, then another one would crow. They continued like that until all roosters in the vicinity sent their calls.

Over the years in this very life, I found that some people, even some who live in a spiritual community, an ashram, are resentful towards rising as early as 4.30am or earlier. Actually, the requirement is for rising before 4.30am so that one begins spiritual practice at 4.30am.

If for instance one has to do puja ceremonial worship at 4.30am, one must take bath, put sacred marking on the body, say prayers, approach the altar, do duties to a deity and then begin the ceremony at 4.30am. This would mean rising before 3.30am.

If for instance one does yoga postures with breath infusion and meditation, one can rise at about 4am and still have time to begin at 4.30am. This is because for just doing personal yoga one does not have to do many preparatory actions as in the case of approaching deities on an altar.

Either way, one will have to rise before 4.30am to begin whatever practice or worship one should do at that time.

I used to be head of household with four children and their two mothers. Even today people marvel that I did that especially in the current monogamous cultures of the developed countries.

Two women in one house?

Unheard of!

People think, "How did you do that? That is against female nature. No woman would put up with that. You abused them."

Anyway, no sense crying over the past.

I awoke the family early every day, children included.

Were there resentments?

There sure were.

Even today I still catch flack over it. There are still energies, resentment forces bubbling up from the psyches of household members which reach me like daggers stabbing though the body on a dark night.

Right now, I am alone, cooking for myself. It is a breeze when compared to the days when I had a family of four children and two women to manage, with me putting on the daily early rise pressure. Day after day there was that push back, that collective hostility which I endured. Now as a free as a bee, I do not have to absorb that.

It is interesting how that negative energy will stand its ground for years and fight to the finish, winning in the end, when one sees that it sticks with one's family and as soon as they are out from under it, they resume the late rising.

What is it in human nature which commands that early rise is unwanted, undesired and disliked?

Right now, all alone and blue, with no one to take care of me and cook my meals, I am happy as a lark as the saying goes, meaning that after morning practice, I settle down, cook a meal for the day, sit and take it.

This causes my whole life to change where early in the day, all the digestion for that day takes place. Everything shifts upwards. There is no negative energy to deal with, to mix in and slow the progress.

Living single as a yogi is wonderful indeed. A student should enjoy solitude whenever providence allows it. You never know when providence will pull the rug of easy spiritual life from under you.

- There are three kinds of people who live in ashrams and who rise early. There are those who love to rise early and who do so with a smile on their faces, who look forward to the opportunity to practice spiritual discipline before sunrise
- There are those who pretend to rise early, who do so because they have to, because it is an imposed condition for living in the ashram. Those who hate to rise early and who have no pretenses about it. These persons honestly admit that it is the worse feature of ashram life.
- Those who pretend that they like rising early but who in fact would not do so if they were not prestige-hungry. They get up early so as to boost their status in the ashram, to become known as the most austere people. These are insecure inmates who discover that one way to gain a reputation is the rise early. They have no sincere interest in it but do it to acquire honor.

The pretense ascetics feel that everyone in the world should rise early even women, even though traditionally in ancient times, most yogis were males. If you read the *Ramayana* and the *Puranas* you will hardly read of women ascetics. In fact, even some wives of Lord Krishna were annoyed every morning when he would rise early to do meditation and deity puja worship ceremony of God. They would wonder what got into his head.

If your husband is God, why should he rise early to worship? But it may be and we may conjecture on this, as to Krishna having to do that, because after all, God cannot afford to be an atheist, to not believe in God, in Himself.

But in the Mahabharata, there is one special woman who turns the negative responses of Krishna's wives on its head. That person is *Draupadi*, a woman who managed five princely husbands, the Pandavas. When asked about her magic over these handsome and capable men, one of the attributes which she described was her rising first before any of her men and her eating meals last. Draupadi was up and at it. She prepared the meals, did the deity puja ceremonies and managed numerous servants for the royal household. A super woman is indeed!

Rising early is the best of my day, my favorite time. I enjoy it.

Encounter with the Astral Pacific

Last night in the astral world, I was with some aborigine people from Papua, New Guinea. Exactly how I was shifted with these people, I do not know. I did not trace the cause of this.

These were a seafaring tribe. A leader spoke about how they live and how modern incursions affect their people. He was at a loss about what to do to prevent the onward march of civilization into their lifestyle.

Because I was in the astral world, I suddenly left the land area of their bush camp and were with this leader and his two sons in a boat plying across the Pacific. This was the astral Pacific which is just as frightening as the physical ocean.

This was a large canoe with an outrigger bar to one size. It was intimidating to be in such an insignificant craft in the large Pacific Ocean. The aborigines had no idea of the actual size of the Pacific. To them there was nothing dangerous about being in the sea.

The leader was in the bow of the canoe. I was seated in the middle. His sons were in the stern. The eldest held a crude rudder bar which was used to steer. There was no food in the canoe, nothing. They were nude except for the leader man who used a small loin cloth. I wore British khaki clothes with no hat, nothing to deal with the sun shining mercilessly down over the Pacific, except that the sun was cool because it was the astral sun. The seats were so small that only one person could sit. If you had to move forward or backward, if a person was seated that person had to tilt to the side to allow passage.

The leader spoke about their situation in modern times. Suddenly, we looked as the rudder bar floated way. In that astral place, we all knew that it was seized by the astral Pacific. The leader looked at his son with stern eyes, relating that the son should not have allowed the ocean to take the rudder. It floated away quickly. The boat was carried away from it by an undercurrent which we could see.

However, the leader got his wits about him. He sat behind me in the center of the boat. He used magic to steer the boat according to a sun shadow which his body created. His sons looked on because for them this was a learning incidence of what to do when the ocean confiscates a steering mechanism.

Soon after this we reached a caged area which was supported by four posts which were stuck in the ocean by someone. There was food in the cage but the leader could not get into it because it was enchanted by the person who built it so that no one could enter it.

Understanding that he could not break the enchantment, the leader sat down again. He did some incantations. Suddenly we found ourselves on an island somewhere in that astral place. The leader and his sons were happy about this. They ran away down a dirt path, with the leader outpacing them. I ran behind. My astral body could not run at their speed.

After this I reached an area where I saw a man. He directed me to use a path to meet them but I could not reach them. They disappeared. After this I came back to my physical body.

Relationship with Krishna

If some person, any person, relates to Krishna in a murti sculpture or in painting or photo, that is based on a specific relationship that person has with Krishna. The issue then, or the investigation as to the whys and wherefores of this, should be about the relationship with Krishna. Is it direct?

Is it true that everyone has a direct connection with Krishna?

If that is true explain why many people during the time of Krishna could not directly approach him? When Sudama Vipra, the poverty-stricken brahmin went to visit Krishna at Dwaraka, the poor guy found all gates open. No restriction was there. But when Brahma, the planetary creator went to see Krishna he had to wait, even though he had important matters to discuss.

When Duryodhana made gourmet food for Krishna, the Lord refused to dine. When Vidura made a poor man's lunch, Krishna eagerly accepted it.

When the hunch-backed woman Kubja invited Krishna into her place because she was in love with him, Krishna went there and fulfilled the lady's desires and even made the woman into a beauty queen but when Shurpanakha who was somewhat ugly by contemporary standards pleaded with Rama (a *Vishnu* divinity) to be accepted as a lover, Rama ordered his brother to mutilate her nose.

It is a matter of relationship. The communication is allowed through the gate of relationship. What relationship does someone have with Krishna? This is provided he actually has a relationship with the real Krishna and not with another deity or with his own imagination about Krishna?

- Arjuna has the relationship of a friend.
- Devaki had the relationship of a mother.
- Pradyumna had the relationship of a son.
- Subhadra had the relationship of a sister.
- Sandipani Muni had the relationship of being Krishna's instructor.

Eat as Early as You Can

Eating to facilitate yoga is not a simple matter. Eating beneficially is struggle for a yogi in regards to the effects of associations from others.

Here I speak from personal experience, struggling with diet and the time for eating since I first assumed this body in my father's genitals, all the way into and out of my mother's uterus, to being under the eating direction of a grandparent, and then being under the eating direction of a step mother, then being under the format of a mother, then under that of the US Air Force, then under several employers and friends. Then I was in ashrams and with several other friends.

Then came the big development of having children, for which I lived with women. If a yogi wants to go mainstream and intends to succumb to varied influences, he/she will have no problems with the time of eating. Otherwise, there will conflicts for going against the grain.

Having children is a problem but still that does not mean that one should not have infants. It only means that one must brace for hassles. In as much as I struggled in my father's body, and in my mother's, to rein in their eating habits and to change to what was conducive for yoga practice, my children when they entered my psyche, struggle to switch the adjustment I made to bring my body in line with the yogic eating procedure. This struggle continued for as long as the children remained with me because of their minor status.

Yes, they ate what I provided and at the time that I stipulated but nevertheless that was an uphill battle with me on the bottom getting most of the blows because nature is disinclined to the yogic way as a matter of course. It will give more support to the non-yogic way than it will to the yogi process.

My proposal is that a yogi should eat as early as possible. This means the main meal of the day should be the breakfast meal. That should be soon after the morning breath infusion and meditation.

A mistake that yogis make, is that they fall under the eating habits of their spouses. This is mostly done for convenience, especially if the male yogi has a job and cannot find the time to prepare meals. Some are from a family situation in which they did not participate in the preparation of meals. Thus, as householders they are at a loss of how to prepare meals. They depend on the skill of the spouse, which is based on that person's ethnic background, which more than likely was non-yogic.

Eat as soon as you can. In fact, if you can, prepare the meal. Do not be lazy. Do not be dependent on others who are disinclined to early meals.

Boring Sushumna Nadi

For the kundalini to pass through the *sushumna nadi* into the head, that *nadi* must be cleared. However, as soon as kundalini subsides to *muladhara* chakra, the central passage will invariable become filled with dense astral energy. The more a student practices, the more likely that eventually *sushumna* will stay cleared and will not become congested with dense energy.

Possibly, a more serious concern is if kundalini becomes habituated to going through the central spine into the head. If it is addicted to that, the yogi has the achievement because at the time of final passing from the physical body, it is likely that kundalini will of its own accord move upward. This is good for the yogi.

One does not know what one's condition will be at the time of passing, if one will be in a coma or if one will be occupied with pains and discomfort. In which case, one's ability to make kundalini go through *sushumna* will be suspended.

If one cannot guide or direct kundalini upwards, it will take its instinctive route, like for instance going through the tiny hole at the bottom of the spine, going through the bigger hole which leads through the genitals, or going somewhere else. If it does that the self will find itself in a lower astral environment. But if kundalini is habituated to ascending the spine and if it forgets about the lower portals, even if one is out of commission and cannot control the existential conditions at the time of death, like a good servant who helps the master when the master is inconvenienced, kundalini will do the needful.

Recently when I practiced with students, one man's kundalini rose suddenly. Even though his observing self was out of commission, having be blown into light, his body stood on the knees without falling, just balancing. In that case, kundalini like a good servant kept the body from falling. He looked more like a cobra which was erect with its hood spread.

Training kundalini to ascend the spine results in getting kundalini oriented to going through sushumna as its default passage. In the story of *Puranjan* which is in the *Srimad Bhagavata*, *Puranjan*, that inattentive fellow, passed from the body by going through the anus chakra.

I am not fond of the anus, or of its work dealing with the waste of the body, which is a most valuable service mind you. Still, I have no desire to pass through the anus at the time of death. But if I am not careful, if the system remains as it was when I first got this body, that is exactly what will happen.

Permanent clearance of *sushumna nadi* has to do with lifestyle more than anything else. You can do as much breath infusion as your heart desires. If you do not streamline the lifestyle to suit the yoga aspiration, the *sushumna* nadi will be clogged repeatedly, because it is the cultural activities which generate the quality of energy which is in *sushumna*.

Containment of Energy

Tonight, Buddha explained the importance of the containment of energies. He said that the problems occur because of not keeping the individual psyche from mixing indiscriminately on the emotional and mental planes of consciousness.

He felt that if the entity can have the psychic energy converted into a form which does not require an exploitive environment to function, all traumatic states which are undesirable would cease.

We had a good laugh when I asked him about who was to do the conversion.

Who indeed would do it because the entity is unable to transform his/her mental and emotional energies into any such containment since the energies are disinclined to that naturally and want to be expressed into the world?

Buddha remarked that the breath infusion process is great. He said that he did not know why he did not discover it. I replied that in his case, it was unnecessary because of his brute mental force which was sufficient to acquire the attainments he aspired to.

Bickering and Fighting

A natural outcrop of this creation is bickering and fighting. Using a boy's form during this lifetime, I noticed how people bickered and fought in their families, friendships, nations, and in the world at large. In every part of the world, on every continent and island, there is some life form. Each is involved in quarrel and violence.

There is a vicious under-current in the fight for resources. In a lecture yesterday, I explained how the good guys and bad guys are involved in the same business in the physical world. That is exploitation.

Once this is realized as to our individual participation, the next step is to know how involved we are and how to reduce that. One should realize if it is possible to eliminate that. If because of the parameters of this existence, it cannot be eliminated, the next step is to consider a transit to some other place which is not symptomatic of exploitation and which does not have that as a necessary lifestyle.

Even in the body there is bickering and fighting, like when the tongue argues with the teeth as to how much sugary foods one should eat. The teeth shivered as the body approached sugary food. The teeth said, "Now we are finished. Now we are done. The cruel tongue has no concern for anyone but itself. Maybe it will survive this. Maybe it will not. What will it be if it survives by itself? Why does it not consider this?"

But the tongue thought, "Cowards! The teeth! I will never submit to their restrictions. The purpose of life is to enjoy sugary foods. For something as hard as those teeth, they are terrible soft on the inside, the fools that they are."

In the body, one part fights another. The left hand hates the right one and envies it. The right hand regularly insults the left one and looks down on it. The battle rages.

The heart tells the kidneys, "Get out. This is my territory. You cannot live here. Who needs you? I am the only indispensable organ. You are a scavenger. You are not worth the sewage job which I hired you to do."

The eyes tell the feet, "You should do as I say but execute my instructions quickly, you lazy oafs. Why do you think I have servants? So that they can act at their leisure?' Move quickly! Move quickly! I am in a haste to fulfill my desires."

The lungs speak to the other vital organs in this way, "I am king of this place. You should honor me. Mind you, if I do not work, you are finished. You should respect me. Bow when you see me. This is the last warning. From now if you offend me, I will commit suicide."

And the battle rages inside and outside. In the mind itself there are enemies living side by side. Even though these should work cooperatively, they disagree. That brings insanity. Their boss, the limited individual self, is mentally unstable, and fails to properly manage the psyche.

Chit Akash In and Out

Based on instructions given by Lahiri, I had small developments in the kriya yoga practice. It is slow going recently due to circumstances which are beyond control, due to imposed associations enforced by fate.

However, better to be slow than to make no progress. In the back of a student's mind should be the idea of persisting with the practice, even at a slow pace, and expecting an acceleration as facilitated by time.

I meditated under the influence of Buddha recently. He does not interfere with my obligation to other teachers. In fact, he observes the other techniques with interest.

I managed to have the *chit akash* glow within the subtle head. Suddenly there was a light from above which I could see in the top front above but there was a subtle skull cap that prevented my seeing the source point of that light. The diagram below gives some idea of this.

The light of *chit akash* was a glow light. One should not be too eager to pursue these lights. Otherwise, they may disappear. One should be stable when these lights appear, just like a mouse in a corner where it hides from a cat.

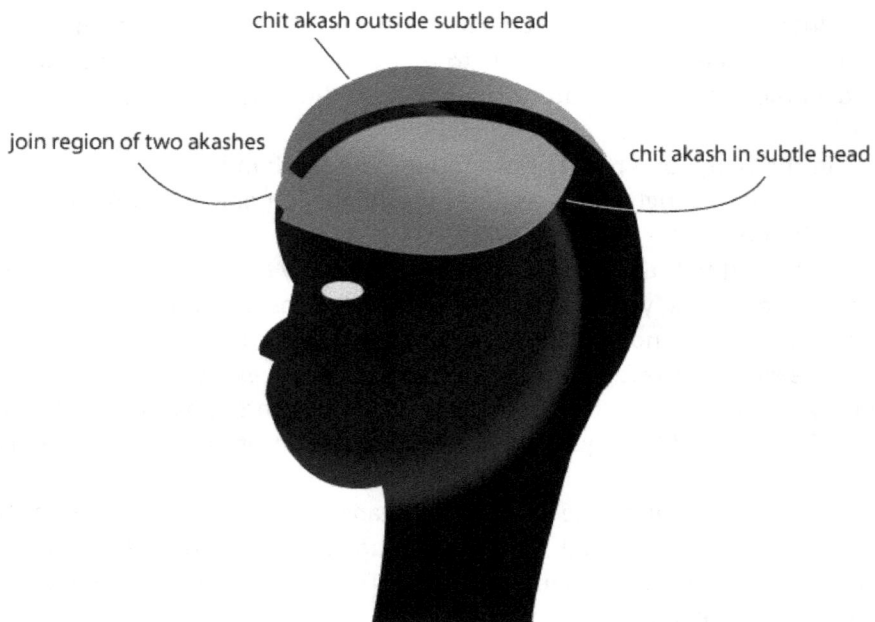

Part 5

Twitches and Chattering

In kundalini practice, twitches and chattering may occur when there is haphazard lock application, where either one did not apply the locks tightly and efficiently or one applies them and then kundalini pried one lose from that control. One may maintain some control but not all.

Because the loss is partial, the energy does not completely disengage the observational power but it vibrates the body. When that happens, be careful the next time, either during the same session or in future sessions, to clamp the locks and keep the mind inside the psyche monitoring whatever kundalini does.

Meditation

The loud layer of silence in meditation is the background vibration in the psyche combined with the background layer of what level the astral body happens to be on. This is similar to if one goes into a swimming pool and dives to the bottom and remains still without ear plugs. One will hear some slit sounds as if glass cracks. That sound will continue indefinitely if one remains there listening to it.

The naad sound however is different where it is the sound of the clash between the primal physical energy and the divine world. The causal plane touches the divine energy and wherever that touch is, the naad sound results as a consequence.

However, the loud layer of silence gives one transcendental relief even though it is not the same as the naad sound which also gives a transcendental relief.

Read this verse from the *Hatha yoga Pradipika*:

अनाहतस्य शब्दस्य ध्वनिर्य उपलभ्यते
ध्वनेरन्तर्गतं ज्ञेयं ज्ञेयस्यान्तर्गतं मनः
मनस्तत्र लयं याति तद्विष्णोः परमं पदम्

anāhatasya śabdasya dhvanirya upalabhyate
dhvanerantargataṁ jñeyaṁ jñeyasyāntargataṁ manaḥ
manastatra layaṁ yāti tadviṣṇoḥ paramaṁ padam

anāhatasya – of the naad supernatural sound resonance on the causal plane in the personal psyche, śabdasya – of sound, dhvanirya – reality, upalabhyate – perceive, dhvaner = dhvaneḥ = reality, antargataṁ – what interspaced, jñeyaṁ – what is to be known, jñeyasyāntargataṁ = jñeyasya (of what is to be known) + antargataṁ (what interspaced), manaḥ – mind, manas – mind, tatra – there, layaṁ – absorption, yāti – goes, tad = tat = that, viṣṇoḥ – of God Vishnu, paramaṁ – supreme, padam – abode

On the causal plane in his psyche, the yogi perceives that the reality is interspaced in the naad supernatural sound resonance, and the mind is interspaced into the reality of what is potentially knowable. The mind becomes absorbed there which is the supreme abode of the God Vishnu. (Hatha yoga Pradipika 4.100)

Nutrition Handicap / Kriya Yoga

From recent detailed studies about why a student cannot reach the *chit akash* spiritual sky in meditation practice, and also for those who do reach it periodically, as to why they are unable to reach it consistently, the main impediment is the nutritional energy in the subtle body.

Initially one must deal with the converted nutrition energy. One should get that under control, because there is no prospect of tackling the neutral stage of the nutrition energy in the beginning stages of the practice.

Because of a deep-rooted urge for consuming the environment in order to survive, even on the subtle level, one cannot grasp the nutrition system itself when one begins the practice. One has to use the system as it is and come to grips with it as it operates.

This is similar to if one finds oneself on a wild horse. Taming the animal initially is out of the question. One has to try to survive by clinging to the animal and trying to get some grip around its neck so that one does not fly off the back of the animal to a disabled condition or to death.

Controlling the kundalini and its supply of hormones, begin with many stopgap measures. Some of these become handicaps for the student, especially for the stubborn unyielding student who comes to the practice with preconceived notions and theoretical opinions.

Many students come with a simplistic view of spiritual life. When they find that their view does not fitting in perfectly, they criticize the path of yoga and harangue the teacher. It is quite natural that people who are simplistic would find the kriya process to be burdensome, inexplicable, complicated and questionable.

In the advanced stages one realizes that those yogis, who reduced nutrition to the very least, were advanced because in the case of the wild horse, if you do not feed the animal, it cannot buck you to a disabled condition or to your death. It will be too weak to do so.

The problem with the nutrition system is that it becomes charged with one phase or the other of the passionate energy and the dulling force, which are the two lower energy levels of physical nature. The other level is the highest which is the clarifying mode. This clarifying mode supplies insight. In other words, if we do not take help from the clarifying mode, we cannot see what to do, at least we will not see how to act in the long-ranged interest.

Acting in the short range on the basis of passion and stupor, will not serve the purpose even though it may provide some enjoyments and fulfillment.

As the nutrition energy goes down in the trunk of the subtle body it creates an energy which suppresses the clarifying influence. When the nutrition energy descends, it acquires a survival aspect, which reinforces a non-liberated way of perception and consideration.

Instead of working with the energy after it is charged and trying to remove, alter or neutralize it urges, it would be better to capture it before it is charged.

If the energy is lifted before it descends or even while it descends and is given a neutral charge or is left in a neutral condition and then used in that way, one would quickly reach the *chit akash* during meditation.

Breath infusion is one way of doing this, where the air is used to uplift the descending energy, to absorbed it upwards into the highest part of the trunk and then into the neck and head.

If one can consistently cause this to happen by any means, the *chit akash* consciousness would be continuous for oneself even though that would provide no access, for any other person.

This has to do with practice, not with opinions, with results not with arguments, with effective process, not with mental plans, only with what nature will actually respond to.

What is the use of opinions, reasonable statements, plans and the like, if nature ignores that?

Relationship

Any type of sexual discharge is a form of bleeding.

One way to look at this is that usually we do not recognize certain body liquids as blood. These come out of the body in a color other than red.

Is breast milk a form of blood?

Is semen discharge a form of blood?

Is non-red female sexual discharge a form of blood?

Once I heard Yogi Bhajan say that one drop of semen equals about 80 drops of blood. He said that semen was blood concentrate.

It is natural for the subtle body to seek former relationships of any type, not just the sexual type. It is relationship not the flavor of sex or otherwise, which causes these repeat astral encounters. If there was a relationship, the subtle body will at some time in the future make efforts to relive it.

The information about past relationships is in the subtle body. With or without one's permission the subtle body will remember these connections and try to reproduce them.

Astral Influence

Why highlight sex when other expressions happen just as well, and just as frequently, to conjure future incidences?

Recently I was with an aunt whom I grew up with in Guyana. She is deceased and left her old body while it was in a deformed state. After about five years after the subtle form was freed from the physical casing, her subtle body assumed its youthful form on the basis of what her last physical form was when it was about twenty years of age.

Somehow because of relationship with her based on being a nephew whom she helped to raise while an infant, I was with her astrally. I was amazed at her skin beauty. Seeing her body from an adult perspective was different to how I related to it as a boy of nine years of age.

I said to her, "Aunty, good Lord, you really look nice." (Creolese English).

She smiled. Then she said that I should leave my body and reside in the astral place where she was where everything was ample and where we would live without modern amenities and hassles. I neither consented nor denied the request.

I have no plans to live in that astral place but I could not tell her because our culture is that you do not deny the elders. I replied, "Yes Aunty."

The point is that relationships of any type causes repeat astral encounters. The subtle body does not forget the relationships. It will seek to re-enact an event in the future. This even applies to discomforting incidences.

Compulsive Astral Encounters

About a week ago, I was in the astral world with Kirtanananda Swami (deceased) and a Hare Krishna devotee, who was a gurukula teacher but who was convicted for sexually abusing a boy whom he taught in a boarding school.

The teacher was hostile to me on occasion. Kirtanananda was too. Still by force of fate, my subtle body is sometimes compelled to meet and associate with them.

It is not a question of why the subtle body does this. It is more an acceptance that it did this, does this and will continue like this in the future.

Attainments

Traditional kundalini yoga concerns the sushumna nadi central channel which is the subtle counterpart to the central spinal nerve. This system has a series of energy gyrating centers called chakras.

Besides this there are other systems and methods of dealing with the subtle body but these are mostly unknown and are practiced privately by adepts. These are done in the *Siddhaloka* environment by advanced yogis.

Why is it necessary to do advanced practice?

It is because an adept realizes that the attainments from the traditional methods only take one so far. To go further one must practice other techniques. In fact, as the subtle body is upgraded, new systems of operation within that form come into play. The adept realizes these and gets help from *yogaGuru*s in mastering and refining the psyche further.

Students may cry when they are told that their attainments are minor compared to higher yoga. This happens because of the over-confidence which one has, and also due to the simplistic and naïve expectations about what one should do to attain spiritual upliftment.

Many begin with the notion that we are perfect or that we are a potential Christs or Buddhas, they reason that we should not earn spiritual accomplishment through a complicated guru-advisory which takes years of practice, or lifetimes to complete.

Neck Nadi

After noticing that the *chit akash* inner and outer space became available after a click sound was heard in the neck, I investigated and found that there was a baffle flip part which shifted causing the energy from in the trunk to move through the neck without being constricted or regulated by the neck. In addition, instead of there being that *sushumna nadi* central channel in the middle of the spine, passing through the neck, there was the entire neck acting as a *nadi*. Everything in the neck was gone, as if the neck was tunneled completely and the energy from the trunk passed freely.

I continued with the meditation. Due to some associations, I was unable to consolidate the progress. It was a tiny bit of progress each day, if any. It accumulated. Lahiri re-appeared yesterday but he remained at a distance. This morning during practice he came closer at about three hundred feet in astral distance away.

He showed that the psyche, without kundalini, operates in a different way. The neck itself becomes the nadi, the central passage. It is cleared of obstructions. It has nothing in it; it is like an empty cylinder in which transparent energy passes freely from the trunk into the head.

Back of Head Clearance

One area which is difficult to reach, but which is must in higher meditation is the back of the head. Generally, this is a dark area, having heavy dense astral energy. When kundalini comes through the spine into the head, it usually wants to attack the intellect which is in the front part of the subtle head. Kundalini will rarely go to the back area.

It comes through the neck and darts to the intellect organ. It avoids the back of the head. It may if the head is tilted forward, go through the back bottom of the head. But even then, it avoids the dark area in the back of the head.

Using breath infusion combined with regular listening to naad sound in the back of the head, one may direct kundalini to go into the back of the head and to shatter the heavy astral energy which accumulated there.

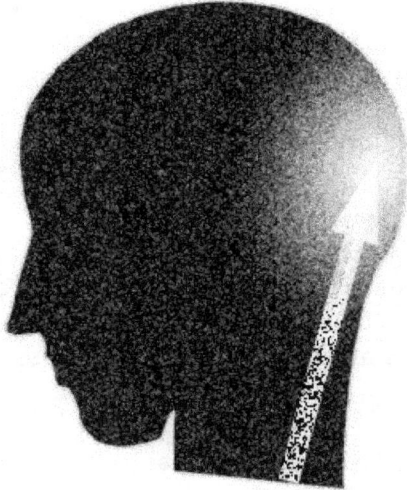

Recognition in the Astral Regions

Early this morning during meditation, as the physical body was seated in a lotus posture, the astral one met with some ex-Hare Krishna devotees whom I knew and served with in the New Vrindavan gurukula. There were at this place which was on the astral side in West Virginia. Even though the two persons were expelled from the society, still on the astral side they are still in the society and still go and live at this location where the gurukula building was when I was with them in 1980.

The head of the gurukula was there. His main assistant was there. In the astral place the assistant sat to my right and the principal was on my left.

The principal showed a paper which had on it the service I rendered to the society while I was resident. There was a column of my books listed but these were crossed out. I looked through the list as I read through the paper. I told him that those books were not published even though I wrote them years ago and that other books are currently in print. He shook his head. Then the assistant looked at me with a look of understanding.

It then occurred to me that they wanted to say that my books could not be listed because the books were not authorized by the society. Bhaktivedanta Swami established rules of publishing which disqualified my books.

I then said to principal that he should do whatever he wished and write the article in any way he wished if that was the requirement of the society.

This experience is valuable in understanding that the karmas or resulting energies of our associations come back to us later either while we have the current body in which such acts were perpetrated, or in some other body in the future or in the astral world when we have no body besides the subtle form.

As Shakespeare wrote:
The evil that men do lives after them;
The good is oft interred with their bones.

Even though I am done with that group, still to resolve energies from past association, my subtle body is with them on occasion. This is not desired but it happens.

People sometimes ask why, in dreams, they must meet certain people whom they dislike.

The answer is:

It is a psychic law of nature. No one has to impose such meetings. Nature itself will see to it that these encounters occur because of past energies which were lodged in nature. Everything has a flyback effect.

These activities of the subtle body may occur even without the knowledge of the individuals concerned who may have no memory of the incidences and who may on the basis of no recall even deny the situations.

Naad / *Chit akash* Combination

After doing the naad meditation under instruction from Lahiri, he switched me to *chit akash* waiting practice. He gave an impetus for a combination of these practices, where one does *chit akash* waiting and while doing that one links into naad but without going backwards into naad sound.

This may be compared to having two wives (husbands) who are agreeable to each other and who assisted in chores which are necessary for the upkeep of the family. In meditation practice, one should sure not get into a situation of many wives (husbands) and only to have one, because it does occur that one technique may not compliment another; in which case the meditation will be conflicting.

For instance, suppose I tell someone to meditate in silence. Then another guru tells that person to meditate using a mantra. How will that happen that the student will be in silence and also say a mantra at the same time. Methods when combined if they are not compatible may cause failure.

Suppose on the other hand I said to someone that he should meditate in darkness, then another guru told the same person to meditate with his physical eyes open. That would not be a contradicting instruction unless the student was told that he would have the eyes open and look at a physical object.

When methods are combined, when a student takes one instruction from this person, and another method from someone else, and then some idea from yet another teacher and combine these, because of conflicting processes he may not get the result intended.

Naad sound actually facilitates the *chit akash* sky of consciousness access. Naad is complimentary to that achievement.

In this practice the student waits for *chit akash* energy to manifest. After a little time, the student begins to pull *chit akash* energy into the psychic plane the student is on. This has to be done, otherwise the wait for *chit akash* to happen may take forever.

If an accomplished teacher gave one permission to do this, on the basis of that person's supernatural authority, one can imbibe *chit akash* energy. Once tiny bits of that energy may flow in, the student should reach to the back of the subtle head and make contact with naad sound. However, in doing this he/she should not let go of the connection with the *chit akash* pull.

While I did this, suddenly a lighted area appeared to my left within the psyche chamber where I was located. Without shifting in any way, I became aware of this luminescence which was about thirty inches across and four inches deep.

Dull Start Kundalini Practice

In kundalini yoga, a dull start-up happens especially during the early morning session. Due to the laziness of the physical body, there will be a stupor energy in the psyche but this should be viewed as an opportunity to burn a lower grade of energy and to move from a lower level to a higher one, to observe how this is done and be willing to do so on a daily basis.

How do we move from a lower energy level to a higher one?

Can one do so by thinking that the self will shift from stupor to wakefulness instantly?

Using breath infusion, the same lazy energy, the same stupor, the same hesitation-procrastination force can be changed into a higher grade of energy. That can be used to catapult the attention of the psyche into the highest quality mento-emotional energy.

A lazy stupor energy is an opportunity to do breath infusion practice which is effective in using that negative energy to attain a higher level of consciousness.

The Vedic system gave a three partitioned mixed energy system as

- dulling influence *(tama guna)*
- passionate influence *(raja guna)*
- insightful influence *(sattva guna)*

These are subtle energies which we rely on. Breath infusion can use the dulling influence for converting that into either the passionate or insight energy. It can take the passion force and convert that to the insight force.

Alcohol for instance can take the insight force and convert that in either the passion or dulling force. For the meditation practice, the objective is to move the psyche into a state of having a majority insight force in the psyche with a small quantity of passion and dulling force. The more the lower levels are evacuated from the psyche by any which means, even by means other than breath infusion, the higher the level the individual will experience.

Recognition that I am on a lower level is praiseworthy, provided I take that as a challenge and take an effective action to elevate myself.

Reason for Ignoring Impending Death

Last night in the astral world, I was with a few relatives who use bodies which are over sixty years of age. The conversation swung to the fact that each of us were left on earth without parents or grandparents, and that we were the elderly generation.

These persons are Christians who do not accept the idea of reincarnation. In the discussion, to get some idea of their rationalizations, I said this:

Why do we ignore impending death?

One person replied:

"It is because of attachment to status as elders or seniors in the family and at the place of employment. There is a subtle pleasure one gets from being a senior. That is enough to keep one focused on the society or community which supports that senior format, so much so that one instinctively avoids considering impending death. I did that. I still continue to do that. It is to be seen what illness will force me to face my impending death."

Another relative said this:

"For me it is not important when my body will die. I focus on my interests, on the things which I enjoy, on what I achieved and on how to develop further. Death is the last consideration. I cannot conceive that I will get a terminal disease or become incapacitated at any point. I feel just as if I will live in a healthy condition forever."

Despite this, there was a feeling that these relatives felt that we should stay together after death, come what may, to be together as relatives just as we were as infants with young bodies in the family. They felt that the sense of kinship which we inherited should continue after death.

Limitations of Celibacy

Lahiri Baba said this:

Even though initially celibacy is a priority, in the long haul it has little value because it is the overall attachment to certain realms, and the bodies acquired in those realms, which will frustrate the effort. If a student has attachment to certain realms, or to the bodies in those realms, what does it matter if he/she is sex resistant?

There are many materialistic lower dimension entities who are not involved in sexual indulgence. They are condemned to lowly existences regardless. The development out of the lower places is based on something other than mere celibacy.

It hinges on being able to translate to other dimension, on giving up the advantage of those lower places, and leaving those aspects aside to go to higher places which are devoid of what one wants to exploit in the lower zones.

It does not matter what a body does or wants to do or what the ascetic does with a body. What matters is if the ascetic can leave that aside if he/she is given an opportunity to go elsewhere. Can the ascetic suddenly leave everything behind?

For instance, let us assume that a certain person is celibate. He/she achieved that. But then when offered the opportunity to translate to a higher dimension that person hesitates on the basis of some other attachment, what then is the value of this celibacy?

But suppose for instance there is this other ascetic who is not celibate but he is called by a deity. If he leaves aside whatever he does or whoever he is with, he will translate and become a new body which is suitable to the place of the deity who summoned him. He will not have to bother with celibacy or with any other aspect from the old location or from the body which was designed for use in that previous place.

An able-bodied seaman has to be seaworthy, which means he should be a swimmer. He should know how to use a lifejacket. He should know how to hoist a life-raft. Yet all of that has no use if he is cast off in the middle of the Pacific Ocean. How long will he survive if he is dumped into the middle of the Pacific with the best lifejacket? The seaman's qualification has little or no application in a situation like that. Likewise, these moral stipulations are limited in the final analysis, because they hinge on the type of body and the type of environment one will be placed in by providence. It is very easy for nature to erase one's achievements in the next body by putting one in a condition where one must do whatever one desired to do, for whatever reason, in the last existence. Hence, abandon pride in moral principles.

Is one ready to abandon whatever one is attached to? Even a slight attachment to something moral could be an impediment that will prevent one from translating to a higher place. Morality may be the biggest impediment.

Chaurangi

This morning Lahiri gave information about a siddha named *Chaurangi*. He is mentioned in the book I translated, the *Hatha Yoga Pradipika*. I published this book under the title of *Kundalini Hatha Yoga Pradipika*. In as much as the *sex you!* book was an important contribution to the annals of transcendental literature; this translation and commentary is a major contribution to the practice of kundalini yoga.

Lahiri said that *Chaurangi* freed many *dakinis* from lower astral regions by giving them buttocks adjustment procedures which caused the lower torso of their subtle bodies to be full of clear translucent light, that freed them from lower lusty energies which were in their subtle forms.

Pull Zones

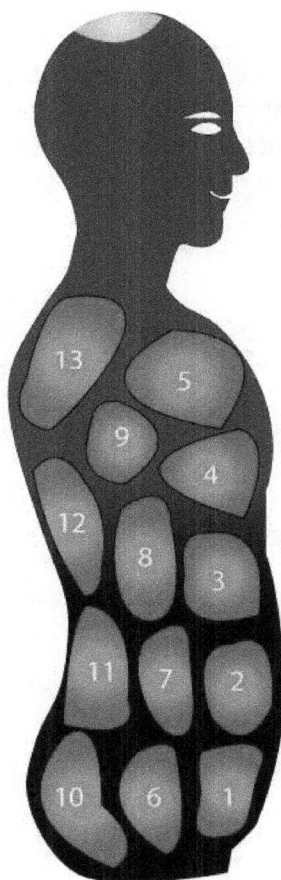

This diagram gives the various pull-up zones which are tackled by yogis who are proficient in the kundalini reform techniques and who find it necessary to flush the trunk of the subtle body. Each zone contains energies which are supportive of the gravity-influenced hormone system of the physical and subtle bodies. The student does this practice in the order of the number of each zone, gradually lifting the energy.

One begins with zone 1. After pulling that up for a month or for a year as required, the student moves and pulls zone 2 and then does the rest in the numerical order. Breath infusion is the method of the pull. The benefit is access to the *chit akash* and completely clearance of the neck so that the entire neck functions as a *sushumna nadi* passage.

Neck Clearance

Lahiri explained the necessity for whole neck *sushumna* clearance which is in contrast to the tradition *sushumna* spinal center clearance. At first one is told to focus on the spinal center only. Later however when one has some success, one should graduate to clearance of the entire neck which would then serve as a larger *sushumna* central passage.

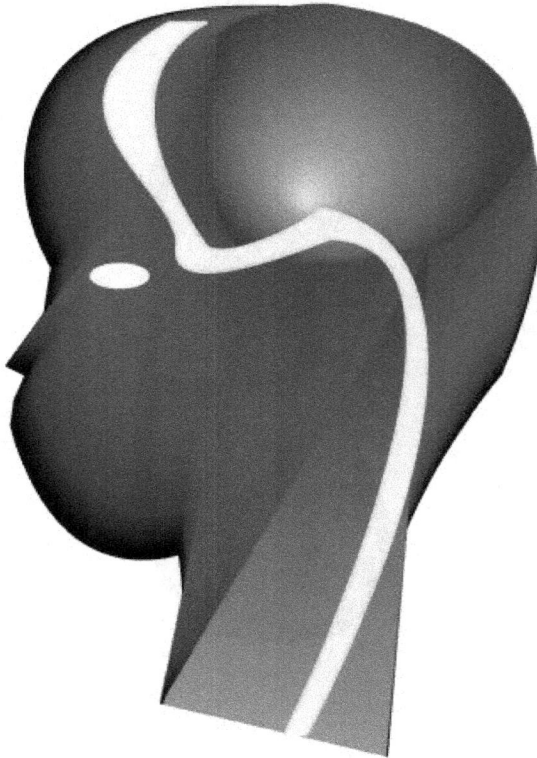

traditional sushumna nadi
narrow pass

The spinal column is not the whole psyche. Its clearance does not mean that the whole psyche was altered even though there would be noticeable changes in the psyche due to the clearance of the spine only.

Sex Energy / Hormone Uplift

Lahiri said this morning that the celibate effort would have to go for about five to eight years of consistent effort with kundalini yoga, rising kundalini through the spine every day, before it can be thorough. It is best if the yogi/yogini is single and is away from various sexually liaisons but being single is not a guarantee all by itself.

One can be single and still be unsuccessful in the effort. One can be with a partner and be more successful than someone who is single.

What is necessary is sincerity and the removal of personal interest in exploiting sex pleasure. The presence or absence of sex pleasure does not mean that there is or is not a personal interest. Someone may be sexually involved and still have little or no personal interest in its exploitative feature. Another person who has no sexual access may have a latent or hidden interest in it.

Not having sexual access either voluntarily or involuntarily does not in any way show if a person has interest. One has to descend through the psyche to see its actual and potential attributes. Actual attributes which are not present may be present as potentials, which the yogi/yogini fails to recognize.

The entity using a psyche and using a body is not the psyche itself. Nor is the individual empowered to completely remove the tendencies of the psyche. The psyche will have to manifest some of its tendencies irrespective of the aims of the entity. What the entity needs to do is to carefully watch its interest. At some point one has to let nature do what it has to do or what it wants to do, while one secures one's interest. What is to be protected is the interest not the organ or sense activity of the psyche. Initially one is trained to pay attention to the organ or sense activity because in the beginning the interest is too abstract to be apprehended.

Lahiri commented on the issue of nutrition hormone energy uplift. This is for advanced students who already mastered the sex energy uplift after five to eight years of practice. For them after about fifteen years of practice, they should focus on the hormone energy uplift and abandon concerns with the sexual energy.

Once the interest is withdrawn from the sexual energy, there is still some problem which is the hormone energy. That is the last effort to make with breath infusion. This does not mean that the ascetic changed nature because he/she can achieve that. Nature will continue in its own way irrespective of what an ascetic achieves.

The Sleep after Death

Today I began what is known as *the sleep after death*. This is where after death of the physical body, the subtle one, being released from the chore of maintaining the physical form, sleeps for some time, for weeks, months or years, depending on how exhausted and worn it became in that life time.

Why did I begin this before death of the physical body?

The answer:

To get a head start on the death of the physical body process and to begin the rest and recuperation of the subtle one even before the physical system collapses. Instead of scrambling to go on living physically and planning around that, I shift my accounts to the subtle plane. To help me with this providence produced severe complications of destiny which are a warning about the physical world and about the endless harassment which a living being must deal with in this environment and its social occasions.

Even a yogi can be worn as a result of social involvements. In which case, he/she will have to *rest in peace* (R.I.P.) hereafter as the first thing to do after the final astral displacement from the physical system. But if the yogi can rest in peace in part or fully before leaving the body, that is all the merrier.

After death if the subtle body is emotionally worn, the yogi will fall asleep just after the death occurrence and who knows when he/she will awaken and where in which dimension, he/she will be in.

Will he awaken like a man in a nursing home who on a certain morning knows neither his name nor number?

Will he awaken with memory of everything but the yoga practice?

Will he awaken in an astral heaven or astral hell?

Will he awaken with the hostile thoughts of his social relations who want to argue over what he did which displeased them?

Will God be in the surroundings?

I will practice the *sleep after death* process, for the rest of the use of the present body. In that way the subtle body will be rested even before the final astral projection. That will free me from having to stay with other entities who will have to sleep for a time hereafter.

Astral Compulsion

Last night my subtle body somehow or the other was in an adjacent astral world on the island of Trinidad. I was there with a lady who was a girlfriend of mine when I stayed on the island in 1966. At the time some ancestors of mine considered if this person would be their mother. This inspired me to have a liking for this person.

Later after I left the island, I abandoned the relationship because it was not practical. There were changes in our situations which were objections of fate which we had to observe. You could imagine that after over 40 years, I met that lady in the astral world. It was because another lady who was a girlfriend in the same country met with that lady astrally and alerted her to my astral vibration.

After getting equipped with my astral frequency, the lady, due to my knowing her before, attracted my astral form to the island. She could not do it alone. She pooled her power with that of some others who wanted me to be on the island.

At first, I was circumstantially forced to eat some non-vegetarian food. Then I did some chores for a man and his family. Then this lady came there with her brother and sister. This brother and sister must be at least around fifty years of age but their subtle bodies assumed the same child forms which they had when I was on the island before.

They greeted me cordially.

"We are happy to see you. We missed you. Why did you not return? Our sister loved you. You are different to others. Stay with us."

After this the woman in question, their sister, dismissed them. She spoke of the affection we had for each other so long ago. She said that she was fond of me and was robbed of the opportunity to consummate it. I did not reply but I thought that these relationships happen frequency in each life, in each childhood. These have endless consequential playbacks. If one were to try to satisfy each of these relationships, trillions of years would not be enough to do so. Someone would be hurt in the process. Someone would be neglected. Someone would be abandoned.

In the back of her mind was the idea that somehow after death, I would be with her perpetually. Can you see that, where as a yogi, I would spend the hereafter with this person fulfilling her desire for relationship?

Where would that end?

Who would be dissatisfied if providence ends that in one or two or more astral years?

What about other persons who may feel the same way about me?

Sex Hormone Uplift

Lahiri shared some diagrams. Persons, who do hatha yoga, Gorakshnath style, or kriya yoga with *urdhvareta* intentions to lift semen or sex hormone energy, may find this useful.

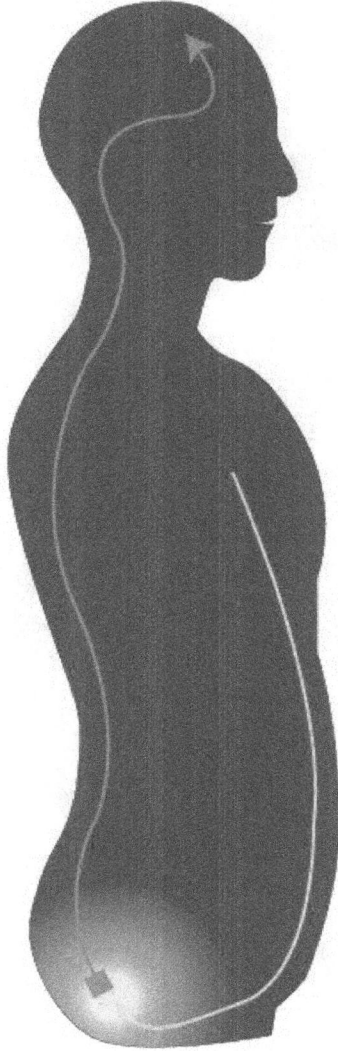

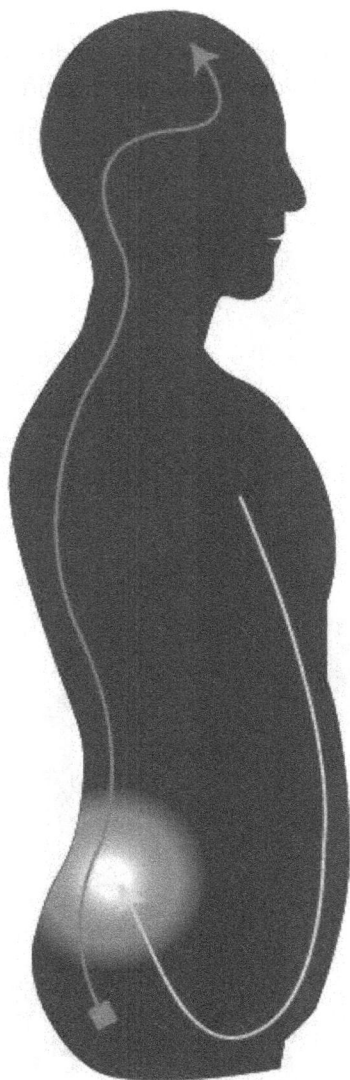

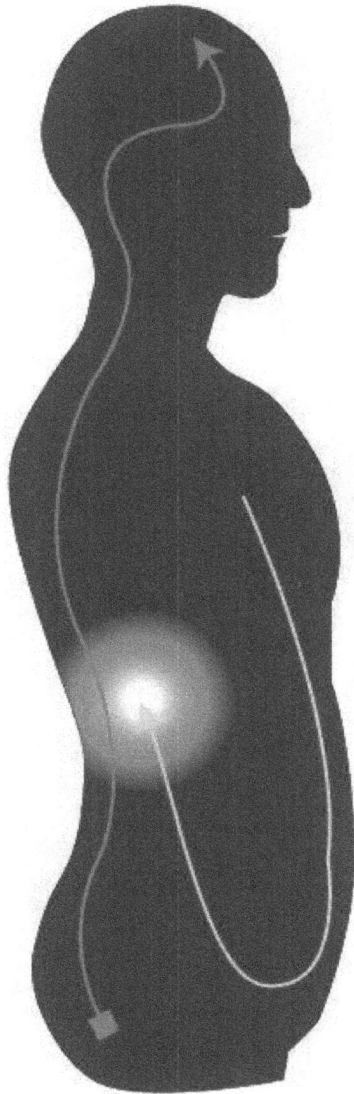

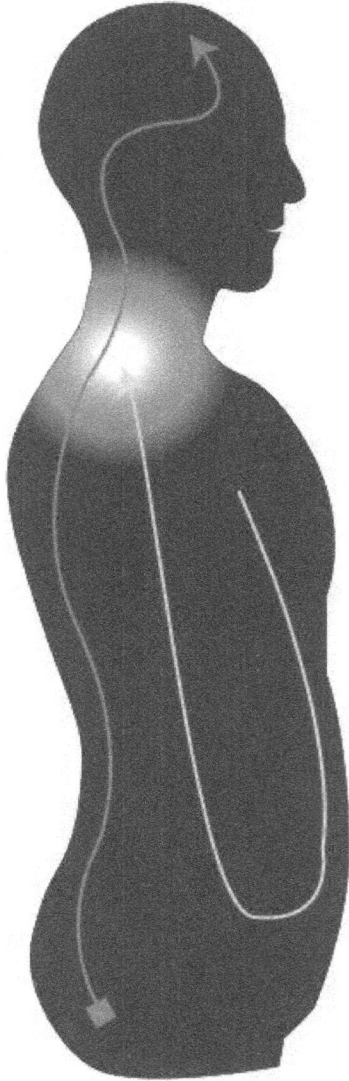

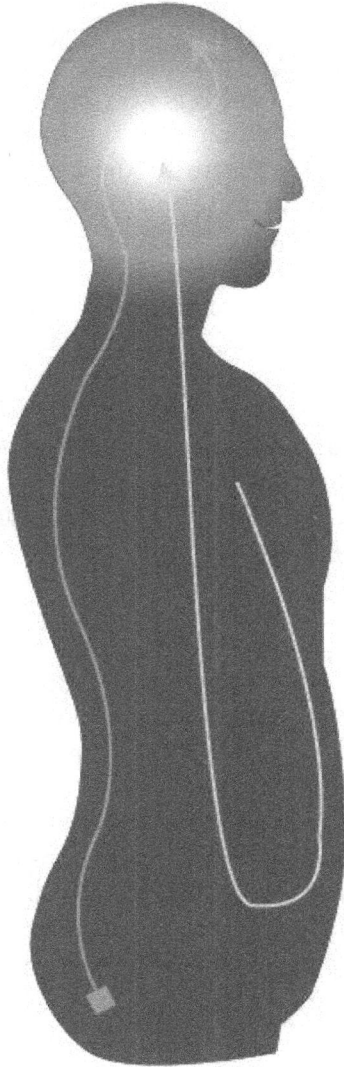

As to the hydraulic methods used to achieve this, it is *pranayama* practice, particular *bhastrika* breath infusion process.

The key to this is to begin where you are and work daily to adjust the system upward so that at first the sex hormone energy naturally flows upwards due to a mystic uplift force which acts like a hydraulic pump in the subtle body. Later when this is established, one should study how the nutritional energy is converted into various types of hormone energy and how it is charged with sex impulse and other types of survival basics in various parts of the body, in glands and regions.

Once this is understood by internal insight-study of one's psyche, one can lift the nutrition energy. After one gets a grip on that, one can check to see if the nutrition energy still reaches the sex hormone storage and charging system in the groin. Inevitable because of the laws of nature, one will discover that this is still happening because that is the way it is. At that stage of practice, one can use the diagrams.

There will be no absolute changes in the laws of nature because these are fixed for the duration of any creation. All that is left *to do* is to extract one's interest from the system. After a certain amount of effort, one will be awarded with a lifting of one's interest in nature's concerns.

It is at that point that one reaches the stage where in the *Yoga Sutras*, Patanjali wrote that the system of nature continues for the others. They remain with it in their miserable profiles which are saturated with trauma. This is an individual practice. With the help of the superior souls each person must achieve whatever is to be achieved for himself/herself.

Ape-Posture Yoga

There is a part of yoga, where a student discovers certain postures which were not taught to him. With this there is the discovery of the special features of postures which were taught by the yogaGuru. Legend has it that there are as postures as they are species of life. That means species which are extinct, those which are current and those which may be displayed in the future.

Lahiri showed me the silverback gorilla release posture which is like that of an ape using the fist on the ground as the forepaws. This is an important posture because it is the posture which causes an evolution from the four-legged animal to the human one. It allows an approach face to face for sexual liaison between the male and female of the same species.

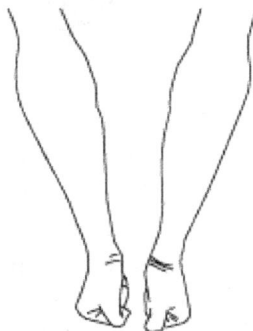

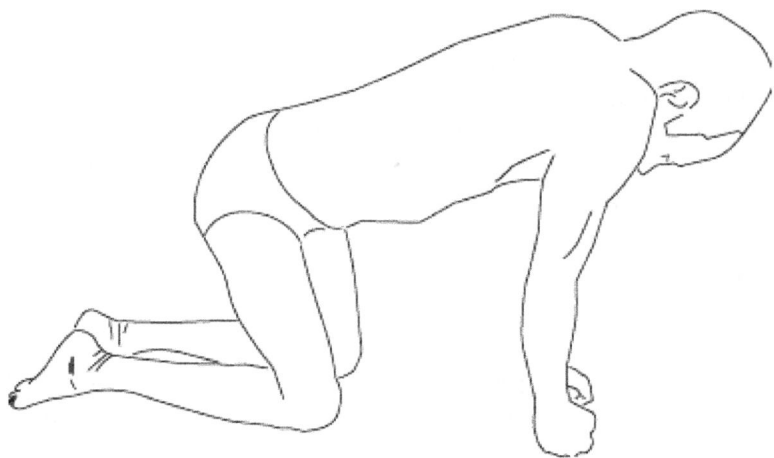

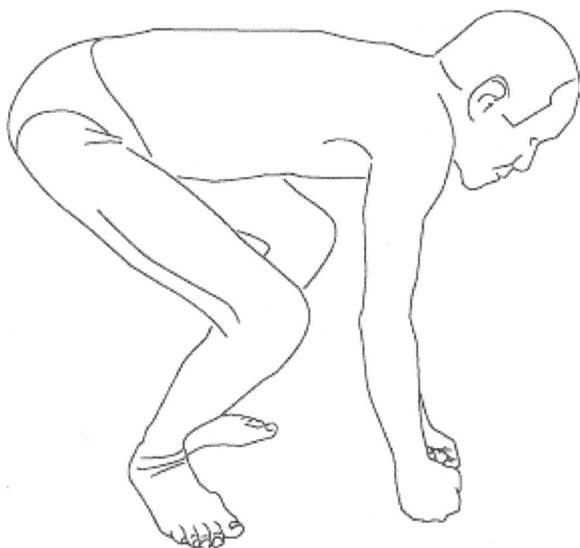

Most animals have sexual intercourse for reproduction. They do not have the facility for enjoying sexual intercourse for its own sake. That is not a choice for them. It happens because the bodies are so constructed that the incidence of sexual intercourse just for pleasure rarely arises.

Even though the potential for it is there, still because there is no memory facility through which to dwell on past sex pleasure experience, they do not think of having sex only for pleasure. The brain of the animal does not support that. Just think of how much we humans like sexual intercourse. Now think of a situation where one had intercourse and retained no memory of its pleasure. How would one desire it repeatedly without that recall?

Suppose I had intercourse with a woman to whom I was irresistibly attracted. Then I had no memory of the act, no pleasure recall. What would be my chance of having that experience again if I did not meet that person again and did not become attracted to that person afresh again.

This inquiry could give insight into the value of memory for sexual acts. I could write an equation:

0 x memory of sex = 0 x repeated sex

Or stated in a sentence:

No (zero) recall of sexual pleasure means there would be no repeat incidence of sexual intercourse.

In the animal species there is sexual pleasure during acts of intercourse which are done based on nature's reproduction system, but the problem is that the creature is not allowed to remember the pleasure. In the human form there is the same reproductive intent driving initial sexual acts, particularly at puberty, but with it there is memory recording of the acts. These recordings allow a human being to reconsider the pleasure and decide to pursue it for its own sake.

In the ape species, this sexual memory apparatus is there in a slight way and with it is the stand-up feature. Due to standing the ape can have intercourse from the missionary position, something which in other quadrupeds is not permissible because of the construction of the life form.

But there is another part of the standing position of the ape, which is that it causes a tension in the lower torso in the sacral region of the spine. This in turn causes deep reflexive thinking in the brain.

While doing breath infusion with focus on the sacral region in terms of the ape posture, one can explore what happened some millions of years ago when one transferred from the lower quadruped forms into the ape form which is just before the peak of evolution, which is the human form.

The ape is that last stride before standing on the top of evolution. When meditating on this while doing breath infusion on that region, one can feel the pride and pleasure of it. The pride is that the ape form is the most superior of the quadrupeds. The pleasure is that one can face the partner while engaging in the act for begetting children. In the ape form there is also the sexual pleasure but there is no focus on it for its own purposes. The only focus one has there is for sexual fluid discharge. When doing this posture during breath infusion one can see how one felt about sexual pleasure for that purpose. One can estimate the differential between that and indulging for its own sake.

Neck-Open *Chit Akash*

This morning's meditation was a two-hour session. What is required is at least a twenty-minute practice. After doing that for a time, one may increase to thirty minutes and more, and then later to forty-five minutes.

It is important that one be properly rested before doing long sessions of meditation. Otherwise, one will be drowsy which is not meditation. Patanjali listed sleep as an indication of what is not yoga. Recurrence of non-yogic memories is another indication of that. So is imagination and reasoning during the session.

For the breath infusion session, it was short charges of energy from the very beginning with no big spinal kundalini rises. These short charges are important in the advanced stages when one should target *hard to find* places in the subtle body. These places are locations where usually one does not feel the bliss force as when kundalini rises through the spine into the brain. There is cell kundalini which means that each cell has a micro lifeForce which may be aroused. When that happens if one is not sensitive it will be like it never happened in the first place.

As one persists with breath infusion, one will become more sensitive to where even the slightest arousal of energy in the tiniest of cells is perceived. But for a beginner such flows of energy have no impact on the consciousness and the big rises of kundalini is the aim in practice.

During breath infusion, I breathe rapidly for a little, sometimes even for as little as eight rapid breaths, then I hold the locks while looking down into the body. Sometimes there would be twinkling pixels of colorful translucent energy here, there or everywhere in the torso of the subtle body. These I mentally arrest and hold. When that energy fizzed, it disappeared. I begin another series of breaths. I repeated that. In the advanced stage every slight movement or collection of energy is noted, regarded and handled. This is in contrast to the procedure for beginners where only the sensational and very obvious movements of kundalini are observed.

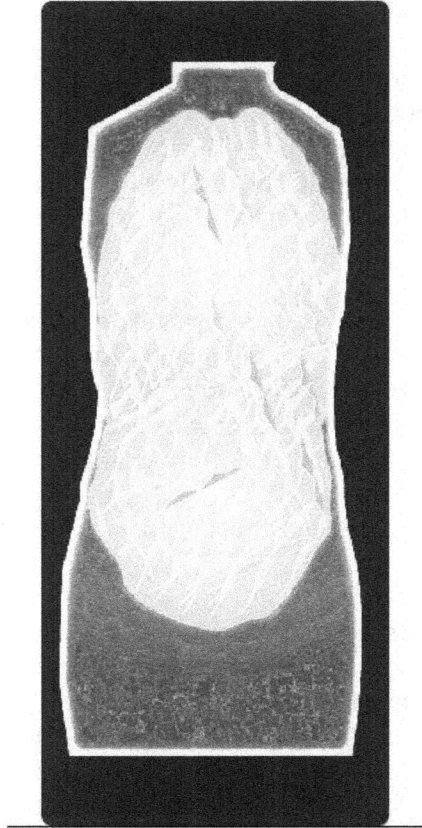

Later in the session, there was no arousal of kundalini into the head, but this is a special practice to get the energy to pass through the neck not just in the spinal column in the neck but using the entire neck space as a conduit. This facilitates *chit akash* contact in the meditation session which occurs immediately after.

During the meditation session, I had difficulty adhering to and entering naad sound. This happens when one forsakes naad for one reason or the other. It is usually due to association with people who are not interested in meditation practice or with those who are but who are bogged with insecurities. If one is in touch with either materialistic people or with student yogis who are distracted with emotional issues, that may degrade the practice and cause one to lose contact with naad sound.

It is no wonder that in every yoga book of worth there is mention about doing yoga alone and in isolation. Tons of practice, years of effort and progress, can be wiped out with one dose of negative association either with materialistic people or with yoga students who just cannot stay away from lower levels of consciousness.

Anyway, whatever will be will be! What is to happen will occur. A yogi can advance in so far as providence permits.

After eight minutes of meditation, I stayed close to naad, very close, but I was not in it. I knew that I was out of touch with naad and should again reinstate myself to complete the instructions of Lahiri about meditation with bringing energy from the *chit akash* sky of consciousness.

Naad was in the back part just outside the subtle head, like in a gulley, in a rectangular gap. I was outside of it, keeping contact with it. I got an instruction which came from another dimension which said that I should take the slant across. It had a diagram like this:

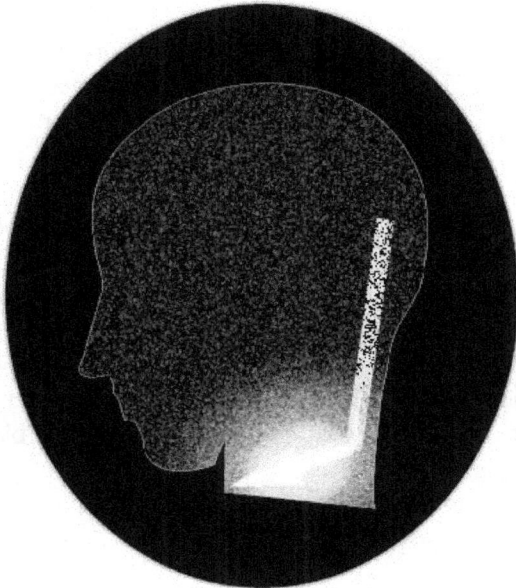

That meant to take the action which is in the diagram. First one has to connect with naad sound. From that position and holding to naad as if it one's very life, as if it is one's mother and one is a scared infant, one should go into the neck at a slant angle. Once in the neck, midway in it, one should send a lift energy across the entire cylindrical neck and open the neck so that the energy can pass up through into the subtle head.

This causes one to shift to a plane of existence where one can absorb *chit akash* sky of consciousness energy.

Sex Pleasure Elsewhere

Breath infusion this morning was highlighted by a set of falling stars. These burst from compressed twinkle pixel energies which were from individual cells structures rather than from the kundalini shakti in the spinal column. I would on occasion while holding locks after a series of breath in a particular posture, twirl to one side, feel the energy being compressed and then being released, and then twirl to the other side.

At one stage, the energy reached up through the inside of the trunk of the body and entered each side of the neck and caressed the cheeks.

That felt like when one is a newborn infant with a new body, with smooth skin, and one's mother, on the third day after one's birth, holds one's face. At that time her hand is as smooth as glass and as tender as a new sprig from a vine. Her emotions are about concern for her infant.

A very important development occurred this morning, where I noticed that some individual cells, voluntarily yielded their bliss energy to the yoga practice. This is a change of pace and a desirable adjustment in the present configuration of the subtle body. The people I got this body from had no interest in yoga. The genetic structure of the body I received from them was hostile to yoga. It is encouraging to see that the configuration of the body may be changed even down to the cell level. Here I mean the psychic cells in the subtle body.

The physical body, like an old but useful shoe, may be confiscated by nature at any moment. The teeth are either missing, patched or worn. The heart is near its last throes. The feet feel as if they are made of stone. The brain races to its last burn-out.

By nature's habit, the cells are willing to contribute their bliss force to the reproduction sex function. During sexual climax, we find that every cell in the body, contributes its bliss energy which gives a large bliss experience in the genitals, thighs, breasts-chest and mouth especially. As humans we hunger for this experience and would do anything to have it.

Thus, it is a feat for a yogi, in the effort to develop a *yogaSiddha* body, if he/she can get the configuration of the subtle body changed so that all parts willingly yield bliss energy irrespective of the sex force.

Try to imagine what it would be like, if the genital pleasure was available with the same intensity elsewhere in the body, like say in the right side of the torso, or in the middle of it, or in an arm pit or anywhere else?

Siddha Yoga ~ *Surya Namaskar*

Surya namaskara has come to mean a series of graceful postures which are salutations to the sun. It is interesting that this flourishes in the developed countries with people who deny the idea of many gods and God, people who believe in oneness of everything and in the fact that there is, to their view, no supreme individual.

This *surya namaskara* is popular among people who think that *asana* postures are yoga. In the *hatha* yoga of Gorakshnath, yoga has six procedures of which the *asana* postures are one only, not the whole thing and not the most significant part either, but the elementary procedure.

In pranayama practice *Surya* is a deity, an actual person. His energy emanating from the sun planet is used to help the yogi to alter the habits of the kundalini lifeForce and change the configuration of the subtle body. A yogi who uses a physical body begins using the solar energy to change the attitude or mood of the two types of energy, namely, the bone marrow and the sexual reproduction energy.

When doing the breath infusion if one pulls in sun-charged energy, and if one can make it enter the psyche and mix with the subtle bone marrow and the subtle reproduction energy, that is a psychic *surya namaskara*.

Namaskar means the action *(kar)* of obeisance *(namas)*. For a yogi this is not a ceremonial procedure. It is not a show of graceful bodily movements. It is an inner transformation and influence where the energy of the sun enters the psyche and upgrades it so that it becomes compatible to the sunlight body used by the persons who live on the sun planet using bodies which are sustained by that power.

Push against Naad Sound Kriya

Meditation this morning was inspired by Yogeshwarananda whom I have no seen for some months. He looked into my subtle head but did not comment. Recently due to some non-constructive association, my practice regressed.

However, I was absorbed in naad sound when Yogeshwarananda arrived. He gave a technique which is the *push against naad sound* kriya. This is used when a yogin, for some reason or the other, was thrown from naad sound and cannot get into it.

He gets help from a yogaGuru who gives an authority to push the coreSelf against the naad sound and to link into naad in that pushing way. To understand this, think of two lovers who become estranged, where one partner feels that he/she cannot live without the other.

When that needy one tries to communicate with the other, there is rejection. What should that needy person do?

In this case, the yogi is the needy one. The naad sound is the detached one. The needy yogi pushes his/her energy to the naad sound. This will feel like pushing against a reinforced concrete wall. The yogi keeps pushing. He finds that this serves to connect to naad. From that pushing action, the meditation continues.

I pulled *chit akash* energy while pushing against naad. Yogesh disappeared after giving that hint. I assume that he sensed my difficulty. Out of compassion, he gave a solution.

Talk about love from the old fathers, the yogaGurus. Sometimes I compare the love I have for a woman with the love I have for the old fathers. I rate that the love for a woman is trivial in comparison.

Working for Money Hereafter

Most astral communities which are directly adjacent to the physical existence are reminiscent of physical life. While in those places, one feels physical even though there are slight or major differences in those locations as compared to physical life.

During the last fifteen minutes, during a two-hour period in which I sat for meditation, I was in an astral place which is a crossworld from Guyana in South America. My physical body sat on a bed with the spine of it supported by a pillow and resting upright against the bed head.

I was with some men who drilled for who knows what. After migrating to Brooklyn, New York, these two persons departed from their physical bodies.

Now in the deceased existence, their astral bodies are in a place which is adjacent to Georgetown, the capital of Guyana. They drilled with a 3 inch bore contraption through the subtle earth place where they resided. While speaking to them, suddenly as it does in the astral world, the scene changed. Some women walked on one of the main streets in Georgetown. It is called Water Street. There were three Indian women with baskets carrying food for sale. One was stopped by another woman who was dismissed from work at noon. The vendor with the basket said she had three rotis with curry. The working woman told the vendor to follow into a store which is a famous store called Fogarty even on the physical side.

After this I was back with the two men but this time we were in the earth in a tiled basement where water seeped through the tiles. The two men carried to the astral world, their memories of working in Brooklyn, New York, in the underground rail system. They dug under the ground in Guyana and tiled it, except that the land there is so water logged, that water sprung from every place it could in that basement. I was struck with wonder at how determined they were.

After this I returned to my body which slept in a room in South Florida. I checked a clock and noticed that two hours passed since I first sat for meditation.

I did not research it. It did not come intuitively as to how my subtle body became attracted to the men and the vendor. The two men used black colored astral bodies. The vendor used an Indian (India descendant) based astral body.

In the astral world there is no need to get money for commerce. Still, on the basis of our physical conditioning, we may venture to the hereafter with the materialistic culture of working for money. Religious beliefs and philosophies aside, people who think that it is important that one should work for money, will definitely do that after they are deceased.

Twinkle Energy ~ Breath Infusion

During breath infusion, I had a thorough energization of the torso, especially the *hard to reach* upper parts, under the shoulders. There was a twinkle dangling spring-like energy which dangled from the scapula which is the bone which runs across the shoulders. When this happened, it was like tiny stainless-steel springs jumping up and down, dangling with a translucent energy vibrating from them. At one point it threw the body to the left side and tilted the body off balance. I had to control the body and reposition it.

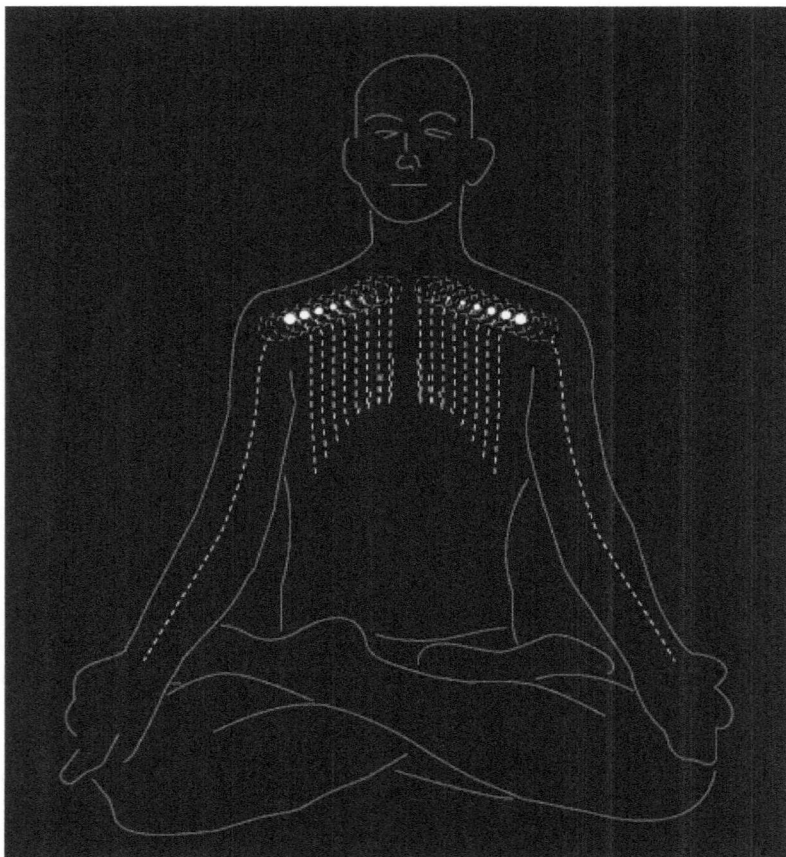

I thought to the energy,

"O no you will not take the body and do as you like. Behave! I will direct you."

The force which tilted the body was not spinal kundalini. It was the infused breath energy which was lodged under both collar bones. It was more concentrated on the right side. This caused the body to tilt to the left. It felt as if the body would keep tilting until it upturned. I stopped this action. The energy which caused the tilt, retreated into a bunch of energy under each collar bone. I began a series of rapid breaths and used that to capture the energy and to force more breath energy into it. This caused it to lose its power over the psyche. I took more control.

During this experience, there was bliss energy scattered everywhere within the trunk of the subtle body.

Before this there was a light green energy in the trunk, a pixelated energy which tried to fluff itself. I took control of that by doing more rapid breaths and by infusing the energy which accumulated into a compression force.

Part 6

Buddhism in China

My observation after study of the original instruction of Gautama Buddha, is that Buddhism as it was originally practice is part of the yoga process. What is missing perhaps is *pranayama* practice, but even that is included in part. The other parts of *ashtanga* yoga system are present in Buddhism.

One should note that Buddha learned to meditate in India from Indian gurus, whom he surpassed but his graduation from that did not mean that he gave up meditation. He took it to a higher level.

Buddha was from a brahmin caste family which had Gautama Rishi as its family lineage (gotra). Just recently within the past year, I met a certain Vishaka who was a caste brahmin from South India and who identified himself as being from the same Gautama Rishi lineage. The name which Buddha has as Gautama is not his first name. It is the lineage caste family name, like a surname in Western culture.

The question is not if yoga and Buddhism can co-exist but rather that since Buddhism is adapted from Indian yoga, it requires a careful investigation to see what was adapted and what was developed further.

When Patanjali listed the applications of *samyama* (three higher stages of yoga), the list contains many of the accomplishments of Buddha which Buddha described to his disciples when he explained what he experienced in the meditations just before and just at the time of his enlightenment into the cause of trauma.

Let us not get carried away with generalizations. We should be specific that his enlightenment is not the same at that of Jesus Christ or some other religious celebrity like Yogananda or RamaKrishna. His enlightenment was about the elimination of trauma (emotional anguish).

My observation in 2006 in China in Beijing and Xiang is that Buddhism for the most part is not concurrent. Few Chinese practice it. In fact, I did not observe any big religious influence and also no big communist influence even though the government was communist. There was a silence that I notice about religion and ideology, like a lull period between storms.

I saw people come out of apartment buildings after sunset and also before sunrise, to practice Tai Chi in large groups with each person doing his session side by side with the others.

I visited both Buddhist and Taoist temples. The popular ones had many Chinese visitors who were more like tourists than religious devotees. I noticed that at some places there were government agents. Some of the religious literatures were sold in book stores on the premises which were run by government people. The literature itself was tainted by government people, as I could tell from the way it was written.

Two Taoist temples, one was in Xiang, were just like something out of an ancient time with only one or two monks or caretakers and no visitors, no government agents. The agents were only at the popular locations which were frequented by tourists who were mostly Chinese.

Sometimes in Beijing there were Tibetans and Mongolians, here and there in small groups. One could tell by their goldish complexion as compared to the whitish-cream complexion of Chinese. The Tibetans looked lost, stunned, like something hit them.

One thing that deserves consideration is the fact that Buddhism was an incursion into Tibet and China. It replaced as well as fused with Bon religion in Tibet and Taoist process.

In time I feel that Buddhism will again become rooted in China. It is just a matter of time. Communism will wear itself out. Some ancient systems will be reestablished. Entirely new processes will emerge.

Kill the Body

A few days ago, Yogesh reminded me of the *kill the body* process which is used by yogis on the psychic side, when providence pulled all time energy away from a physical body.

This is done in cooperation with the natural withdrawal system just before the astral body leaves the physical one for the last time. It is based on two achievements which are the advanced detachment practice of a yogi and the consequential-tally system of nature whereby the energy for purpose of a certain body is exhausted.

As one lives this physical history, one may find that gradually the account closes so that there is no more purpose for a particular body. Of course, if a person is materialistic, the day will never come when that stage is reached. This is because of tag-on desires which link themselves into the initial purpose for taking the body.

Some entities, who have little or no potential for yoga practice, may never ever experience a terminal process regarding the use of a certain physical body. This is due to the fact that they are hemmed in with the packages of desire.

Desire and hope energies are eternal, or so we were told by Patanjali. These by their very nature, unless they are squelched will not allow anyone to realize a termination of purpose for a body. These will cause fresh impetuses to manifest.

A yogi should be careful with association. Otherwise, he/she will play the loser's game, which is to prolong the self on this level through hedging the self with desires as a barricade against time.

Yogesh instructed that I look for cues from fate about how it will terminate the body. Once one becomes sensitive to that, it is a downhill race in which one must be an expert glider who is not afraid if that downhill run terminates at high speed into a stone cliff.

On the other side of tomorrow is the day after. Come what may.

On the other side of any death of any body, is the astral realms which are no different if the body is smashed to death or dies peacefully.

Since the physical existence is a losing battle. Since resentments are ongoing. It makes sense to take cues from fate about ending the interest in physical history.

The energies which are native to this place, will remain here. There is no need to hang on to these energies or to feel that they are one's own. Whatever is nature's, is nature's, now and forever. There is no need to claim it.

The monkey should release the peanuts, so that its hand can be small enough to be extracted from the narrow-mouth bag which holds the nuts.

The peanuts belong to the bag not to the monkey. Let those who feel the peanuts are theirs, hold the peanuts. Nature will encourage the attachment and may even reward those who keep grasping.

Interest Absence

I did a mystic procedure which I practice for a test-procedure given by Lahiri.

The stress on this is complete loyalty to naad sound, such that even if one has that and then one loses it for whatever reason, one cannot do this practice, until one reestablishes the loyalty to naad.

Currently due to stress coming from numerous sources but mostly from pest associations, I lost the full loyalty to naad. This situation is intolerable but the way out is the method of more practice.

Who owns the physical body, is the old question which again raises its ugly head. In addition, there is the bigger issue of who owns the subtle body. Suppose, I get your phone number, I call you. Then I suggest that you do me a favor by taking a package some distance. Then immediately after before you even have time to decide, a mutual friend, calls you. He insists that you meet him in faraway place to rescue his friend who is imprisoned in a labor camp. Then another friend sends you an email stating that you should come to a remote place to plea for his release after he was captured by insurgents.

What should you do? Which of these persons owns the body? Desires are so prevalent that they do not let up in this world. On his death bed, a man who was over seventy years of age, told me that he was not ready for the death of his body. He said his desire was to live on. He had so much more to be purposed for in physical existence.

Who owns the body? There are so many lay claims for services from it.

As a kid in Guyana, someone said, "Do this."

Then someone else said, "Do that!"

The body itself was reluctant to do either task. From within, it said, "Do neither task. Resist! Resist!"

Who owns the body, the seniors or the body itself? Can the body control its circumstance to an absolute degree? Does the body have the power to fully resist the demands of others?

Lahiri gave a process for reaching and absorbing *chit akash* spiritual energy. This is not for transferring to chit akash sky of consciousness. It is for remaining on this side of existence and bringing tit bits of that energy, pixels of it, into the subtle form, so as to transform the subtle body into a *yogaSiddha* form which is similar to but which is not a divine body.

What is the value of such achievement?

It is for making the yogi becomes compatible to the divine existence, because that is the first step in becoming qualified for transit to the divine world.

First one has to be in naad in full loyalty to it, as practiced and achieved before. Then in the meditation while in naad in the back of the subtle head, the coreSelf should look forward in the subtle head from the position of the intellect. It is a blank stare from within the subtle head where the yogi feels that there is no interest energy exuding from the sense of identity which surrounds the core. It is a looking but with no energy exuding towards the object which is the focus.

Point the gun at the target. Pull the trigger. Nothing happens if the gun is not loaded with viable shells. It is blank. It has no charge, no explosion of energy, nothing.

Feeling blank energy at the intellect and realizing that the interest ceased completely, the yogi marvels at first. This is because he/she tried for years to bring an end to the outward coursing of the energy from the coreSelf through the intellect. He/she had no success except for a few moments now and again during practice. But now he/she realized the result in fact and is surprised.

The eyes feel like those of a dead man, blank, empty, lifeless.

Soon after noticing this and staying put in the center of the subtle head, the yogi notices that the naad sound increased in volume to a blare-frequency which is noticeably louder. It has a ping frequency but it is not distracting. It is more like honey-music. But then there is this energy which oozes in from the *chit akash*. The yogi should let that energy enter and sooth his troubles away.

He will hear no more bickering from the earth natives, the condemn people who make no progress, who must remain materialistic come what may.

Kundalini Maintains the body

Naad sound resonates for all eternity but we do not hear it because of a lack of focus on its dimension. Sometimes it imposes itself upon someone and is considered a nuisance. But there is an inner ear sound which is similar to naad and which may be mistaken for naad. That is heard when there is a disease in the ear or when the sound chamber is changed in shape due to rupture of the ear canal.

A yogi/yogini should trace and hear naad or cause the self to hear it even in the worse conditions. When we hear naad we do so after transiting from one plane where naad is not heard to another plain where it is perceptible. One should observe this transit and learn how to reach naad at any time.

There was a man who frequently visited a religious place on occasion. Once a stranger approached him and wanted to know where he was from but when the stranger asked about the route used to get to the holy place, the visitor said,

"I never gave it any thought as to where I was from and as to how I would get here. I usually walk and then I may reach here. Then I walk and I may return to my place. I have no firm mapping between here and there."

Unlike this traveler a yogi should note how he/she reaches naad sound and as to how he/she is made to be unaware of naad sound. These inner observations should be made.

With more and more practice there should be more and more objectivity in any altered state of consciousness. With a little help from its friend, the coreSelf, the kundalini maintains the human body. On occasion we find that the kundalini can maintain the body, even without the selective input of the core. Even if the coreSelf disagrees, the kundalini may continue to maintain the physical body. If you find that the body remained in an upright or partially upright position when you have lost proprietorship of it, the conclusion should be that the kundalini maintained it.

Naad/coreSelf Tight Embrace

There is what may be termed the naad/coreSelf tight embrace, where a yogi finds that he/she is in naad as if glued there with the most powerful adhesive. This is like when a boy meets a girl and they fall in love at first sight. They feel drawn to each other by a spell-binding exotic force which neither of them understands but which is so compelling that neither of them can maintain objectivity.

It may be compared as to when there is a strong attraction between a man and woman where the woman becomes very possessive of the man and takes an aggressive move to arrest the man in her arms, which is something that males are famous for doing.

When this happens with naad, the coreSelf is usually facing forward, looking to the front of the subtle head but seeing nothing because there is no interest in sensing anything besides naad. The core in this condition has for the time being lost interest in the sensual pursuits and is only concerned with its beloved naad sound.

But then suddenly sometimes, there appears in front of the core, a cobalt-blue dull shine energy which irradiates everywhere around the naad sound but which is predominantly in the front part of the subtle head. In that state, the core, if it was alerted by an advanced yogi, could pull in chit akash spiritual energy into its psyche, so as to accelerate the progress for developing a *yogaSiddha* body.

Kundalini Shoulders-Down

This is an experience which I had three days ago. Due to pressing concerns, I failed to publish it. Even if they are unable to make notations on occasion, it is important for students to persists with practice.

This kundalini shoulders-down experience happened during breath infusion, where there were no spinal kundalini arousals. These are cell kundalini arousals instead of spinal arousals which go into the head. To begin with doing breath infusion, spinal arousals are everything. But after doing that for about five to seven years, one should graduate to cell arousal. Some students may have such experiences early on and should cherish them along with spinal arousal.

The big value of cell arousal is that it deconditions one from sexual energy expression. Being celibate when that means simply having no sexual indulgence does not in any way cause one's psyche to be deconditioned from sexual indulgence even though it does cease the memory of the indulgence for the time being for the number of months or years, one is able to maintain that by the grace of providence. And who knows when providence will take a turn to relocate one into an environment where the memory will be reactivated? Can you remember when in any past life, you ceased sex desire? Then in a new life, it began with full impetus just as if you never curbed it?

Sad is it not, if one cannot remember?

What does that say about the celibate aims?

Being celibate when it means that one lifts the sex hormone energy from the genitals and causes it to be distributed all over the psyche and to reach into the head, deconditions one from genital sex experience but does not necessarily prepare one for a spiritual body in which every part of the body has pleasure potency expression equally.

Everything should be learnt step by step. Students who feel they know it all because of being taught what is preliminary but which to them is a credential of authority, will stall because of arrogance.

In my experience from the start of the breath infusion session, there was cell kundalini going, darting in all parts of the psyche randomly. There was a twinkling dangling springs-like energy falling from the shoulder blades and scapula. It has a silver shimmer. It hung and shook. It was with a bright silver color and hung down like lose flexible stainless-steel springs with coils of about three-fourth of an inch in diameter. It was intense. It caught me off-guard. I did not expect it.

It tried to get the body away from me by throwing the body to the left. I looked down on it, like a giant standing over a dwarf, peering down. I thought it was funny that such kundalini energy would try to take control of the subtle and physical bodies. I could feel its throwing force which was great. I held the body so that it did not move to the left. The force which was thrown moved alone without the body.

It had no effect on the subtle head but it had bliss traces which were felt in the torso. I looked down observing it, smiling.

Sex Taxation in Yoga

I was inspired to write about the sex taxation system as it applies to advanced yoga practice. This system of taxation is run by a tight genetic and primal survival system which cannot be changed except by migration from one level of the subtle body to another. It is not an easy acchievement for a yogin. The evidence of this is that only siddha yogis experience a closing down of this sex taxation system.

What is this system?

It is the method of nature where a subtle and/or gross physical form is purposed for reproduction. The living entities exist but they require matching forms for environments. They can manifest only by doing so through the bodies of others. This applies on all fronts even as vegetation, where one type can reproduce seedlings of its own kind.

The sex taxation system is a tight revenue service like a bully government's extraction of taxes from its poor citizens. In this system the energy is the sex chakra on the spine and the sex organ chakra in the center of the pubic area. These two outposts cause the rest of the body to contribute a portion of energy for the accretion of concentrate cell energy which is used in the manufacture of sex hormones which in turn is used in the manufacture of sexual pleasure and then harmful emotions, along with life forms if fertile conditions are present without contraceptives.

A yogi should get to the stage of insight where he/she can see that sexual pleasure is not the only composite which is manufactured. It is the obvious most desired composite but there is another part which is the harmful emotions composite which does not become visible until the pleasure aspect is experienced and the person waits for more of it. Then there is an attack from within the mind which brings on numerous impractical desires and the resulting tensions which those produce.

In the breath infusion practice, there is a stage, where the cells which are victim citizens in the city of the body, get up in revolt and decide that they will no longer send the requested payments to the sexual chakra system. At this stage there is a hush energy from the sexual chakra, where it becomes shocked at this declaration. Then the sexual energy engages in a conspiracy where the student feels that he/she conquered sex desire, even though that idea is totally impractical at that stage. If the person is unfortunate, there will be no temptations provide by providence and the person will float in arrogance until providence decides to provide an effective assault.

In dealing with this in the siddhaYoga process, a yogi, during breath infusion, extracts the hormone energy from the victim cells and compressed it back into those very cells. Instead of the energy going to maximize sex experience, it bursts in the victim cells, who then feel like victim citizens who no longer must pay takes to an oppressive government.

While initially the way to deal with sex expression through the genitals is to cause the expression to go up through the spine into the head. In time, in the more advanced stage, the secret is to not have the energy be accumulated in the first place. To do this the kundalini of each cell must be actuated where the cell is located. It is not sent headlong through the spine after directing the sex chakra to deposit its energy and its tax-stolen energies into the kundalini life force at the base chakra.

Shivers-Quivers Knee Energy

During breath infusion, there was a shivers-quivers knees energy experience which cause the knee area to send its kundalini energy downwards through the legs. There was a little hump at the bottom of the knee. From it a light split downwards with shining rays angled outwards.

The physical body began to shake and quake but I held it together looking and allowing the energy to do as it desired.

This is part of the creation of a *yogaSiddha* body which is a virtual spiritual form, even though it is not a spiritual form in fact. It is a preparation for a spiritual form and for getting used to the way of existence in the divine world as contrasted to what we do and desire here.

The legs and feet, the forearms and fingers are the last parts of the subtle body to be brought into full astral purity of energy. These areas are hard to target even for the most stalwart ascetics. The feet, legs and thighs are slaves to sex desire. The hands, forearms and arms are the instruments of the reproductive faculty.

These areas should be brought under yogic submission by any which means, but especially by special asana postures and breath infusion.

Why a Yogi Wants a Long Life?

There is no point in staying in a physical body after one reaches a certain stage of advancement. This is because at a certain stage the physical form is useless as a tool to stabalize and realize the subtle body. Just as to manufacture an aircraft one needs a hanger on the ground but to fly the machine one has to exit the hanger, so to gain control of the subtle body a yogi may need a physical form. That is not true for all yogis but it is true for many.

The more important issue is fame and disciples. As soon as a yogi becomes famous his progress is more or less finished. For instance, in this lifespan, I am not famous. That is the mercy of fate. If however, I become famous, I will be so occupied that my practice will be nil.

It is possible to make advancement if one is famous but only if one can secure isolation all the same. This means isolations on the physical and astral levels. Merely to be isolated physically has no meaning if one is open to association on the astral planes.

As soon as a yogi becomes famous, he spends hours with people who want to know this and know that or to get a blessing or hear of his experiences and opinions. That means that his personal practice is suspended.

In the case of Gautam Buddha, we hear that after enlightenment he left places if there were disturbances from disciples. He got his robe and bowl and sneaked off, leaving disciples wherever they were. This indicates that disciples are the bane of personal advancement.

There is also the factor of resentment from people whom one knew before or whom one knew even in past lives. Those from the current life have live-memories of things they perceived as being done to them by the yogi. These will pursue a famous yogi to insult him. I endure this from time to time. Relatives sometimes, hunt a yogi to make demands of him or to express disapproval or condemnation of him for real or imagined reasons.

If the yogi is not famous, he has a chance to escape most of this, because people get little satisfaction from cursing someone who seems to be condemned by circumstance.

There are associations from previous lives. These people do not remember knowing the yogi but they remember him through an instinct energy which surfaces as a particular attitude of disliking or criticizing him. Many of these people approach as soon as a yogi becomes famous. They harass him.

I remember around 1974-1975, there was a period when people came and riled at me even though they had no idea if I was a yogi of worth or a fake ascetic. They felt that they should insult me through and through.

If I was famous then this kind of attack would have increased exponentially.

Why should a yogi keep a body for as long as nature will allow him/her to?

There are two reasons.
- to make further advancement
- to share yogic techniques.

It depends on why the person took the body or why the person had to take the body. Some yogis take a body by choice. Some do so because they are compelled.

In either case if the yogi needs the physical form to make advancement, he/she should use a body for as long as possible.

If the yogi has a mission to give information, he may go with the body for a long time so long as his message remains relevant.

In my case for example I wrote books but as the English language changes, those books will sooner or later become irrelevant. There was a sannyasi who said that his books would last for at least one thousand years. Who knows why he made that statement? The fact remains that languages evolve. As soon as the language becomes outmoded the books are overlooked, unless one gets someone to rewrite them faithfully while one is in the hereafter or unless one takes another body and writes again in the new language or in the new format of the same language.

I wrote much, but due to the rapid changes in the language and because of the influence of technology, most of it may be trashed as irrelevant in a few years.

Why do I write?

Because I must do so to expend the energy which I have in my psyche for purposing this life. I cannot take that energy elsewhere. It must be deposited here even if it will be wasted. Regardless of the efficiency, what is for this world is for this situation?

Knee-Contained Body

The bubble body was introduced by Siddha Swami Nityananda. It involves the trunk, neck and head of the subtle body. In it the energies are homogenous with no part having any special cells or special pleasure energy which some other part does not have. In other words, there is no genital value in any specific organ or part of the body. In such a form there is no genital, no sexual organ.

In a more advanced stage, Lahiri introduced the knee-contained body. This is the same bubble body but instead of being the trunk, neck and head, this includes the thighs up to the knees. Even the knees have the same pleasure yield as any other part of the body.

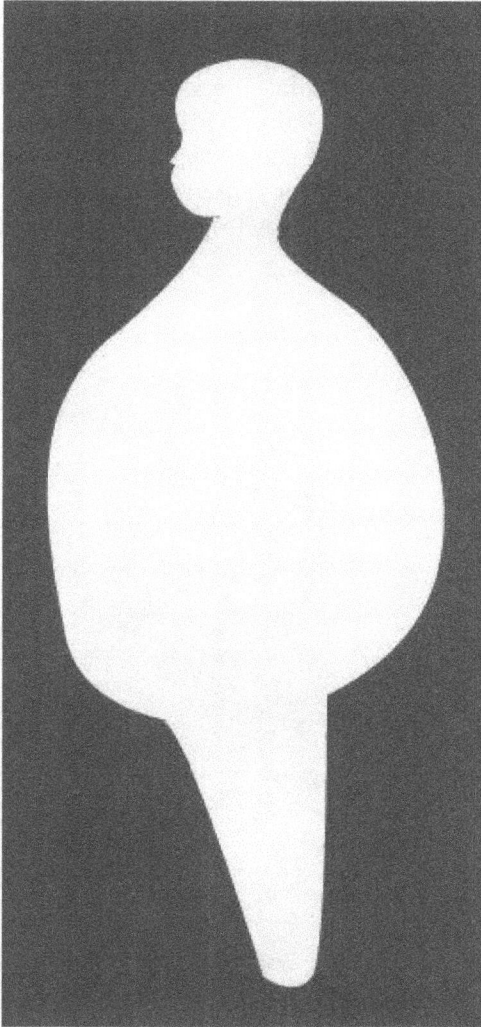

The progress of this does not end there, because if the yogi keeps at the disciplines diligently, especially breath infusion with inner focus, eventually this will include the legs up to the ankles and then the feet up to the toe-tips, and further to the arms, forearms and finger-tips.

Naad Meditation Failure

This morning during the meditation after breath infusion, Lahiri entered through the top of the subtle head in a miniature subtle form. He directed me in how to use naad for a procedure. This concerns the naad sound and being ripped away from it or being prevented from finding or hearing it by other psychic forces which penetrate the psyche.

Lahiri showed a double panel diagram which I include below. This shows that on the front side of one panel, the side nearer the face of the subtle head, there is a layer of thought energy. This energy is so charged that as soon as it latches on to the coreSelf, it causes the core to be segregated from the naad sound. It produces a resistance force on the back side of the coreSelf. This force further peels the core away from the naad sound which is the back of the subtle head.

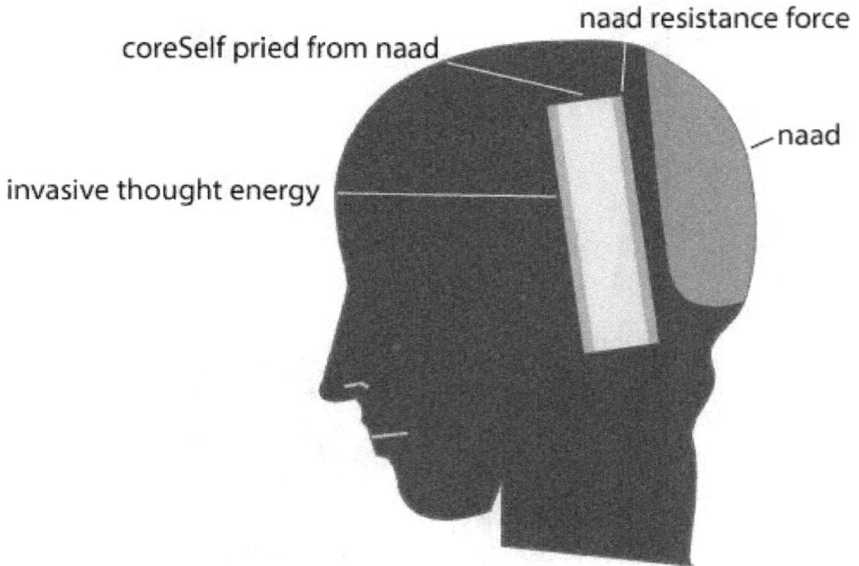

The result of this is that the yogi finds that he/she can neither latch to nor find the naad sound. In some experiences the yogi has no memory of naad until after the meditation session is over. He realizes that he was in a farce-meditation where he was under the control of the energy of some other person or persons.

Who are these persons?

It could be anyone that the yogi associated with. Mostly these are relatives and friends, persons who have a relationship with the yogi in a confidential way. Even when he is not in their physical proximity, they have access to the psyche of the yogi.

Relatives and friends are a necessity in the physical world. I cannot have a physical body unless I get it through physical relatives. They are compulsory and yet, through the history of yoga, we found that the most obstructions to practice came from relatives. Friends, even friends who are yogis may send obstructions into the mind of the yogi.

Due to selfishness and pure massive ignorance, relatives and friends send obstructive energies to stop a yogi from making progress, to detract a yogi to themselves, to their interest, for their maintenance.

Progress Severed

This is true, where one finds that relatives and friends drop all cordiality and love and begin a vicious raspy assault if they think that yoga practice of the yogi causes a reduction in the attention, they get from him. The yogi also is due to perform certain services for relatives and besides these mandatory obligations, there are additional charges levied by relatives. They feel that the yogi owes services which are needed for the fulfilment of desires. If the yogi does not show an interest or if he stubbornly ignores the requests, a disruptive energy is emitted from the psyche of these persons. This enters his psyche and rips him/her away from the spiritual objective.

There are many beginner-yogis, who have grand ideas about being freed from such obligations but these persons are unaware of the power of these impositions. They fail to understand the up-hill struggle which awaits them when they get serious about practice.

So far, I made a little progress in yoga. Some students think that I am an advanced yogi and still I write these episodes to bring it to their attention that even for me, it is a battle which I may lose in the final analysis. I may be a good warrior. I may have killed many enemies of yoga. Still, the battle rages. It is one against many. It is one against another one in some cases, where I lose my armor and sword. Then I am left for dead on the battlefield after being cut down by a thought energy which entered my psyche and altered it away from naad focus.

The worse association a yogi can get is from those who are dear to him and who turn against him and his spiritual progress or who think that they are interested in his spiritual progress but who in fact are destructive to it. There is nothing worse in meditation than an envy or demand from someone who is dear to a yogi or someone who at one time was dear to a yogi or who was in confidence with a yogi.

Such a person is apt to do the perfect hatchet job on the spiritual progress of the yogi. Then the yogi is left with a failed practice. Sometimes years of meditation effort are wiped out by one act of resentment from some person who was or who is dear to a yogi. Some opponents have a sharp axe which cuts the yogi's progress once and for all. Then the yogi is released from the obligation and must begin the practice again. He must painstakingly put it back together.

But there are other opponents who carry a blunt axe. They chop a yogi but the wounds are not neat and precise. These are like a primitive butcher cutting with a stone axe. These torment a yogi for a long time, for months or even for years. Finally, from trauma and emotional hemorrhage he is killed. Putting himself back together, takes many lives and many sojourns in the astral hereafter.

This is the reality. That is why I provide this information.

Irresistible Goddess *Pushti*

Today during breath infusion, I worked on returning the hormone formation energy to the goddess *Pushti*. This person is a *Lakshmi* entity who sponsors nutrition in human bodies. She carries the prototype breasts and female sexual generative organs. Her mission is simply to sponsor reproduction so that entities using infant forms are nourished fittingly.

She is so effective that some infants in a poverty situation are well nourished while one whose parents are wealthy may have an impoverished body. When *Pushti* nourishes someone, it does not matter if he/she is in a poverty-stricken or wealthy family. The person's form will be well-designed and will grow fittingly in the right places by the nourishment provided.

For this goddess, everyone praises her because no matter if the parents are rich or poor one requires, as a basis, a healthy nourished infant body. Any buxom woman from any class or caste, from any poor or wealthy situation, from a friendly or hostile nation, is a representative of goddess Pushti.

Sometimes other women observe how such a desirable woman is treated. They are surprised. They wonder why the fuss. Some other women simply envy it because of the persuasive powers of these representatives of the Goddess. A woman is not required to have an exceptional intelligence to have a buxom form. It does not matter because the language of nutrition has intelligence. It communicates itself to most male humans. The statement of such forms to males is this:

- *I am nourished. I can nourish.*

A yogi must at some stage return the hormone formation energy to the goddess. If he fails to do that, it will cause his *yogaSiddha* body not to be developed.

In the human body this hormone formation energy begins as energy for collection of nutrients from the stomach and higher intestines. Later as the human body ages through adolescence, this energy begins the construction of sex hormones. Later in the elderly years of the body, this energy begins to close out its operations. This is manifested in what is called menopause in women and sexual impotence in men. The closing of this system means that it becomes dormant.

There are some ascetic women and men who feel that they have no sex desire after the manifestation of menopause and impotency. These persons are mistaken and indulge in self-delusion. Dormancy of a tendency means that the tendency is suppressed for the time being. It will re-emerge powerfully.

A yogi should return the hormone formation energy to goddess *Pushti*. When he does so, he should do so with smiles. It happens that anyone who approached the Goddess must smile broadly while doing so. This is because her environment causes one to smile when one sees her.

Even though nutrition causes the yogi to go crazy, still when he approaches this goddess he will smile. Her buxom shape, her ample well-formed upward looking breasts, everything about her is pleasing to the eyes.

With her milking yielding full breasts where creamy milk exudes, she is everything to infants. She is everything with her skin which is smoother than glass. Her tender touch causes the hairs to stand on end in ecstasy.

The yogi pulls the hormone formation energy up through the front part of the chest. He returns it to the goddess. He says thanks repeatedly. Without that there would be no opportunity to experience the physical world.

There is another side to the goddess. That is her flip personality who is the goddess of death. According to the Puranas, this goddess of death was instructed by Brahma to kill living bodies by any which means including old age and disease. She refused to do it and went away crying. Her thought was that no one would like her if she was the person who did this. After hiding for thousands of years, she again saw Brahma. He made the same request. This happened more than once, until at last she yielded when Brahma said that no one would see her or know that she was the cause of death. Hence no one would resent her. Brahma repeatedly said to her that it was her duty to do so. When she asked him to assign another more palatable task, he refused to change the mission of her existence.

During the appearance of the *Ma Pushti*, the buxom supernatural woman, there was a split second when goddess death *(Mara)* appeared. With her there is an attempt to smile but it was immediately squelched. No one likes the approach of death. No one likes diseases and infirmity. Goddess Death wanted to talk to me but there was no speech as the speech energy in my psyche immediately disappeared and hid. Nevertheless, I produced a smile under my cheeks, under my unwilling skin. I greeted her with respect.

She waved, smiled through a heated light in her eyes and went on, indicating that she would overlook me for the time being.

Chit Akash Naad Pull-In

Today I did a chit akash *naad pull in*. This is for using the naad sound to pull *chit akash* energy. Consider the naad sound coming in from a border between two countries. One country is the physical world where we are located. This includes the subtle energy or astral dimensions. The other country is the divine environment.

From the border a person can go in either direction, but that is if he/she can reach the border and become established there. While listening to naad and turned towards naad, away from the frontal part of the subtle head, being surrounded by naad resonance, the yogi can pull *chit akash* energy into the psyche.

No Kundalini Spinal Arousals

Breath infusion this morning was great with no kundalini spinal arousals. Mainly, the focus was to get to *hard to reach* places in the thighs, legs, feet, arms, forearms and fingers. At some stage, these areas must be attacked or the *Siddhaloka* body would not be assumed.

There was an infused energy which ran up inside the thighs but which did not curve to the genital region. Instead, it leaned away from it and went straight up into the body without attraction to the pubic area.

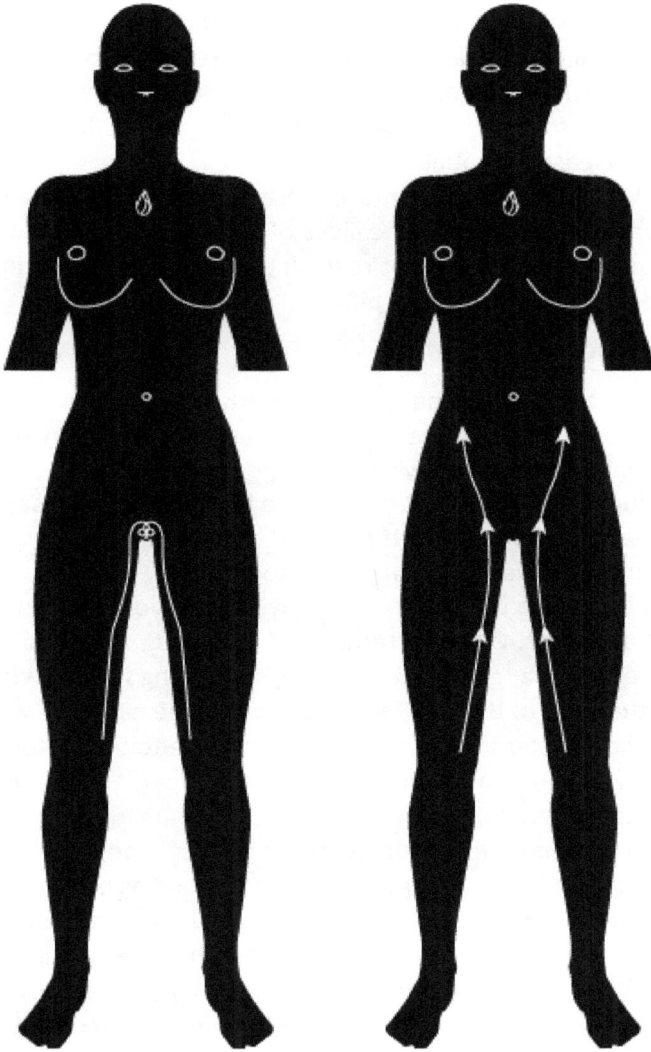

In the normal configuration of a human body, the thigh energy curves into the pubic area to provide supports for the reproduction center. However, if a yogi does not intend to continue in material existence in many lives to come, there is no need to support this natural configuration. It should be, if possible, erased from the psyche.

This does not mean that every student can achieve this. In fact, most cannot. They are not finished with the course through physical existence. Still, it is of interest to understand what the future holds, even if that future will be billions of years hence.

Impetus for self-realization to the full extent may take hundreds or thousands or millions of years to fructify. It depends on the evolutionary status of the person. Sometimes people want to know if they can do advanced mystic focus. The answer may be yes or no. It depends on the evolutionary release potential of the yogi.

There was one burst of infused breath energy combined with cell kundalini where it ran through the sides of the neck into the shoulders, into the arms and forearms. It did not reach into the fingers but it tingled under the shoulders and above the arm pits.

Preparing for Death

A student questioned about final departure from a material body. It is not an easy topic because the techniques used depends on the action of providence in bringing the body to an end.

Assuming for instance that one loses a body suddenly in say an aircraft crash, the method of final departure would be a bit different to if one passed on from a body that was terminally ill for some time.

Fate has much to do with it. Fate may on occasion, give one an alert in the form of a portent. On the afternoon of March 10, 2011, from the house in South Korea. I saw a red sunset. I felt that something strange would happen because of the color of the sun. The next day was the big event which caused the Fukushima disaster in Japan which is very close to South Korea. For that matter if the earthquake was on the west side of Japan, then perhaps I would not be here to say anything about it.

What to do to prepare for death of the physical body?

To tell you the truth, your guess may be as good as mine.

When I was asked about it today, I admitted that I carried an energy in my psyche to deal with such incidences as death. I already died more than once while having this body. Once when a car I drove flipped, my subtle body was hurled out of the physical one by the spinning action of the car when it left the highway and flew over a deep embankment. One other time was when I was with Frederic R, a friend who was in Tech School at Lowry Air Force Base, Denver, Colorado.

We were travelling to a rock concert for Led Zeppelin sometime in 1970 at the Denver Coliseum. Both of us took LSD pills. Frederic was a seasoned druggie who could do anything normal while taking hallucinogens. I could handle the stuff too because it is all about how it affects the kundalini *shakti*. While we travelled there, I reconsidered why I took the body. Seeing that it would be a loss cause for the most part, I thought to kill the body by throwing it out of the car.

A voice from the sky, said that I should finish the mission anyway and that I would implicate Frederic if it happened while he drove the car.

I had another instance with death once when I was on a small freight ship going from Guyana to Martinique, when a series of huge waves crashed over the ship during the night. The ship actually went under completely because the waves were bigger than the ship. Somehow the vessel came out of the water and continued. Seasoned sailors were scared to death. We felt that the ship would be down under, once and for all. In such a situation life rafts and life jackets are meaningless. At the time my body was about fifteen years of age.

There was another incidence when I was in Trinidad. There was an earthquake which lasted for about 20 minutes. An earthquake for about a few minutes is one thing but if it goes on for more than five-minutes then one must face the fact that one's body may be killed. There is total insecurity. You live with that, feeling that Mother Earth abandoned you.

When I used this body, when it was eight years of age, I had a near-death experience, where I was towed on a bicycle by my paternal aunt. It was late at night. I sat behind her on the bike. I fell asleep while holding her from behind. My hands fell away. My body fell from the bike. My aunt was a big lady. I was a skinny boy. She had no idea I fell from the bike.

I then realized what happened when I become conscious of my body crumpled on the road. I look and saw that my aunt rode away with no hint that I was not on the bike. I ran to the bike. I jumped on the carrier seat. This was a death experience, because when I realized that the physical body fell from the bike to the road; I did so from an astral experience which I was in at the time. Death is similar in that it may happen even when one is not in the physical body. A body can die while one is astral projected from it. Then one must realize that one was evicted from the lifelong residence which one used to identity as a physical self.

From infancy through about thirteen years of age I had many near-death experiences. I would be out of my body and be unable to assume control of it. Or I would be in an astral existence and then I would not get back rapidly into the physical casing. That would cause anxiety regarding if I could be the physical body again.

It happened that sometimes when I would return to the physical body, it would be dead for all practical purposes. The heart would be stopped. Its breathing stopped like if something pulled the main breaker from a circuit. When I would return into the physical body, it would act as if it was not there as it was blank. Then by my astral presence, it would have a jerk action. Then the heart would begin and the breathing would begin the way a car starts then the ignition switch is turned.

The first step in preparation for death is to understand that there is nothing which one does, nothing which is important which is one's property or absolute possession. This is hard to explain to people who feel that they must always act physically. Nearly everyone feels that this must be done and that must be done and this much time is needed, therefore death should stay at bay. It should not approach today.

Like a good sport, a yogi should play in the game of life. He/she should not take his/her life seriously.

King Yudhishthira set a nice example for everyone when he left aside everything when he heard that Krishna and Balaram departed from their bodies. He left even his dear wife, the beautiful most desirable woman Draupadi but she was intelligent enough to follow him into the lifestyle of a total nobody.

His attitude was simple:

If God is not concerned, why should I be?

That is the first step in preparing for death.

Urdhva-Reta Precharge Pull

This procedure is an advanced one which should be kept in the back of the mind for later use; just in case one advances enough before leaving the body and can implement it.

It is useless for beginners and also useless even for advanced students who were unable to completely pull up the sexual hormonal energy from genital discharge and pooling. In the *Hatha Yoga Pradipika*, a big deal is made about lifting seminal fluids by male yogis. Little is said about female yoginis in that book but there is mention there about male yogis lifting both male and female secretions during sexual activities.

That book is not for the peevish, simple-minded students of yoga. It kicks aside the traditional ways of considering spiritual advancement. It gets down to the essentials of what happens within the nature of the psyche.

In working with the sexual energy in the psyche, one must first deal with it as it is. This takes tons of observation and realization. The first part of this is disappointment at that stark truth which is that one cannot control the sexual energy. The reproductive force in the creation is a conjoint system which is bigger than any limited being. For as long as it will prevail, there is no hope for fully confining it but if one gets a reprieve by fate, one can escape from its grip.

Initially when confronted for battle with the willpower of the yogi, the sexual faculty repeatedly wins the struggle. Some students go away in disgust. They declare that they cannot subdue sex desire.

I was in a spiritual society where they would ridicule yogis who were reported to succumb to sex desires, even in cases where these fallen yogis surmounted it later for themselves and in some cases for their sexual partners.

Why do people rile a yogi who is observed to give in to sex desire for one reason or another, or because he could not resist the force of it?

Lahiri spoke to me this morning during practice about what he termed to be the *urdhva-reta up-ride*. This is when the hormonal energy which usually goes to the genitals to be charged for sexual activities there, does not reach that area and instead is pulled up through the front area of the body. Instead of this energy going down, it drops a little and then it reverses and moves upwards through the front of the neck into the face.

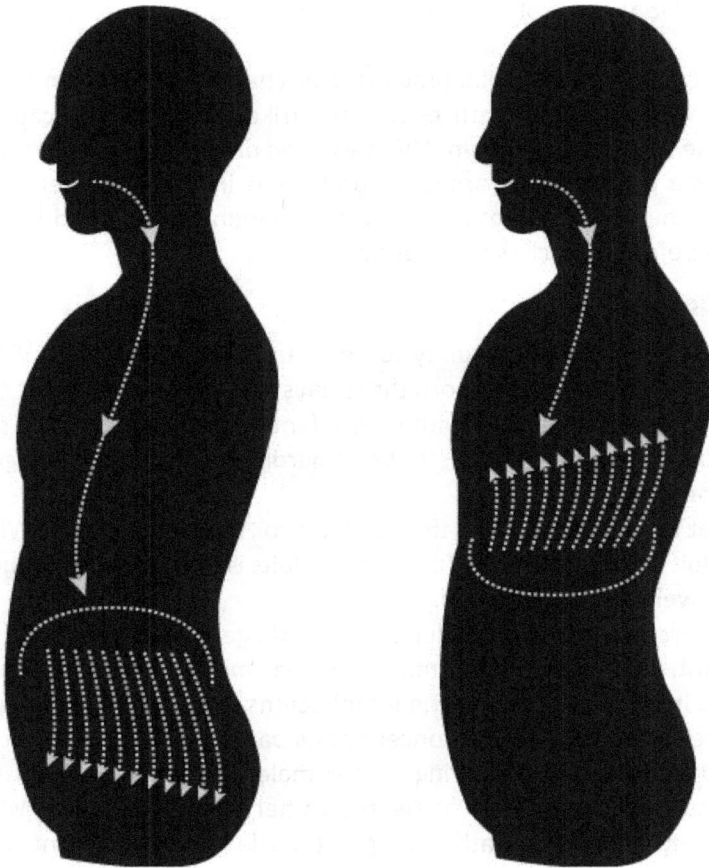

When felt or seen by the yogi in meditation, this energy has a cloudy-white color as compared to when it would be sexually charged where it would have a yellow-orange color. In females it assumes a pink-red-crimson color.

When this happens in a yogi, initially the sexual area of the body assumes a depressed mood. In the case of women, it assumes a super-depressed mood. If this mood is tolerated as an energy phase, rather than as a mood, if the yogi does accommodate this depression, it soon passes.

What is the value of such a complicated kriya which goes against the grain of nature?

It is that the yogi will not have to deal with kundalini energy which is sex-charged. He does not have to do yoga to process sexual energy. That is one less chore for him which means that he has more time to focus on meditation practice in a deeper and more meaningful way. Most of all, he can hang with the *mahasiddhas*, people whose subtle bodies do not carry a vulgar sexual interest.

The traditional kundalini practice uses charged sexual hormone energy in a mix with infused breath energy to strike the kundalini, causing it to ascend the spine into the brain. This advanced practice has no charged sexual energy as a part of it. No aroused kundalini is involved. The energy which would be charged does not reach the sex charging system and is utilized in the body before it reaches those areas.

Love of Body?

Today I had the opportunity to be in an office where there were eight infants. One look as if it was born three days ago. In the developed countries it is rare to see both parents with their infants here and there. The society is so segmented and partitioned, that one hardly sees all the ages together on most occasions.

What is for infants is just that. What is for teenagers is that. What is for young adults is that. What are for mature adults is that. What is for the elderly is that as well. All is partitioned.

The infants I saw were under one year of age. It was interesting because one parent, a male, kissed his infant who was merely days of age and could not focus its eyes just yet but the infant seems to know what the father did and appreciated the love and concern of its parent.

One mother was endearing to her male infant. I wondered who the infant was, how the infant was related to her from its past life. Was it her grandfather, great grandfather or great uncle? Did the infant serve her ancestors in a servant capacity in its past life?

If he was alive during her teen years how did she treat him? Was her love for him dependent on the age of his physical form?

If he had an elderly body of say about seventy years of age, could she love him in that form just as well?

Is the love between two persons reliant on the age of the bodies used by them?

Containment of Energy Satisfaction

This is an advanced practice for meditation with containment of the energy of the psyche, where that energy gives the yogi a full satisfaction as it is without input from anywhere else. It is an unusual satisfaction. It is a completely different type of satisfaction. Either of these is complete in themselves while they occur in the meditation.

This containment of energy satisfaction occurs when all of the carbon dioxide is removed, say about at least 98% of it, even from the *hard to reach* places. This occurs when kundalini is abolished and the system of energy is no longer based on pooling of sex hormones and the use of that by the kundalini life force.

This is a lust free, sex free, bliss energy which in comparison to what one enjoyed before is like no happiness, even though it is really happiness in its purest form. Appreciation for this bliss energy comes after having forgotten the sex pleasure type of energy.

Kundalini Dominance Terminated

In the long range, for all that the kundalini is, and all that it can do to increase insight into the realities and provide bliss energy to offset the insecurities of being a lone limited existence in infinite seas of realities in which one has no control, the kundalini has to be discarded.

It will never truly be subservient to the coreSelf which it is allied to. Any opportunity it gets to rebel and to proceed with a physical survival course it will take. Hence it can never be trusted absolutely except by the naïve students. At any moment, it will abandon the quest because it does not have a sincere interest in spiritual self-realization, a course which is a threat to its very existence and which will reduce its autonomy.

How to terminate kundalini's dominance?

Get rid of it!

Free its slaves!

How to do that?

Work hard to raise kundalini through the spine on a daily basis for however long it would take to habituate kundalini to that. Once kundalini is habituated and when it forgets the pleasure it gets from linking with the sex drive mechanism, draw kundalini up the spine into the brain, instead of pushing it up the spine from the bottom by using breath infusion.

Once you can pull it up, it will make itself into a stub energy which hangs from the bottom back of the brain.

Once this is achieved, study the system of nutrition which is the feed system for the sex drive.

Once you commit that study and understand how that works, think and think again about living somewhere else, in a place where there is no need for a nutrition/excretion type of existence.

Could there be such a place?

Where is that realm where one will not eat, digest and excrete?

Where one will not inhale, absorb, utilize and exhale?

What is that place?

What is the you which would be in such a place?

Once a yogi finds the other locations, he/she should consider how to change the subtle body so that it no longer sends nutrition energy to the sex organ chakra. But if the nutrition energy no longer goes there where would it be?

If the cells of the body no longer have to contribute energy to the sex organ mechanism, where would that energy go?

Would there be congestion as a result?

Would the body bloat like a person who overeats and who is obese?

In this practice one pulls up the nutrition energy as compared to sending it down through the sex organ area to strike the kundalini at the base chakra. When one does this, the cells are infused directly and do not require the kundalini to stimulate them to arousal. They become drunk with their bliss energy like freed slaves on a sugar plantation who break into the rum cellar and drink as they please.

Before the rebellion, they made run but never drank it. Now it is at their disposal. Confused, they enjoy themselves. They run here and there and are merry. They do not know how to rule themselves because they never did that before. They act like unsupervised silly kids in an ice-cream parlor.

Can the coreSelf supervise everything the way the kundalini did?

Does the core have the required survival intelligence?

Sensual Energy Withdrawal Advanced

The first part of sensual energy withdrawal is a misunderstanding but it is a necessary step in getting to know something about the components and construction of the psyche. In kindergarten, one and one equals two for sure but there is hardly anywhere in the creation where that is actually true. For instance, if you can get a horse to do a certain amount of work, and you can get another matching horse to do some work, that does not mean that if you hitch them together to an implement, they will do double work. Invariably they will do less than double work which means that one and one does not equal two.

But again, if you put two equal quantities of radioactive materials together, they may explode. That blast would more than likely be much more powerful that if you exploded them separately and tallied the combined force. This would prove that one and one is more than two.

At the kindergarten level, there is no way to diminish the important of believing that one and one equals two. A student insulted me because I told him something and then contradicted that teaching a few years after. Or I may give a technique and then say that it should not be practiced.

Kriya yoga is not for childish adults who cannot accept that the world is full of paradox, that this is true here and this is not true over there.

At first for pratyahar practice, we tell people to pull in their sensual concerns, pull it all back into the head into what you feel is the existential center of consciousness.

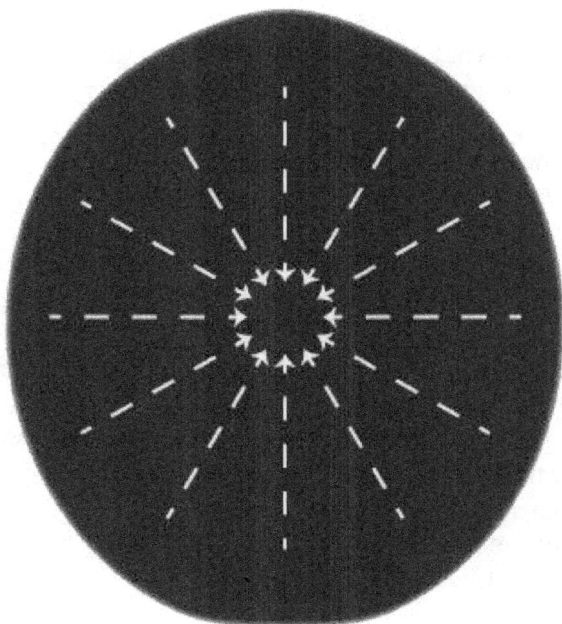

Some persons can do this. Some cannot. If this is done consistently for a time, the yogi will feel as if energy is no longer pouring out of his/her head into the world, into the physical, mental and emotional world. It feels as if energy comes into the head from the physical, mental and emotional worlds. But then after a time, the student will face the fact that when the energy comes into the head something else happens within. A whole set of new operations happen in the psychological environment which is in the head. There will also be the realization that energy comes into the head from the parts of the subtle body which are below the neck.

This is like when a person escapes from a busy situation which he does not like but then he finds that the place where he sheltered is even busier. In meditation one shuts down one's interest in the noisy and bothersome environments but then one finds that one's mind and emotions have a turmoil all of their own. These get louder and louder as one meditates. Then one runs to the meditation teacher and complains.

What should one do now?

If one seeks peace and quiet within, what should one do if within the mind there is turmoil with no peace and quiet.

As soon as one does that first pratyahar and one internalizes one realizes that the internals are chaotic, that the problem is not the environment around the body but the one inside of it.

One must sort what is inside. One must get the self out of the phony oneness which one considered oneself to be before one did any serious meditation.

What are the components of the psyche?

Are these aspects in an organized structure?

How can one reorganize the components for a cohesive sensible self who has some satisfactory degree of self-security? It will not ever be 100% secure because it is infinitesimal in an infinite existence but it can find its security maximum. It can train itself to be satisfied with that.

When the components of the psyche become ordered and there is relative peace within, irrespective of the environment on the outside of the body, then the self should locate some quiescence within its psyche but this pertains mostly to the head of the subtle body.

The questions are:

What about the rest of the subtle form, the parts below the neck?

What about distractions and disorder in those areas?

Can we reform those energies?

Can we extract and expel polluted subtle energy from those areas, replacing that with fresh energetic subtle force?

Affection and Happiness as Social Commodities

For the past month, I am with a family who has two dogs. I noticed that the animals use affection to gain favors and to induce me to do as they desire. I am wondering if we use affection in the same way in the human species. So much of what we do as humans is disguised or sophisticated animal behavior.

These dogs present affectionate attitudes and approaches and exhibit great happiness so as to induce me to take them for a stroll or to get them a doggie treat or even to pet them. They come, wag their tails, jump and spin, lick, waggle their bodies in anticipation that I would become happy and be induced to fulfill their desire for a stroll, a treat or a pat.

In the world of social relations with dogs or humans, is affection or happiness a commodity which is traded for much desired services?

Is affection a form of influence and persuasion?

Which is better to outright be frank and tell someone what I desire or to exhibit affection for that person first, show happiness and then subtly induce that person to give what I want?

Seclusion from What?

A recurring theme in the teachings of Buddha is that of seclusion from sensual desires, unwholesome states and the rapture which results from the successful completion of that.

This occurs so frequently in the Buddhist texts like the *Majjhima Nikaya Middle Length Discourses* that one may read that and continue reading without grasping the method of achievement.

Usually, seclusion in yoga means isolation from human society, like going to a faraway place, a remote forest, an inhabitable mountain or any such place where humans do not frequent. It could well mean isolating oneself in an apartment in a modern city like New York.

Here however on close inspection, Buddha spoke about another type of seclusion which was seclusion from sensual desires and upset moods in the psyche.

How on earth can one become secluded from desires which are innate to the psyche?

How can one become removed from moods, feelings, compulsions and habits in the psyche?

Vision Energy Draw Back

A big investment that must be made when a coreSelf makes contact with the physical energy is the outstretching of the vision energy. If for instance I had a form which had an appendage like a trunk, then the one which represents the vision energy would outreach further than the longest snake.

It would come out of the center of the forehead and go into the world grabbing anything that had color or shape.

One or two persons accused me of liking pretty women. If that is true, then it would mean that my vision energy is way out there, as the vision energy would be if it is to find its satisfaction in color and shape. I have some artist friends. Even though I am a mock artist, still I appreciate the skill of my friends when they weave colors to produce shapes which the vision energy appreciates.

The extension outwards of the vision energy is a major problem for the student yogin, not only for beginners but for the advanced ones as well. This energy is a big event in the struggle for survival. Imagine yourself as a unicellular organism in a pond somewhere. See how you would survive in such a situation if there are things around you which see you as a meal. If you have no way to extend your vision interest through eyes which catch light, then how will you protect yourself? How will you know when something approaches, as to its shape, color and movements?

Obviously, you would be greatly handicapped and would be an easy meal for many other life forms, especially for the ones which developed eyes. What does this have to do with *pratyahar* sensual energy withdrawal which is the fifth stage of yoga?

By the grace of Lahiri, and due to a kriya practice which I observed some advanced yogis doing some years ago in the astral world, I began to focus down into the subtle body. At first this was completed only in the chest-abdomen region of the body with the sexual energy being like a huge brick wall at the bottom. Once the sexual energy was vision penetrated, the abdominal cavity and groin area of the body were curbed with the vision energy penetrating those zones.

After this the student is told that he/she must access the knees and then the ankles and tip of the big toe. Then suddenly one realizes that while doing this, one was inadvertently reeling in the vision energy which was going outside the body through the subtle eyes and even through the third eye. Imagine the trunk of an elephant going back into its body down through its chest, abdomen, groin and into its thighs, legs and feet and remaining there and not ever protruding to pry into the external environment.

What is the advantage of this?

It facilitates reaching the *chit akash* sky of consciousness, because there is a complete shutdown of the psychic facilities which are focused into the physical world and into the subtle counterpart of that world, so that the interest of that particular self, now courses to divine situations.

Immunity of Buddha

Meditation and breath infusion practice this morning was part of the progress of the method which I currently develop. As instructed by Lahiri. I was to complete this months ago but one thing after the other occurred which forestalled this.

A yogi must be sure that progress is made no matter how slow it is. Do not be stagnant. Do not digress. A little regression will occur from time to time, as negative consequences find a yogi and as justified or unjustified, fair or unfair resentments surface and sabotage a yogi's psychic circumstances and destroy the quiescence of the mento-emotional energy.

The mento-emotional body is fragile. It cracks at the slightest shift, but a yogi can learn how to endure its fickleness, and still make advancement.

Recently by divine grace, I had a direct communication with Buddha where he showed that certain associations are dead-enders, where no matter what a teacher does, he/she cannot make those persons to be liberated now or in the near future, not even in one million years. Buddha showed a gap between where he is right now and the current history-content of planet earth, where the energy from the earth cannot reach him even though he can put energy into the earth realm.

That gap he termed as immunity for him from having to experience the mento-emotional agonies which arise in the earth's history. This is reduced to the statement that it is not who you are but where you are. It is all about location. Of course, who you are has value when you are in the wrong location because through having the right identity you can do something to relocate but until you actually do, the troubles will find you.

There are many people who want to be successful at yoga. Some are monkeys disguised currently as human beings. Some take pride in finding fault in Buddha.

How desperate is one for liberation?

Does it matter if the pilot of the aircraft is black, white or yellow?

Does it matter if he is Christian, Muslim or New Age?

Suppose he is of your religious persuasion but he lacks the skill to safely land the aircraft?

Suppose he is your religious enemy but he is skilled and will get you to earth safely?

Chit Akash within Reach

In meditation there was a light up above, which gradually came into partial view as I looked up through the third eye opening. Then there was a light just outside of the eye opening up ahead a little to my left. The light above shimmered but was focal. It was like moonlight but it has a bliss feature to it, the way one would feel a cool air making contact with one's skin. The feel of it may be compared to when a boy meets a girl he loves or a girl meets the boy she loves, and there is skin contact which is extremely pleasing.

Both of these lights were in the *chit akash* and shined through the third eye opening to enter my psyche. This is auspicious in the real sense, not in the superficial ritual belief sense of pujas, *havan, aratik* ceremonies and such.

The light above shined only for about five seconds for the most and then it moved to the back out of sight. The light out-front stayed longer but I could not time how long it was there.

What is supposed to happen?

The light above is supposed to remains in focus and then it gradually appears to dissolve the covering membrane of the psyche, so that there is no inside or outside where I am in a psyche and the *chit akash* is outside of it. The membrane which keeps the *chit akash* out of the psyche is described in no uncertain terms by Lord Krishna. Study these *Bhagavad Gita* verses:

तेषामेवानुकम्पार्थम्

अहमज्ञानजं तमः ।

नाशयाम्यात्मभावस्थो

ज्ञानदीपेन भास्वता ॥१०.११॥

teṣāmevānukampārtham

ahamajñānajaṁ tamaḥ

nāśayāmyātmabhāvastho

jñānadīpena bhāsvatā (10.11)

teṣām — of them; evānukampārtham = eva — indeed + anukampā — assistance + artham — interest; aham — I; ajñānajam — ignorance produced; tamaḥ — stupifying influence of material nature; nāśayāmy = nāśayāmi — I caused to be banished; ātmabhāvastho = ātmabhāvasthaḥ — situated in the self; jñānadīpena = jñāna — knowledge, realized + dīpena — with light, with insight (jñānadīpena — with realized insight); bhāsvatā — clear, shining, clarity of consciousness

In the interest of assisting them, I who am situated within their beings, cause the ignorance produced by the stupefying influence of material nature, to be banished by their clear realized insight. (Bhagavad Gita 10.11)

Just in case, you do not get the point, here is a direct description of our existential situation:

अर्जुन उवाच
अथ केन प्रयुक्तोऽयं
पापं चरति पूरुषः ।
अनिच्छन्नपि वार्ष्णेय
बलादिव नियोजितः ॥ ३.३६ ॥

arjuna uvāca
atha kena prayukto'yaṁ
pāpaṁ carati pūruṣaḥ
anicchannapi vārṣṇeya
balādiva niyojitaḥ (3.36)

arjuna — Arjuna; uvāca — said; atha — then; kena — by what?; prayukto = prayuktaḥ — forced; 'yaṁ = ayam — this; pāpaṁ — evil; carati — commits; pūruṣaḥ — a person; anicchannapi = anicchan — unwilling + napi (api) — even; vārṣṇeya — family man of the Vṛṣṇis; balād = balāt — from force; iva — as if; niyojitaḥ — compelled

Arjuna said: Then explain, O family man of the Vṛṣṇis, by what is a person forced to commit an evil unwillingly, just as if he were compelled to do so? (Bhagavad Gita 3.36)

श्रीभगवानुवाच
काम एष क्रोध एष
रजोगुणसमुद्भवः ।
महाशनो महापाप्मा
विद्ध्येनमिह वैरिणम् ॥ ३.३७ ॥

śrībhagavānuvāca
kāma eṣa krodha eṣa
rajoguṇasamudbhavaḥ
mahāśano mahāpāpmā
viddhyenamiha vairiṇam (3.37)

śri bhagavān — the Blessed Lord; uvāca — said; kāma — craving; eṣa — this; krodha — anger; eṣa — this; rajoguṇasamudbhavaḥ = rajo (rajaḥ) — passion + guṇa — emotion + samudbhavaḥ — source; mahāśano (mahāśanaḥ) = mahā — great + aśana — consuming power; mahāpāpmā = mahā — much + pāpmā — damage; viddhyenam =

viddhi — recognize + enam — this; iha — in this case; vairiṇam — enemy

The Blessed Lord said: This force is craving. This power is anger. The passionate emotion is the source. It has a great consuming power and does much damage. Recognize it as the enemy in this case. (Bhagavad Gita 3.37)

धूमेनाव्रियते वह्निर्
यथादर्शो मलेन च ।
यथोल्बेनावृतो गर्भस्
तथा तेनेदमावृतम् ॥ ३.३८ ॥

dhūmenāvriyate vahnir
yathādarśo malena ca
yatholbenāvṛto garbhas
tathā tenedamāvṛtam (3.38)

dhūmenāvriyate = dhūmena — by smoke + āvriyate — is obscured; vahnir = vahniḥ — the sacrificial fire; yathā — similarly; 'darśo = ādarśaḥ — mirror; malena — with dust; ca — and; yatholbenāvṛto = yatholbenāvṛtaḥ = yatho (yatha) — similarly + ulbena — by skin + āvṛtaḥ — is covered; garbhaḥ — embryo; tathā — so; tenedam = tena — by this + idam — this; āvṛtam — is blocked

As the sacrificial fire is obscured by smoke, and similarly as a mirror is shrouded by dust or as an embryo is covered by skin, so a man's insight is blocked by the passionate energy. (Bhagavad Gita 3.38)

आवृतं ज्ञानमेतेन
ज्ञानिनो नित्यवैरिणा ।
कामरूपेण कौन्तेय
दुष्पूरेणानलेन च ॥ ३.३९ ॥

āvṛtaṁ jñānametena
jñānino nityavairiṇā
kāmarūpeṇa kaunteya
duṣpūreṇānalena ca (3.39)

āvṛtam — is adjusted; jñānam — discernment; etena — by this; jñānino = jñāninaḥ — educated people; nityavairiṇā = nitya — eternal + vairiṇā — by the enemy; kāmarūpeṇa = kāma — yearning for various things +

rūpeṇa — by the sense or form of; kaunteya — son of Kuntī; duṣpūreṇānalena = duṣpūreṇa — is hard to satisfy + analena — by fire; ca — and

The discernment of educated people is adjusted by their eternal enemy which is the sense of yearning for various things. O son of Kuntī, the lusty power, is as hard to satisfy as it is to keep a fire burning. (Bhagavad Gita 3.39)

इन्द्रियाणि मनो बुद्धिर्
अस्याधिष्ठानमुच्यते ।
एतैर्विमोहयत्येष
ज्ञानमावृत्य देहिनम् ॥ ३.४० ॥

indriyāṇi mano buddhir
asyādhiṣṭhānamucyate
etairvimohayatyeṣa
jñānamāvṛtya dehinam (3.40)

indriyāṇi — the senses; mano = manaḥ — the mind; buddhir = buddhiḥ — the intelligence; asyādhiṣṭhānam = asya — if this + adhiṣṭhānam — warehouse; ucyate — it is authoritatively stated; etair = etaiḥ — with these; vimohayatyeṣa = vimohayaty (vimohayati) — confuses + eṣa — this; jñānam — insight; āvṛtya — is shrouded; dehinam — embodied soul

It is authoritatively stated that the senses, the mind and the intelligence are the combined warehouse of the passionate enemy. By these faculties, the lusty power confuses the embodied soul, shrouding his insight. (Bhagavad Gita 3.40)

तस्मात्त्वमिन्द्रियाण्यादौ
नियम्य भरतर्षभ ।
पाप्मानं प्रजहिह्येनं
ज्ञानविज्ञाननाशनम् ॥ ३.४१ ॥

tasmāttvamindriyāṇyādau
niyamya bharatarṣabha
pāpmānaṁ prajahihyenaṁ
jñānavijñānanāśanam (3.41)

tasmāt — thus; tvam — you; indriyāṇyādau = indriyāṇi — senses + ādau — initially; niyamya — regulating; bharatarṣabha — powerful man of the Bharata family; pāpmānaṁ — degrading power; prajahi — squelch, destroy; hyenaṁ = hy (hi) — certainly + enam — this; jñānavijñānanāśanam = jñāna — knowledge + vijñāna — discernment + nāśanam — ruining

Thus regulating the senses initially, you should, O powerful man of the Bharata family, squelch this degrading power which ruins knowledge and discernment. (Bhagavad Gita 3.41)

इन्द्रियाणि पराण्याहुर्
इन्द्रियेभ्यः परं मनः ।
मनसस्तु परा बुद्धिर्
यो बुद्धेः परतस्तु सः ॥ ३.४२ ॥

indriyāṇi parāṇyāhur
indriyebhyaḥ paraṁ manaḥ
manasastu parā buddhir
yo buddheḥ paratastu saḥ (3.42)

indriyāṇi — the senses; parāṇyāhur = parāṇi — are energetic; āhur (āhuḥ) — the ancient psychologists say; indriyebhyaḥ — the senses; paraṁ — more energetic; manaḥ — the mind; manasas — in contrast to the mind; tu — but; parā — more sensitive; buddhir = buddhiḥ — the intelligence; yo = yaḥ — which; buddheḥ — in reference to the intelligence; paratas — most sensitive; tu — but; saḥ — he, the spirit

The ancient psychologists say that the senses are energetic, but in comparison to the senses, the mind is more energetic. In contrast to the mind, the intelligence is even more sensitive. But in reference, the spirit is most elevated. (Bhagavad Gita 3.42)

एवं बुद्धेः परं बुद्ध्वा
संस्तभ्यात्मानमात्मना ।
जहि शत्रुं महाबाहो
कामरूपं दुरासदम् ॥ ३.४३ ॥

evaṁ buddheḥ paraṁ buddhvā
saṁstabhyātmānamātmanā
jahi śatruṁ mahābāho

kāmarūpaṁ durāsadam (3.43)

evaṁ — thus; buddheḥ — than the intelligence; param — higher; buddhvā — having understood; saṁstabhyātmānamātmanā = saṁstabhya — keeping together + ātmānam — the personal energies+ ātmanā — by the spirit; jahi — uproot; śatruṁ — enemy; mahābāho — O powerful man; kāmarūpaṁ — form of passionate desire; durāsadam — difficult to grasp

Thus having understood what is higher than intelligence, keeping the personal energies under control of the spirit, uproot, O powerful man, the enemy, the form of passionate desire which is difficult to grasp. (Bhagavad Gita 3.43)

Mission-Incompletion Return-Energy

During meditation this morning, near the end of it, I found myself in some of the mission energy for this lifetime which I had not used and cannot use because of not having the opportunity to use it in the early part of life.

This energy was to be used between the years of 1969 and 1984 but I did not have the opportunities to use it. It remained sealed and untouched. It was a beautiful feeling to be in touch with this energy but I returned it to the source who was Buddha. This was an energy for me to colaborate with Tibetan yogis but I never got the opportunity to do so except on the astral planes.

As I was in this energy in meditation, it had a good feeling but I released it to Buddha who had invested it in my psyche long ago. This energy came out of his wisdom nature and is a bliss energy which has a color like that of purified camphor. It was a nice feeling being inside his wisdom body. It was like a child in the body of its mother.

This is part of getting a death release from the authorities whom I work for. A yogi must account for the energy they invested, as to how it was used or left aside. Some energy like the energy I was involved in during this meditation, is to be returned unused because of mismatches in the twists and turns of fate.

Never never day

Lahiri created loud laughter among some advanced yogis, when he kept saying:

Never never day! Never never day!

This was a coded message which meant:

There will never be the day when a yogi will be free from claims made by others.

Lahiri explained that the whole idea that a yogi will become freed from the claims lay upon his existence by others, is fallacious. It will never happen that a yogi will be declared free from obligations in the physical world. The nature of this place is to stake claims for animate and inanimate commodities and services. In conclusion, he said,

> *"Even a dead body is claimed by humans. Certainly, it is claimed by insects that enter it through the nose and mouth. They argue with each other about which part to claim.*

> *One bug tells the other,*

> *"This is mine. Scamper away."*

> *Another one says,*

> *"If you bite here, I will kill you. To save your life run away."*

Lahiri suggested this:

> *"Yogis should abandon the idea of protecting the whole body. Part of the body may be assigned to the coreSelf not all of it. Leave the property of others for others. Tend to the part which belongs to the core. Abandon the idea of full proprietorship."*

> *"I ask that you elevate your part of the psyche. It is not possible to own every part of it. Those parts which belong to others should be left to the claimants."*

Analytical Orb Draw-Back Practice

Lahiri showed a kriya which is a difficult practice to achieve unless one did hours upon hours of meditation under the proper guidance. This is the analytic orb *(buddhi)* draw-back procedure. It is part of the *pratyahar* practice but the advanced stage of it after one retracted the sensual energies and those energies lose their lust for participating in the physical world and lower astral planes.

At that stage the sensual energies are parked in the head of the subtle body like limousines which were retired to a junk yard and which have dead batteries and rusted parts. The only active thing remaining is the interest energy which comes out of the sense of identity and even that is disabled, just like the keys of the limousines which were left hanging on a key rack in the office of the junk yard but which were left there some 30 years ago. For sure those keys will still fit into the ignition switches but so what? Those cars will never start again.

In that condition, the yogi within the head of the subtle body, sits in the central place and looks ahead. He sees a faint glimmer of the intellect organ. He looks at it but it is like looking at a coconut which floats near a beach in the South Pacific off some isolate little rock jotting out of the sea.

The yogi looks at it. He wonders,

"Is that the thing that ran my life some years ago or some lives before?

"Is that the most powerful thing in existence, the famous intellect? "

This one little thing, the intellect psychic organ, this one little orb, is the cause of the self's contact with the physical and astral worlds. Remove it and the contact is over. All troubles will come to an end.

In the Buddhist system it is more a method of focusing on not contacting the various elements and substances but in the kriya yoga system it is not contacting the psychic organ(s) which make contact with the elements or substances.

Fire/Ice Kundalini

This was a cell release kundalini not spinal kundalini arousal. I did some mystic actions for Lahiri. This one has to do with bringing kundalini from the legs and feet. This is a reversal of the natural gravity system which supports downward flow of energies as opposed to upward travel.

A big event for yogis is *urdhvareta* stage which means sexual energy going upwards and not downward. That concerns up from the groin area where the sexual energy is urged through the genitals. The energy is brought into the body through the nose and mouth, then it is mixed, then it is sent downwards using the gravity of the earth to help ease its passage to and through the genitals. In the body of the quadrupeds, the energy travels horizontally at first and then it does downwards and out of the body but in the primate and human bodies it begins with a downward flow immediately which makes those hormone compounds much more powerful and makes the human body much more impulsive about sex indulgence.

Urdhva is Sanskrit for upward. *Reta* is Sanskrit for male sexual fluid. If there is no movement of sexual fluids upwards in the male body there will be little vigor except the energy of habit to procure sexual indulgence. When students go to a kundalini yoga teacher, they are lectured about retaining sexual fluids so as to increase vigor. *Tejas* is the Sanskrit word for vigor. It means no fucking, not even flirting, because then the reproductive energy is not retained. On the subtle side, the retention may cause a bright aura to shine from the subtle body of the yogi.

This aura causes increase in psychic perception, otherwise the psychic senses are reduced. The yogi cannot have insight consciousness which means that he will become a materialistic person.

To save students from this curse of having no insight consciousness (*jnanadipa, jnanachakshu*) gurus usually lay down a restriction so that if the student is not married, he is not to have sexual indulgence. If he is married, he may have it with limited permission.

I may say to a student,

"Stay away from sex. Get far away from it. Otherwise, do not waste your time doing kundalini yoga or even meditating. Sex ruins yoga."

But then the student may think,

"He told me not to have sex but I saw him with a woman. What is the conclusion here?"

But then the student should know that sometimes one whose ship sinks can render good advice to others about how to keep their canoes afloat. Do not feel that you are so great that you cannot take advice from someone who fails at the process he recommends. It is quite possible to give good advice even if one cannot follow the very counsel. It can happen. Always look to see if there is a good will coming from the advisor. Do not worry about if the advisor is able to follow the advice.

A man, who was a smoker all his life, did advise some young men not to use cigarettes. It was the very best advice.

Urdhvareta practice is touted in the yoga circles. It is commendable. If one can attain it one is rated as a yogi. Without that one cannot get a rating. It is the basic part of hatha yoga. Still, it is just the beginning of advanced yoga. It is a sensitive issue because of our social condition. Previously, having the sexual fluids flow upwards was basic stuff. In the conservative societies of ancient India, u*rdhvareta* was not something anybody could take credit for developing, because the bodies did that automatically because of the sociology of the culture and the genetic orientation of the bodies of the high caste Indians.

The practice I do is an *urdhva* upward turning practice but this has to do with the sexual fluids and everything else. For this particular kriya, there is no focus on sexual fluids. Instead, it targets the system in the psyche which supports the sexual fluids to cause those systems to change their supportive behaviors. In other words, instead of attacking the energy army right on, we sabotage their armaments and food supply. If they cannot eat; if they cannot get ammunition; the battle is won without firing a shot.

I worked on the ankles. The kundalini of the cells in that area fired through the legs and thighs and then bursts like mini metal springs firing upward at a rapid speed, feeling like fire, then like ice, then like fire, then like ice, then like the space between fire and ice. It shimmered in the trunk. None of it was in the head of the subtle body.

Lahiri thinks that if the bottom of the psyche is cleared of polluted subtle energy, then in the head, *chit akash* will be reached promptly.

Introspective Shut-down Meditation

Lahiri asked me to explain the introspective shut down procedure. Needless to say, this takes years of meditation to master, if not lives of attempts at meditation and then success at last in some life when one has the grace of providence.

This is the pratyahar 5ᵗʰ stage of yoga. Unfortunately, each stage of the eight processes (*ashtanga* yoga) listed by Patanjali Mahayogin are not like steps which one mounts one after the other. This means that one may rise a step, then descend that step, then ascend that step, then again dismount it, repeatedly, going up and down, up and down.

Pratyahar is not completed in one effort. One may do it, master it to a degree and then advance to *dharana*. Then again one may have to return to *pratyahar* master another phase of it and then move up to the related *dharana*. This advance and retreat may continue for years or even for lives of practice.

In the very last phases of the *pratyahar* sensual energy withdrawal process, a yogi feels like a man who is in a dark cave, which has an entrance way in the distance. No light comes into the cave from the outside but on occasion suddenly without warning a gap opens in the cave wall. The man sees something outside of the cave for a few seconds or for longer periods.

It used to be that when the man first found himself in the cave, he used to hanker to go outside into the daylight but over time he lost interest in the environment which was outside the cave. Then he used to stay in the cave for months at a time without going outside. He would have some memories arising about what he used to know outside the cave, but overtime even those mental images diminished and were forgotten.

It was then that he discovered that he had an interest energy which was really the single sense organ which divested into the five senses. Its development of, or spread into five senses, ceased entirely. He is left with that single sense which Sri Krishna listed as the mind itself as one sense.

ममैवांशो जीवलोके
जीवभूतः सनातनः ।
मनःषष्ठानीन्द्रियाणि
प्रकृतिस्थानि कर्षति ॥ १५.७ ॥

mamaivāṁśo jīvaloke
jīvabhūtaḥ sanātanaḥ
manaḥṣaṣṭhānīndriyāṇi
prakṛtisthāni karṣati (15.7)

mamaivāṁśaḥ = mama — my + eva — indeed + aṁśaḥ — partner; jīvaloke = jīva — individualized conditioned being + loke — in the world; jīvabhūtaḥ individual soul; sanātanaḥ — eternal; manaḥ —

mind; ṣaṣṭhānindriyāṇi = saṣṭhāni — sixth + indriyāṇi — sense, detection device; prakṛtisthāni — mundane; karṣati — draws

My partner is in this world of individualized conditioned beings. He is an eternal individual soul but he draws to himself the mundane senses of which the mind is the sixth detection device. (Bhagavad Gita 15.7)

One has to understand that the five senses are offshoots of the mind field, which is itself the central user interface, used by the individual person. De-energizing the five senses is the beginning of *pratyahar* practice, because the root of those senses still remains to be subdued.

When Krishna mentioned six detection devices *(saṣṭhānindriyāṇi)*, we should not think that there are six senses; otherwise, Krishna could not have segregated the *manah* mind as a special device among the six. It is not only special but it is the central controlling principle of the five sensual pursuits.

There are five fingers on each wrist but in a sense the wrist itself acts as a finger too. It is the wrist which operates the five fingers and which causes their coordination. From one angle there are five fingers only and the wrist seem to have no importance. From another angle there is one wrist which has all importance and the fingers are mere extensions. The mind and the senses are so related.

There was a problem however where the man in the cave realized that he would not get full control of this single sense. Sometimes it would obey his will and desire. Sometimes it ignored his mental commands. What to do to gain full control of it, he thought.

As he considered, his guru who was not in the cave but who could speak to him regardless said this:

At first you should relax. Observe how it behaves. Presently it is too wide to be controlled. If you arrest one part of it, the rest will escape your grip. It is spread spherically from your coreSelf and cannot be grasped as one beam.

Like hairs on the body which are sensors for the touch sensation, grasping all of them at once is not possible. To silence them one has to get to their root impulse. The root impulse of all the hairs is connected into one primary sensor root which is the place from which all the hair can be silenced.

It has two types of expression:

- *Operation of sensual activity outside of the cave*

- *Operation of sensual activity inside of the cave.*

Once the yogi closes its external access and reduces its interest in the external world to nil, memories will become the primary enemy. It is by memories that it creates thought-images or conjectures which cause it to become unruly. Shut down memory. Then it will be immobilized.

Part 7

Square Bottoms / Shrunk Breasts

By force of providence, I attended a musical performance for about one hour today. It was called the *Magical Music of the 60's*. These are some titles of those songs.

- Are you lonesome tonight?
- Let the good times roll
- King of the road
- Amazing Grace
- Green green grass of home

The real thing was that this was an elderly community in South Florida. There were about 250 people in attendance. Each was over sixty years of age. Most were females with and without hunched backs. Grey hair was the color of the day. Cosmetics were used even though it was powerless to do anything to improve appearance at that stage.

As I walked in, I remembered that Buddha was frightened by old age. It served as part of the trigger for his full renunciation from social participation. He even abandoned the advantage of his young adult body as a result.

In his time old bodies were here and there, while now in the developed countries, the elderly folks are cordoned in communities. Here I noticed women who were beautiful in youth, with their fancy being taken away by the ruthless deteriorating influence of time. Their once buxom bodies were now deformed.

It was reminiscent of a junk yard where old cars were left so that vegetation grew here and there, as they rusted away.

I had criticisms leveled because people say that I am always attracted to beautiful women and only look at the same, but it is interesting how the same accusers never notice when I am attracted to less than beautiful or to elderly types.

Near the music hall, there was a swimming pool, where some men congregated with their flappy physiques, hanging bellies and fully or partially bald heads. Stripped of the pride of appearance, their heads drooped as they walked the corridors. Some females were there too with their now square bottoms misfitted into the swimming gear; their breasts all but shrunk to just about nothing except for some whose obesity stood its ground.

For a yogi old age is nothing but a reminder that one cannot forever be a physical body. The current address of the astral body which is the physical form, will be taken away by the death of the physical system. A yogi focuses on relocating. This causes that there is little or no despondency when faced with the inevitable health deterioration of the physical form.

By doing breath infusion intensively, a yogi keeps the subtle body from taking the pattern of old age and energy exhaustion of the physical system.

On the stage, they went from song to song. There was a backdrop of Texan small-town imagery. Most songs were about a love gone awry or some other theme of loneliness and other features which one faces in the elderly years.

The singing ladies had their diamond studded cowboy belts and so did many of the supporting males.

The main themes were about sex, love or lost love, and that the social life on earth is the central issue. There was no mention of an afterlife. There were suggestions that one should try to remember the good old days the days of youth when romance flourished.

The audience of grey hairs was thrilled. Most were of Christian orientation with no idea that a new physical body will be necessary as soon as the present old worn-out physical system is confiscated by nature.

Pregnant Woman Influences Embryo

Email Inquiry:

"When a mother is pregnant, the kind of soul she can accept depends on her mental attitude. And then there is another beauty that within the realm of your belly, which is your pregnancy, you can totally transform the soul. The soul is pure and has nothing to do, but the subtle body carries the karma of the previous life. A mother can totally purify the subtle body of the new child."

Could you comment on this statement of Yogi Bhajan?

MiBeloved's Response:

Yogi Bhajan is one of our teachers. There is a rule which is that one should not criticize a guru whom one takes assistance from. At the same time, there is another rule which is that one should answer questions which concern spiritual life if the questioner has a genuine interest.

The mother-to-be is circumspect by an attitude but the construction of that attitude was not explained by Yogi Bhajan.

It is not that the mother invents the attitude. A woman or any human being for that matter who would be a male or female parent, is under influences. Some influences are obvious. Some are abstract so that we cannot determine what those influences are or who they originated from.

Thus, it is, that when a mother is pregnant, the kind of soul she can accept depends on her mental attitude, which is a composite of influences combined with her desires. But this also means that the influence of the soul she would accept may be part of her mental attitude and part of her emotional make-up. To determine what these influences are one would require psychic insight.

Yogi Bhajan's second sentence reads:

And then there is another beauty that within the realm of your belly, which is your pregnancy, you can totally transform the soul.

This statement applies only superficially because the fact is that the tendencies which the soul travels with from many lives, cannot be washed out by a new parent. It is not that simple. Superficially we see that people are credited or discredited as parents for being responsible for the outcome of their kids but the point remains that the child is not anyone's child in the true sense. It is an adult who was honed by nature and induced into taking another body as a dependent of physical adults.

Many children resent being under the authority of parents and society. They sense intuitively that they are adults and should have the rights of adults, to do as they please. Instead, they have to toe the line of parents and society which awards adult privileges only at a certain age of the body.

I know of more than one case, of parents who raised their children as vegetarians and then the children after leaving home became carnivorous. I have also observed the opposite of persons who were raised carnivores and who later converted to vegetarian diet. Thus, the parental influence may not be permanent. It certainly can disappear in another life.

The average woman had neither the insight nor the psychological power to alter the nature of any soul who transmigrates with idiosyncrasies and tendencies intact. Neither does the average man.

However, Yogi Bhajan's statement could be seen as a form of encouragement to the pregnant or potentially pregnant women whom he advised, that they should bear children and should think that they can make an impact in the said children's life.

His last statement is:

The soul is pure and has nothing to do, but the subtle body carries the karma of the previous life. A mother can totally purify the subtle body of the new child.

I feel that the last sentence should read like this:
It is likely that the mother, if she has the insight and supernatural power, may purify the subtle body of the new child.

However, when someone says that the soul is pure, we need to get clarification as to pure what. For instance, glass is pure silica. Tile is pure clay. Yogiji did not clarify pure whatever. In addition, in the statement he did not explain how this pure whatever got involved with the subtle body in the first place.

Suppose we have pure silica which is in the form of a cup. Then we leave it by the blast heat of a furnace. It will melt. Then what is its position? Obviously, it was affected by heat. Yes, it is pure silica but that purity does not protect it from being affected. The fact that the soul took a subtle body which formulates, retains and is conditioned by physical and psychic activity, tells us that the purity of the soul is not an absolute or isolated factor. It is subjected to environmental conditions which may affect the form of its pure stuffs.

Why should the mother have to purify the subtle body of the pure soul? In the first place this accommodates the untruth that this pure soul is a child. The pure soul is not a child. It is a soul who has the potential to be limited by a child or an adult body in any species of life, not just the human one. It is adaptable.

If we dissect his statement, the logic of it will fall apart because in one life the same soul who is the mother of someone may become the daughter of that same person in yet another life. In other words, all souls are adults or are potential adults. We take interchanging roles in varying lives, such that in one life I am someone's son and in the next life I am his father or I am not related to him genetically.

Supposed I grew up under the guardianship of my grandmother. She functioned as a mother. Then she passed on. Then some years after, I got a sexual opportunity. My partner got pregnant. Suppose the soul in that pregnancy is the said grandmother. She emerges and is termed as my daughter. She is a pure soul and so am I. Why did she not make her subtle body pure? Does having an adult body as a parent increase the power of the pure soul so that it can purify its embryo only during pregnancy? Does this pure soul only have that increased power to purify the subtle body when it uses a pregnant female form?

Consider also that initially the pure soul got a pure subtle body or one that did not have tendencies but only potential for tendencies. Why did that subtle body which was under the pure influence of the soul not remain as a pure psychic energy?

This is why I stated initially that Yogi Bhajan's statement is superficial. But we may appreciate that he encouraged women to see the positive side of pregnancies and childrearing. A mother can have a spiritualizing influence on her embryo.

For my view regarding pregnancies please read my book, *sex you!*

Third Eye Meditation with no Vision Force

This was transmitted to me astrally today, March 26th, 2014 by Paramhansa Yogananda, a guru whom I have not seen in years.

During a meditation where I used sun energy to facilitate opening the third eye, he suddenly appeared overhead behind to my left. He said this:

> *"My method requires that there not be a vision energy projected when focusing on the third eye. To know that this is done correctly the student should feel a gap between the central self-energy and the third eye, as if there is a chasm between the two but as if they are still connected.*

> *"If the vision energy is applied, there will be no chasm; it will be a continuous stream of energy. There is a risk that if the vision energy is applied, it will trigger vritti unwanted activities."*

I then asked if he mentioned this in his books. His reply was:

> *"No, it was not mentioned. Even though I did this at the time, I did not verbalize it and did not realize that it should be described. It is an omission."*

Alteration of Sexual Genetics of Subtle Body

This will show what one has to achieve for this process to be complete. This has to do with motions in the subtle body and should not be confused with physical achievements. It is necessary to work on the physical body but the accomplishments on that end may not transfer into the subtle. It is also a fact that what is achieved in the subtle body may not have a full effect on the physical form.

This first diagram shows the sex hormone passage and its termination is where the arrow head is, which is in the genitals of the subtle form.

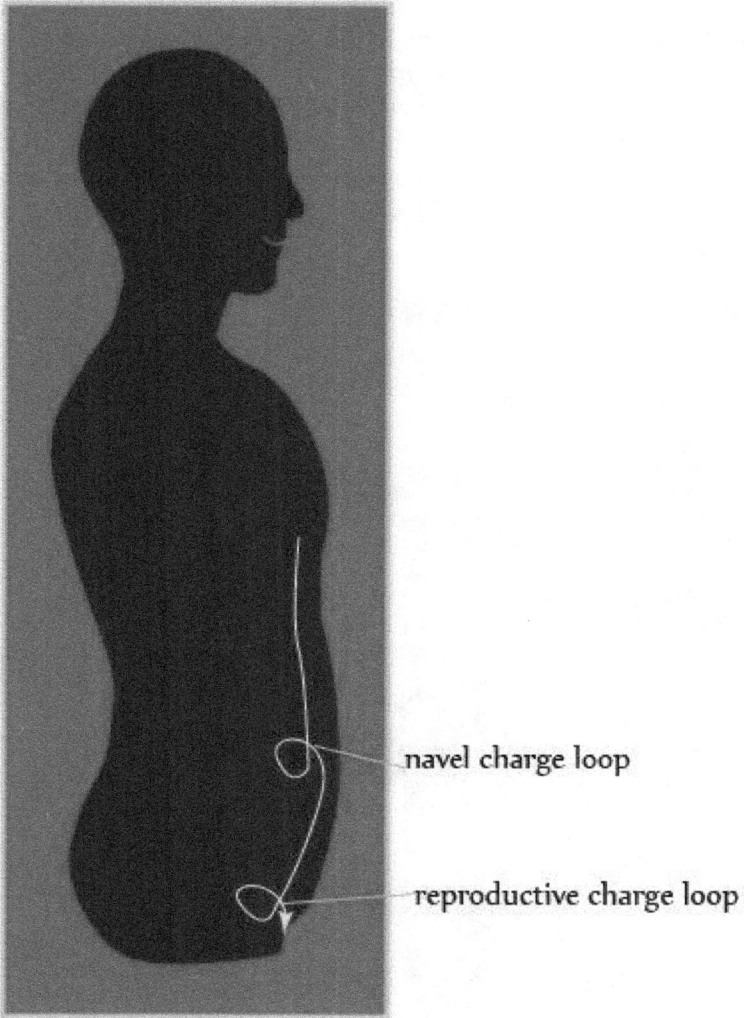

navel charge loop

reproductive charge loop

The diagram below shows the navel and reproductive charge loops but with the energy no longer terminating at the genitals. Instead, the energy terminates at the base chakra, *muladhara*. Causing the energy not to terminate at the genitals is achieved by breath infusion. Some yogis like *Gautama* Buddha achieved this without breath infusion, it seems, but for most yogis it will be achieved only by breath infusion. This is because of the massive willpower control which is required if breath infusion is not utilized.

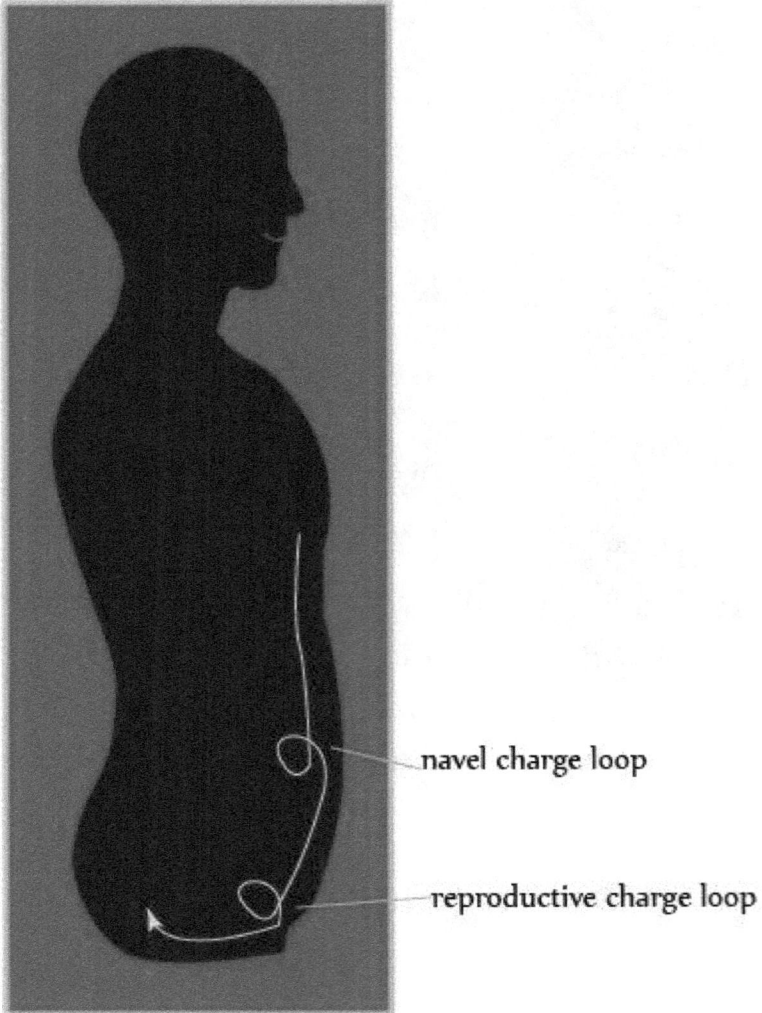

navel charge loop

reproductive charge loop

The diagram below shows that the loops were eliminated even though the energy maintained the same routing. This removal of the loop is vital for the ascetic because it means that the energy no longer has a sex charge or a passionate urge. It will still have an urge but the strength of it is reduced. The energy comes down the abdomen, passes through the groin area and goes to the base chakra but does not acquire a sex polarity charge.

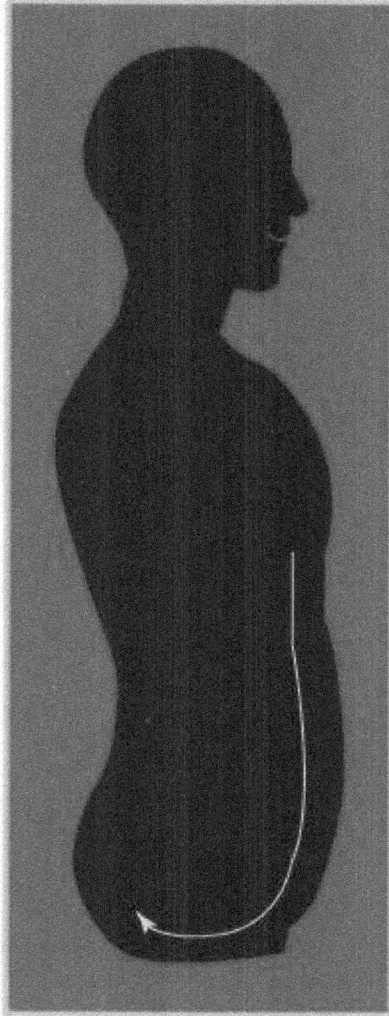

The diagram below shows that the energy reversed direction of flow and is no longer going to either to the genitals or the base chakra. Instead, it goes upward to the chest near the throat.

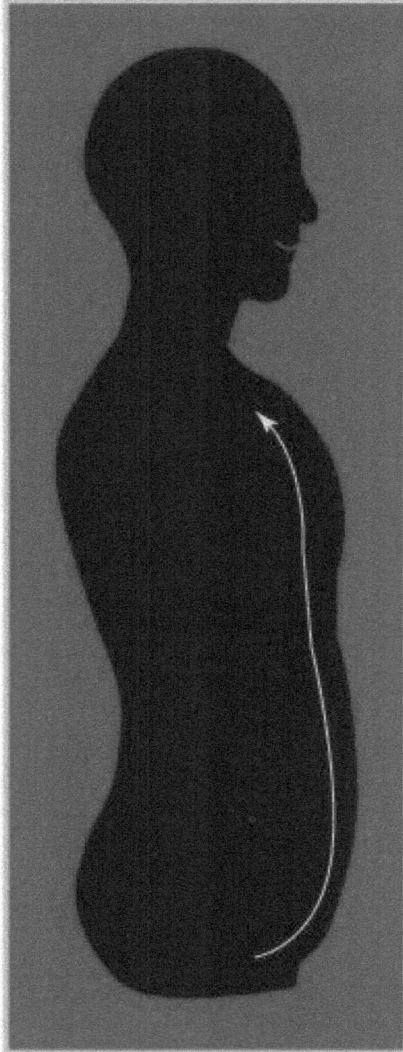

In the diagram below the reversed energy is lifted, so that it does not begin at the genitals but rather begins at the navel. This ocurs by the lift action of breath infusion, or by sheer willpower for those ascetics who can exert that much mental command.

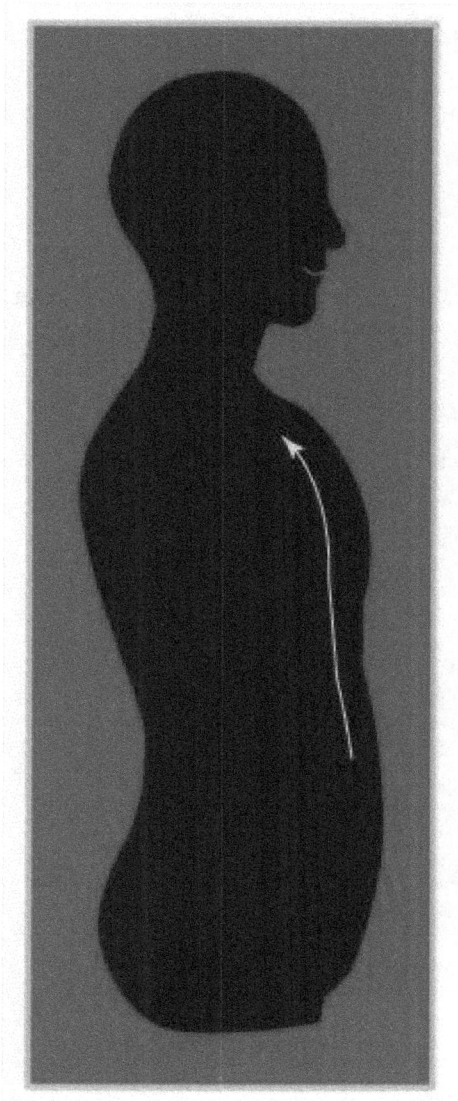

This last diagram shows that the energy reaches into the throat and penetrates even higher into the lower back of the brain. It loops through the throat-kissing orb in the throat where it receives an affectionate charge.

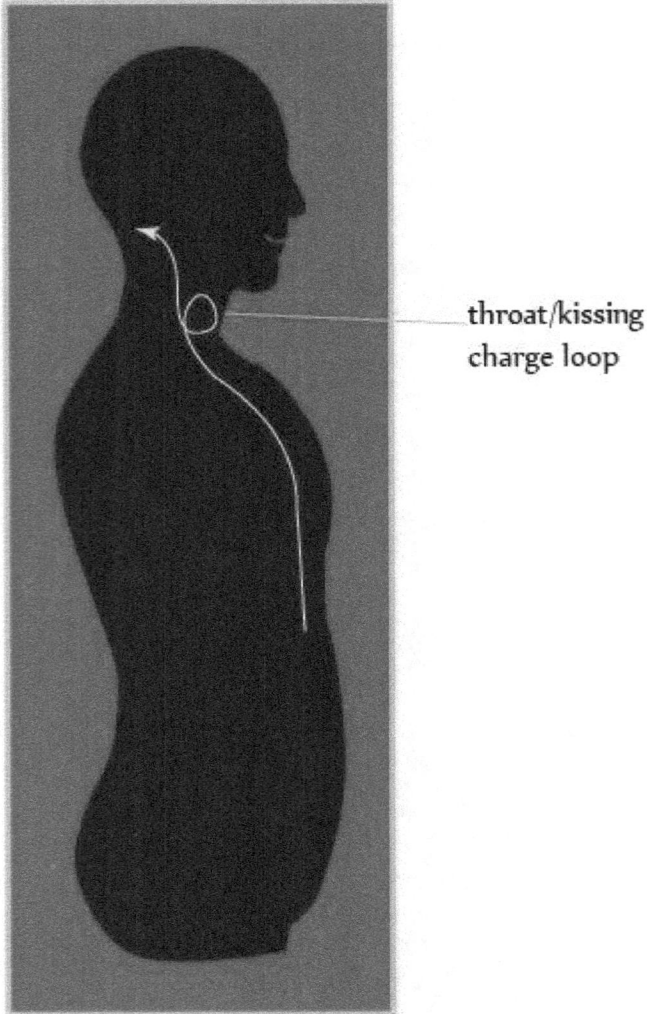

throat/kissing
charge loop

Opinion Mistakes of a Yogi

Inquiry

If a Yogi speaks what she/he believes to be the truth, but it turns out to be incorrect, what does yogic philosophy recommend?

Mi~Beloved's Response:

One of the eight processes for completion in yoga, as defined by Patanjali Mahayogin is *yama* moral restraints. These he listed:

अहिंसासत्यास्तेयब्रह्मचर्यापरिग्रहा यमाः ॥ ३० ॥

ahiṁsā satya asteya

brahmacarya aparigrahāḥ yamāḥ

ahiṁsā – non-violence; satya – realism; asteya – non-stealing; brahmacarya – sexual non-expressiveness which results in the perception of spirituality; aparigrahāḥ – non-possessiveness; yamāḥ – moral restraints.

Non-violence, realism, non-stealing, sexual non-expressiveness which results in the perception of spirituality (brahman) and non-possessiveness are the moral restraints.(Yoga Sutras 2.30)

I translated *satya* as realism but most translators gave it as truthfulness. This is a requirement for yogis. In so far as *satya* is adapted from *sat* state of existence, it means the continuous spiritual under-basis of everything. When applied to the individual limited self in this world, that is reduced to being realistic in viewing situations. It means to understand the potential of this creation and to have insight into what happened, what happens and what will occur within the potential energy and its probable behavior.

Ideally a yogi should be removed from many social concerns because *Bhagavad Gita* has listed *ekaki*, or isolated practice, as a requirement. If the yogi mixes and socializes, his profile changes where he must comply with the karma yoga requirements which Arjuna had to learn from Krishna and apply in social dealings.

If in such dealings a yogi makes mistakes, like for instance saying something that is not true or that proves to be incorrect, then he/she should learn from that not to be involved socially because of the inherent risks of misleading people. This is a bitter medicine for a yogi and should cause him/her to be more cautious in taking a leadership role or an authoritative position.

If I was inspired by God, or even by a great guru, to speak to humanity, how is it possible that I said something misleading or untrue? Either I was not inspired by the deity but I mistook another influence as being divine or I was inspired but I was simultaneously open to some other non-divine influence and did not realize it.

I face the consequences regardless. However, in that there is nothing but learning more about myself, about my inability to sift through subtle influences, about my lack of calibration of my insight capacity.

This should cause me to be more careful in giving advisories in the future and should cause me to go deeper into meditation so that I could root out the inaccuracies.

In relation to *satya* realism, Patanjali gave this instruction:

सत्यप्रतिष्ठायां क्रियाफलाश्रयत्वम्॥ ३६ ॥

satyapratiṣṭhāyāṁ kriyāphalāśrayatvam

satya – realism; pratiṣṭhāyāṁ – on being established; kriyā – actions; phalāḥ – results; āśryatvam – what serves as a support for something else.

On being established in realism, his actions serve as a basis for results. (Yoga Sutras 2.36)

But in respect to being socially involved which causes the demands for opinions and conclusions, he says this harsh instruction.

शौचात्स्वाङ्गजुगुप्सा परैरसंसर्गः ॥ ४० ॥

śaucāt svāṅgajugupsā paraiḥ asaṁsargaḥ

śaucāt – from purification; svāṅga = sva – oneself + aṅga – limbs; jugupsā – aversion, disgust; parair = pariaḥ – with others; asaṁsargaḥ – non-association, lack of desire to associate.

From purification comes a disgust for one's own body and a lack of desire to associate with others. (Yoga Sutras 2.40)

The correction for a yogi who says something misleading, and who said it in good faith, or while in an arrogant mood, is to first apologize to those who were subjected to whatever was said. But more important is the second adjustment which is to delve into his/her meditation and find the root cause of getting that misleading information. This would require deep and sincere introspection.

Mobility Pratyahar

After kundalini was lifted out of the spine, and after the cells of the system yielded their kundalini energy as they are, without feeling they have to contribute to the sex hormone areas, something happens where during breath infusion there is a charge here or there in the subtle body, even in the feet or hands, where the energy does not focalize itself in the spinal column as in traditional kundalini practice.

After the subtle body is full of kundalini potential in every part of it, after the individual cells are freed from the slavery of contributing their vital energy to the grand kundalini in the spine, there is a development which forces the yogi to return to the fifth stage of *ashtanga* yoga which is *pratyahar* sensual energy withdrawal.

Initially this withdrawal concerns pulling energy into the head of the subtle body so as to retrieve badly-needed emotional energy which usually leaks through the senses into the physical world in the exploitive pursuits of creature existence. However as one advances in meditation practice, one will find that repeatedly one must do more *pratyahar* in different variations. In other words, the preliminary stages of yoga remain in force through the higher stages because there are parts of the lower levels which one cannot complete initially.

This should not be a cause for disappointment but rather should be a reason to celebrate increase psychic insight.

There is an interest in mobility for instance. From the time one took life as a unicellular organism like say an amoeba, one was involved in the lack of mobility because a unicellular body does not have the means to do much locomotion. It is highly dependent on currents in rivers and streams. If it finds itself existing in a puddle somewhere or in a placid lake, its mobility potential is nil.

This causes the desire for limbs. This causes one to evolve to more complex life forms which give the mobile facility.

It depends on how one is routed through the evolutionary cycle, and to whether one moves to vegetation species or moves into elementary animal species. If one moves into vegetation species the mobility, or walking/running facilities, take much longer to develop. In fact, initially one's only hope for it is to beget more vegetative bodies, have the insects, wind or rain relocate the seeds and then become mobile through taking bodies through those relocated vegetation-descendants.

The lower animal species have faster access to mobility because of the development of limbs which are used to cart one's body through the environment in the search for food, shelter and relationship.

Mobility is against *pratyahar* sensual energy withdrawal. It is required in the advanced stages that a yogi pulls in or retracts the mobility interest. This is not a direct outward going sense as say the vision sense or the hearing sense. It operates in a covert way. That is why initially the yogi cannot subdue it.

In the advanced states the mobility sense is retracted from the feet of the body. In the case of say a quadruped animal, it would have to be retracted from four instead of from two limbs.

From inside the psyche, the yogi pulls the mobility energy from in the thighs, legs and feet from within upwards into the head. When this is done completely, the yogi loses desire to travel. But this does not mean that he/she will be immobile. It is just that his/her interest in mobility slackens considerably even though the body may still have to move here or there.

This same type of situation applies to other aspects as for instance, sex indulgence.

People who are critical of yogis and who are suspicious that yogis are not genuine and are fakes or failures, hawk on sex indulgence of yogis but there are other areas of restraint such as the mobility tendency which are just as important or even more important than sexual behavior.

If a yogi says that he will squash the mobility tendency, should we redicule him if we ever find him walking? Should we, tell him that he promised never to move again?

Buddha for instance sat down once and did not get up for months. Later he moved about. Should we criticize that? Is that breach less serious than a sexual participation?

The answer would depend on if we rated the action in terms of its social value as compared to its introspective worth. For introspection it is the yogi and the yogi alone which we rate not the yogi in reference to human social relationships.

Sand-Scatter Bliss energy

This morning during breath infusion, there were several spreads of bliss energy in the trunk and limbs of the subtle body, with hardly any in the head. Recently someone complained about not having spine-into-brain kundalini rises during practice but having some energy bursts in the trunk of the subtle body instead.

Bliss energy burst in the trunk of the subtle body and in the limbs as compared to bliss energy burst through the spine and into the head, is to be appreciated by a yogi. One should not become addicted to bliss energy burst in the head no more than we should stick with just sexual energy pleasure as the ultimate enjoyment.

If we do not free ourselves from the sex energy pleasure, we will not be eligible to experience anything higher. Similarly, if we do not free ourselves from the bliss burst in the head, we will stagnate there and will never go higher.

Today during practice, the burst felt like scattered sand which was thrown into the distance and then it felt like a buttery spread of glistening bliss pixels. This happened in the trunk of the subtle body mostly up in the higher part of the chest and near the spinal column but not in the spine itself. It emitted a sound like leaves rustling during the fall season or in the tropics during the dry season.

Naad Sound Resonance Embrace

Today during the meditation session, I encountered naad sound which, recently, was missing in the meditations. It seems that sometimes naad makes itself to be absent from the ascetic even in some meditation which are very productive but which occur mostly at the front part of the subtle head or from the center towards the front.

When I connected with naad it gave a feeling of great relief. It felt like when a girl is first embrace by her beloved but not in a tight embrace like experienced lovers but rather in a lose hold where her beloved holds her hand and holds her waist and then swings her gentle this way and that way to the sound of a waltz.

Naad moved me one way and then the other way like the even swing of a pendulum. I thought that this is the way a girl feels when she is gently caressed by her boyfriend.

Cuddling the Breath Infused Energy

Today during breath infusion there was a rise of infused energy which bundled somewhere in the trunk of the subtle body but which was hard to pinpoint. In any case, when such bundles of bliss energy occur just after a session of breaths, a yogi may cuddle the energy in tight locks in the period when there is no breathing. Then when the breathing commences again, the yogi should pull up the energy so as to move it as it is being impelled inwards on itself. This causes the energy to enter a state of compression where the bliss aspect of it becomes micro-sized or micro-micro sized if it is already micro-sized.

At one stage there was a burst of bliss energy in the back central part of the trunk of the subtle body. None of this was in the spine but was outside the spine scattering on both sides of it outwards.

It felt like tiny flakes of bee's wax falling from the sky and disappearing leaving a shimmering bliss aspect like snowflakes glittering in bright sunshine.

Apana Carbon Dioxide Removal

Lahiri said that it was essential to have the *apana* carbon dioxide gasses removed from the astral and physical systems. The *pranayama* practice is designed to do that but initially student cannot understand the importance of *pranayama* and wants to meditate either without doing it or by doing it in a haphazard or sensation-producing way.

One has to begin where one is but one should advance steadily into the higher yoga as one moves away from corrupt motivations. A pleasure hungry attitude may be there when one first begins yoga. A sense of insecurity may be present. However, one does not have to remain with that mood but should progress from it and become secure in the practice, leaving aside the lower traits.

Pushing down the fingers when doing bhastrika and focusing within on pulling out the *apana* carbon dioxide is a practice all by itself which should be focused on from time to time, to be sure that the lung cells absorb the oxygen. Otherwise, if one does the practice carelessly without being attentive to what happens in the psyche, without mentally directing the cells in the lungs to yield polluted gases, one will make little progress.

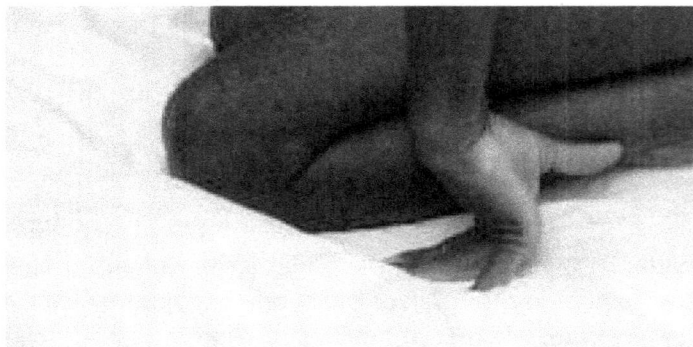

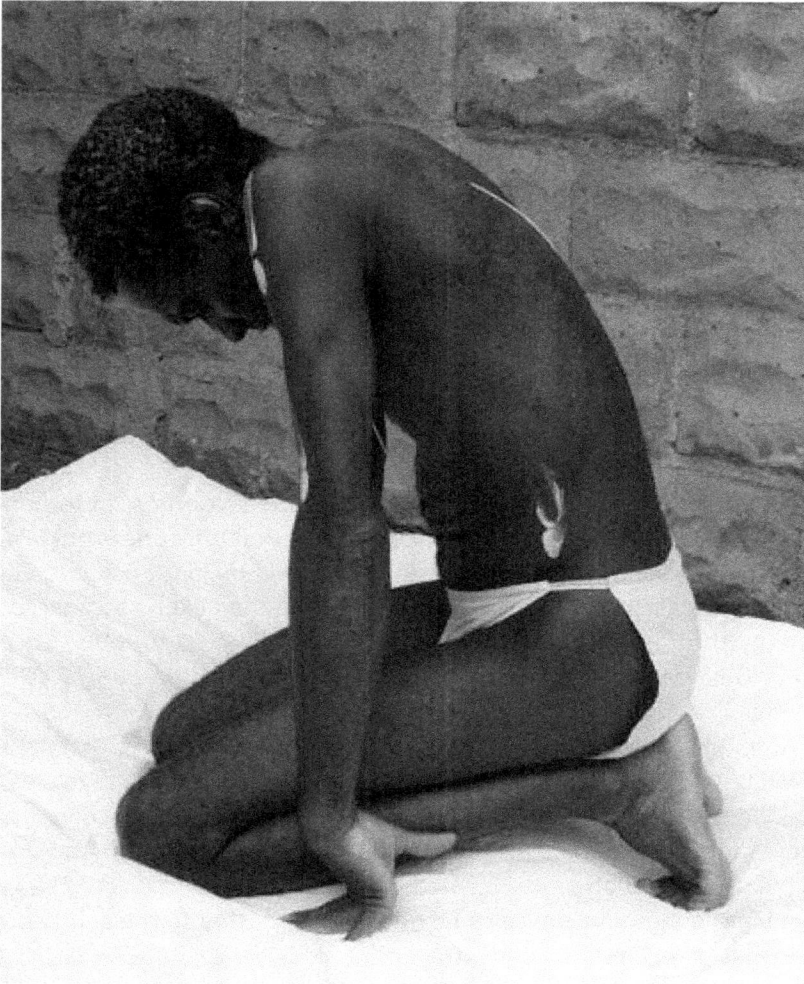

Sex Energy Contrasted

Let us be realistic and understand that kundalini will hoard an energy charge and let it accumulate but only for reproductive reasons which we usually interpret as sexual energy to be discharged. But if a person does the kundalini yoga practice, this hoarded energy can be released up through the spine into the head or through the trunk of the body in some other way and into the head instead of being used as kundalini intended for reproductive expansion of physical forms.

Kundalini's intention in hoarding the energy is for reproduction but we get caught in the crossfire and from our perspective it seems to be hoarded for sexual pleasure.

For the purpose of kundalini energy, in the advanced stage, it becomes necessary to retrain kundalini so that it continuously discharges this energy and does not hoard it, otherwise there will never be a time when we would be free from the addiction of sexual energy discharge.

Since we are stuck with our misinterpretation of reproductive surcharge of energy as sexual pleasure possibility, the only way out is to change kundalini's intention so that it no longer keeps hoarding and it continuously discharges any such energy which comes to it. In the long term that is what happens. This is why there is the term in Sanskrit as *urdhvareta*, meaning upward *(urdhva)* sexual fluids *(reta)*. There is the practice for males of *vajroli* and the one for females as *amaroli*.

If one does kundalini yoga and then for one reason or the other, one ceases doing it say for about a month and during that time one is not involved in sexual expression, then naturally kundalini will build a hormone charge. Then if one begins the practice, there will, more than likely, be a large gush of energy through the spine because of the buildup of so much hormone energy. This would be a pleasurable experience. Pleasure-hungry students enjoy this.

After all, if one is sex-pleasure-starved, and something like that happens, one will be in glee about it. However, in the more advanced stages, we rate this as being undesirable. We strive to have a continuous discharge of the energy through the kundalini, not hoarding it but delivering it in the smallest possible doses as soon as it is formed in the system.

A big secret about the spiritual body as contrasted to the subtle psychic one, is that in the spiritual body, the entire form is a genital. The entire body has a sensitivity which is similar to genital sensitivity. Hence one way to translate to the spiritual body is to cause the subtle one to have a similar construction, where every part is saturated with bliss potential. This can be done by continuous expression of the charged force which kundalini uses for sexual energy discharge.

Naad Divorce

Naad sound resonance can rupture from a yogi, even from an advanced one. We heard of advanced yogis who people assumed remained advanced no matter what. However, assumptions are not necessarily the reality. Being advanced really means that if one departs from it or is forced to depart from it, for one reason or another, one can get back to an advanced state rapidly.

The difference between the advanced yogi and others, is that he will be elevated rapidly, almost instantaneously as soon as he applies himself to get out. Others do not have such rapidity in their favor.

Recently, I would say for about the past four months, I was plagued with some rupture in terms of reaching naad sound resonance. It is there but my confidence and intimacy with it, was breached. This happens because of various types of non-naad associations by being with people who are not intrinsically interested in naad and whose energy has somehow or the other, made contact with my psyche.

During this regression with naad sound resonance, I continued doing some advanced kriyas, even to the extent of making advancement in those methods and reporting on the progress to astral *yogaGurus*. But at the same time, naad ran away, just like when a woman loses her man who is wealthy and reliable and she no longer has access to an easy life and must eke out an existence insecurely on the bottom of the social ladder.

In such a situation that woman regrets that she no longer is with her reliable ward. She longs to be in his presence again. If by chance somehow, she meets that reliable man, she may again apply to be under his care but he may be cold shouldered to her for reasons of his own. He may regard her with disdain, thinking, "This person cannot be trusted. I will not again put myself in a way to be exploited by her."

In that way a yogi is sometimes neglected by naad sound. He/She feels abandoned like a divorce woman who finds herself in a miserable lifestyle after living a comfortable life with a wealthy gracious man. What to do? How to adjust that and get back under the shelter of the auspicious naad sound resonance?

The yogi should pester naad by resuming meditation on naad, by entering naad and staying with it, even if its attitude is one of indifference, just as the abandoned woman may go to her husband's house and begin serving there again in a menial way but bearing with his indifference. Sooner or later even the most hard-hearted man will slacken indifference and resume a favorable relationship with such an endearing and faithful woman.

Naad will again take the yogi and shelter him as if he were naad's baby, nourishing the yogi, making sure that he/she grows nicely and becomes a worthy spiritually-enriched ascetic.

Naad Re-Friendship

One can if one was divorced from naad become reunified through a new sincere effort to be with naad. This can happen even if one was repeatedly separated from naad and repeatedly did things which are contrary to spiritual practice. Naad, it seems has unlimited potential for accommodating the ascetic. It would never totally bar the ascetic from its association.

It is the ascetic's mood that causes the rupture in the relationship with naad. Hence the adjustment of a change in that attitude, results in reinstatement of contact with naad, even though the reconnection may not be as pleasing as desired.

When the ascetic runs from naad and becomes linked to other mental energies, he becomes degraded but that does not last forever. Sooner or later the lowering influence will be lifted. Then the ascetic will suddenly remember naad and consider the breach. He will then make efforts to resume the connection.

At that time naad may or may not be willing to accommodate him but still the ascetic should be confidence that if he resumes the correct meditation linkage with naad he can regain the confidential relationship with it and be elevated to *chit akash* consciousness.

Yogananda's *Chit-Akash* Method

I did and evaluated the process described and recommended by Paramhansa Yogananda who became famous for all time for his book *Autobiography of a Yogi*. The book itself is a fantasy which struck many people whom when they tried to do what was recommended in it, did not get the intended results.

Most people who read that book did not join his society which is the *Self Realization Fellowship* (SRF). Some packed bags and went to India to find the legendary Babaji in the Himalayas but to no avail since they did not have the psychic perception to meet this great yogi, whom they felt was there physically.

Some persons who joined SRF said they reached the culmination but some others went away disappointed after paying for the lessons and trying for years to get into the *nirvikalpa samadhi* as it was described by Yogananda.

It is a fact that the missing factor between the modern kriya yogis and the ancient ones is the proficiency in *pranayama* practice, particularly the *anuloma-viloma nadi* purificatory process, which was done for hours daily by many of the ancient yogis who are now legends in the physical and astral worlds.

What Paramhansa recommended to me today is reduced to this:

- Sit to meditate in an easy sitting posture, preferably sukhasana, easy pose.
- Calm the mind
- Quiet the breathing. Ignore it so that it operates without attention.

- Pull all attention back to the center of the head, especially any attention going to the face part of the subtle head.
- Hunker in the head, like a soldier who hides in a dugout or trench and who is scared to look up because of enemy fire which would kill if he raised his head.
- After hunkering in the center for a little time, and not looking out for any reason, focusing into the center, one will find that the energy in the front part of the head shuts down, as if there was a black out at midnight in a large city and there were no lights anywhere.
- After this is experienced, one should hunker even more.
- One will feel as if there is a pad of energy near the center but just about ¼ inch away from the center, going towards the front. Beyond that there will be a blank space of about ¾ inch in diameter. Then there will be a large space which is dimly lit.

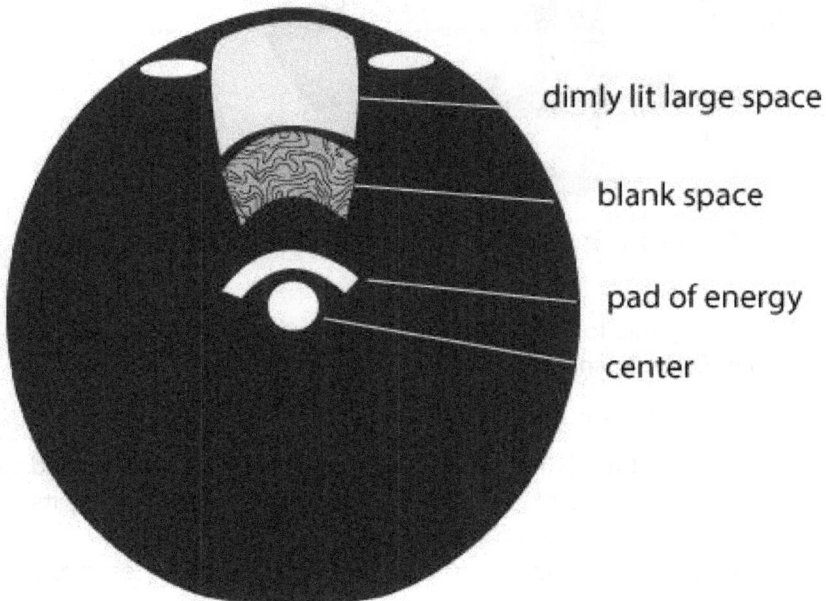

dimly lit large space

blank space

pad of energy

center

- One should be concerned about this dimly lit large space, to place one's attention there but not to have any of the attention go to the ¼ inch space. One's attention should skip over the ¼ inch space and anchor itself in the ¾ inch space. One should continuously let a stream of one's attention go into that ¾ inch space.

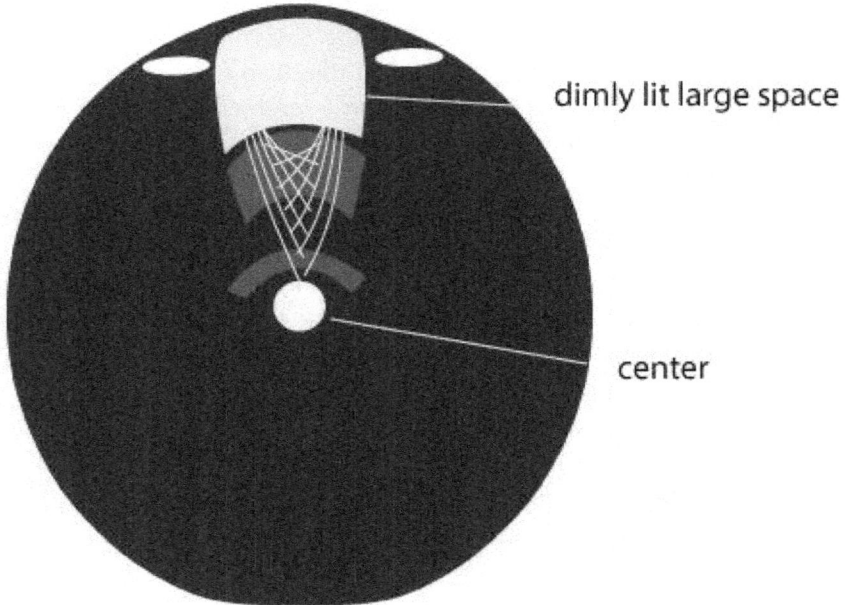

dimly lit large space

center

attention to dimly lit large space

After doing this for some time, one will experience entry into the *chit akash* sky of consciousness.

Naad the Nurturing Mother

This morning during meditation, I was brought closer in with naad sound resonance. There I was a helpless infant in a crib who was lifted by its Mom, cuddled, and placed to feed on the breast.

As a starving baby, I was relieved by this, after becoming estranged from naad for some months now due to various diverse and rather yogically-opposed influences.

The negative influence lasted for some months. It diminishes gradually but imagine what it would be like if it lasted for some lives, or even one whole life time.

Can you see me as a scrawny infant, pissing and shitting in a crib with no Mom to care me, no breast to suckle, living on for a life without dying, without milk, never feeling the tender hands of a mother. What would be my destiny?

Desire

Every desire of every creature, every potential for desire in the creation emerged from the causal plane of existence, which is a level above the astral world.

The physical level of existence is one plane in which there are many realities. Then there is the astral world which has multi-levels. The astral situation is higher than the physical but it has a subterranean level which is denser than the physical even though it is not physical.

Above the astral plane and this is above in terms of vibration, not in terms of north or south nor in terms of the earth's gravitational field, there is the causal level which is one of dense compact supernatural energy.

If it were to be described in terms of sight, that would be difficult because its energy is abstract even to our subtle bodies. Great yogins enter the causal level. To do so they must leave their subtle forms behind.

It is visible but since it is an abstraction to physical perception and even to astral vision, it is better left undescribed with the understanding that it is not lacking in description but we are lacking in the required sense perception.

There was a desire. It was someone else's desire but I was affected. That is not strange. That is normal, that someone's desire affects and commandeers someone else. I can become the pawn of someone's desire.

The desires of others affect me. A human being, an animal, anything, some vegetation even, can become the pawn of someone's desire. Once I was in a city where there were large palm trees. Their lower leaves which were dry and which had the slightest faded colors were trimmed away. They stood like soldiers, clean shaven and crew-cutted to an absolute degree. But then at night they had to endure large floodlights. They never got a chance to be in darkness. Their dried leaves which usually hung to protect their trunks from harsh sunshine were cut away.

Whose desire is that, the trees or the owners of the city?

Talk about freedom to do as desired!

Palm trees - subjects of human desire-

I traced a desire of someone else, a desire which surely affected me, which commandeered me. I traced it to the causal plane. Once there I found it as a single grain of energy like a grain of sand on an infinite beach.

One grain of causal energy was sufficient to produce a desire that may last for a million births, on and on and on, with potency to command the life of others.

Endless desire?

That is what it would be!

That is how this existence is configured.

Tools of desire? Is that what we are?

How does anyone get a desire energy from the causal plane?

Can anyone go there, select a desire, imbibe it into the psyche and use it?

Does the desire latch on to someone like a parasite clinging to a creature?

Naad Sound Resonance ~ Nothing Up-Front

The highlight of meditation this morning was that I am back on track with naad sound resonance.

How long will this last?

That depends on fate. Even if I am determined, still fate may interrupt. In the meantime, however, I will apply myself.

An ascetic has to understand and must accept that fate is finicky. It will support the spiritual practice part of the time only. Thus, when it makes it near impossible to progress, one should not be disturbed but should endeavor and do the needful on the social plane even if such actions contravene yoga.

When the tide moves upstream, one should take advantage of it but when the tide pulls away and one's canoe is beached on a sand bar, one should not be annoyed but should wait patiently until the tide pushes upstream again.

This morning during naad meditation, I was submerged in the naad sound resonance. When I checked up-front in the subtle head, I found that the frontal area, the thought-images zone, was completely absent, as if it did not exist.

- No thoughts
- No images
- Nothing
- Not a whiff of any impression

Like when someone has long moved from a house

This is the advantage of doing a thorough *pranayama* practice before doing meditation, that one achieves the *pratyahar* sensual energy withdrawal achievement all at once with no effort.

I was in naad sound resonance like a fish swimming in water.

Naad ~ Cozy Relationship Resumed

Within the past week, I noticed a resumption of the cozy relationship with the naad sound. This is a promising event in the life of a yogi, where having lost touch with naad, and experiencing sporadic contact with it, one resumes the footing in spiritual practice.

By the grace of providence, the relationship is resumed but that does not mean that there will be no breach in the future. It is likely to happen again that I will be put out of touch with naad for one reason or another, due to a pressing influence.

There is much energy out there which has the potential for disrupting the progress of a yogi. Any of these may suddenly invade the psyche and cause it to go off course, abandoning the high level required for deep meditation. However, whatever will be certainly, will be, and if what is, is favorable, then so be it.

When fate renders an objection to yoga, then we say "Aye Sir!"

When fate facilitates yoga, then we also say, "Yes, Sir!"

This morning, during the cozy relationship with naad, I considered how I could describe how it was as to if it was like romance. Well, it was not so. Naad was more like family members who shelter an infant son who is about 8 years of age, where that boy feels desired, protected and shielded.

Index

prototype breast, 192
providence, 11, 83, 88
psyche, interest, 158
pull zones, 155
Puranjan, 139
purpose for body, 179
push against naad, 173
Pushti, 192

Q, R

quantum female, 52
quarrel, 140
R.I.P. 158
radio wave, 91
Rama, 137
RamaKrishna, 178
rapidity, 239
realm of gods, 122
rebirth, 102, 133
red sunset, 196
relationship, 137
release potential, 196
reproduction energy lift, 49
reproductive energy retract, 29
resentment, 187
residual effect, 87
rest in peace, 158
results, 64
revenue service, 185
riff raff, 18
right hand, 141
rise early, 135
rituals of passage, 6
rolling stone, 125
roosters, 133
rotis, 175
rubber nipple, 19
rule of jungle, 32
rum, 202

S

sacral cage, 107
sailors, 197
samadhi, nirvikalpa, 240
sand scatter bliss, 234
Sandipani Muni, 137

Sariputta, 122
satGuru, 86
satya yuga, 89
satya, 231
Satyaloka, 126, 130
scarf wrap, 118
seaman, 153
seclusion, sensual desires, 205
secret mantra, 86
Self Realization Fellowship, 240
self realization, impetus, 196
self, featureless, 19
self-government, 88
semen, blood, 146
senses, mind, 218
sensual energies parked, 214
sensual energy withdrawal, 202
sewage, 141
sex differential, 168
sex energy composite, 63
sex interest, 157
sex organ chakra, 185
sex taxation, 184
sex, memory, 167
sex, not the cause, 67
sexual climax, bliss, 172
sexual discharge, 145
shaktipat, 75
shave ice, 19
Shiva mantra, 74
shivers quivers, 185
Shurpanakha, 137
siddha astral, 89
silence, layer, 143
silverback, 166
Sisyphus, 49
six months, 48
skipper, 92
slave to sex desire, 186
slaves, 202
sleep, 65
sleep after death, 158
sleep vritti, 129
snake, 205
social rights, 84

X, Y, Z
Xiang, 178
Yoga Niketan, 91
yoga, Buddhism, 178
Yogananda, 240
Yogananda, enlightenment, 178
Yogananda, method, 224
yogaSiddha, body, 95, 183
Yogeshwarananda, 91, 93

Yogi Bhajan, 91, 114
yogi,
   advanced, 239
   death, 62
   feeling, 32
Yudhishthira, 198
Zen Hostel, 10, 113, 125
zones, 155

About the Author

Michael Beloved (Yogi *Madhvāchārya)* took his current body in 1951 in Guyana. In 1965, while living in Trinidad, he instinctively began doing yoga postures and tried to make sense of the supernatural side of life.

Later in 1970, in the Philippines, he approached a Martial Arts Master named Arthur Beverford. He explained to the teacher that he was seeking a yoga instructor. Mr. Beverford identified himself as an advanced disciple of *Śrī* Rishi Singh Gherwal, an Ashtanga Yoga master.

Beverford taught the traditional Ashtanga Yoga with stress on postures, attentive breathing and brow chakra centering meditation.   In 1972, Michael entered the Denver, Colorado Ashram of *kundalini* yoga Master *Śrī* Harbhajan Singh. There he took instruction in *bhastrika* pranayama and its application to yoga postures. He was supervised mostly by Yogi Bhajan's disciple named Prem Kaur.

In 1979 Michael formally entered the disciplic succession of the Brahmā - Madhava-Gaudiya Sampradaya through *Swāmī* Kirtanananda, who was a prominent sannyasi disciple of the Great Vaishnava Authority *Śrī Swāmī* Bhaktivedanta Prabhupada, the exponent of devotion to Sri Krishna.

However, yoga has a mystic side to it, thus Michael took training and teaching empowerment from several spiritual masters of different aspects of spiritual development. This is consistent with *Śrī* Krishna's advice to Arjuna in the *Bhagavad Gītā*:

Most of the instructions Michael received were given in the astral world. On that side of existence, his most prominent teachers were *Śrī Swāmī* Shivananda of Rishikesh, Yogiraj *Swāmī* Vishnudevananda, *Śrī Bābāji Mahasaya* - the master of the masters of *Kriyā* Yoga, *Śrīla* Yogeshwarananda of Gangotri - the master of the masters of *Rāj* Yoga (spiritual clarity), and Siddha *Swāmī* Nityananda the Brahmā Yoga authority.

The course for kundalini yoga using pranayama breath-infusion was detailed by Michael in the book *Kundalini Hatha Yoga Pradipika*. This current book was composed from meditation and breath-infusion notes which were originally shared in staple bound booklets as Yoga Journals.

Michael's preliminary books relating to this topic are *Meditation Pictorial*, *Meditation Expertise*, and *Meditation ~ Sense Faculty* (co-author). Every technique (kriya) mentioned was tested by him during pranayama breath-infusion and *samyama* deep meditation practice.

This is a result of over forty years of meditation practice with astute subtle observations intending to share the methods and experiences. The information is published freely with no intention of forming an institution or hogtying anyone as a disciple.

Publications

English Series

Bhagavad Gita English

Anu Gita English

Markandeya Samasya English

Yoga Sutras English

Hatha Yoga Pradipika English

Uddhava Gita English

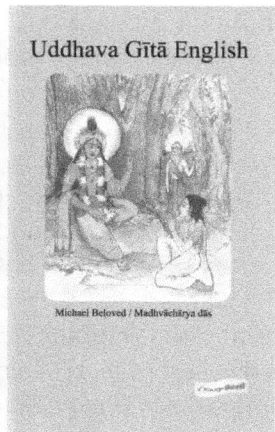

These are in 21st Century English, very precise and exacting. Many Sanskrit words which were considered untranslatable into a Western language are rendered in precise, expressive and modern English.

Three of these books are instructions from Krishna. **In *Bhagavad Gita* English** and **Anu Gita English**, the instructions were for Arjuna. In the **Uddhava Gita English,** it was for Uddhava. *Bhagavad Gita* and Anu Gita are extracted from the Mahabharata. Uddhava Gita was extracted from the 11th Canto of the Srimad Bhagavatam (Bhagavata Purana). One of these books, the **Markandeya Samasya English** is about Krishna, as described by Yogi Markandeya, who survived the cosmic collapse and reached a divine child in whose transcendental body, the collapsed world was existing.

Two of this series are the syllabus about yoga practice. The *Yoga Sutras* of Patañjali is elaboration about ashtanga yoga. Hatha Yoga Pradipika English, is the detailed information about asana postures, pranayama breath-infusion, energy compression, naad sound resonance and advanced meditation. The Sanskrit author is Swatmarama Mahayogin.

My suggestion is that you read *Bhagavad Gita* **English**, the **Anu Gita English, the Markandeya Samasya English,** the *Yoga Sutras* **English,** the **Hatha Yoga Pradipika** and lastly the **Uddhava Gita English**, which is complicated and detailed.

For each of these books we have at least one commentary, which is published separately. Thus one's particular interest can be researched further in the commentaries.

The smallest of these commentaries and perhaps the simplest is the one for the Anu Gita. We published its commentary as the Anu Gita Explained. The *Bhagavad Gita* explanations were published in three distinct targeted commentaries. The first is *Bhagavad Gita* Explained, which sheds lights on how people in the time of Krishna and Arjuna regarded the information and applied it. *Bhagavad Gita* is an exposition of the application of yoga practice to cultural activities, which is known in the Sanskrit language as karma yoga.

Interestingly, *Bhagavad Gita* was spoken on a battlefield just before one of the greatest battles in the ancient world. A warrior, Arjuna, lost his wits and had no idea that he could apply his training in yoga to political dealings. Krishna, his charioteer, lectured on the spur of the moment to give Arjuna the skill of using yoga proficiency in cultural dealings including how to deal with corrupt officials on a battlefield.

The second Gita commentary is the Kriya Yoga *Bhagavad Gita*. This clears the air about Krishna's information on the science of kriya yoga, showing that its techniques are clearly described for anyone who takes the time to read *Bhagavad Gita*. Kriya yoga concerns the battlefield which is the psyche of the living being. The internal war and the mental and emotional forces which are hostile to self-realization are dealt with in the kriya yoga practice.

The third commentary is the Brahma Yoga *Bhagavad Gita*. This shows what Krishna had to say outright and what he hinted about which concerns the brahma yoga practice, a mystic process for those who mastered kriya yoga.

There is one commentary for the **Markandeya Samasya English**. The title of that publication is Krishna Cosmic Body.

There are two commentaries to the *Yoga Sutras*. One is the *Yoga Sutras of Patañjali* and the other is the Meditation Expertise. These give detailed explanations of ashtanga Yoga.

The commentary of Hatha Yoga Pradipika is titled Kundalini Hatha Yoga Pradipika.

For the Uddhava Gita, we published the Uddhava Gita Explained. This is a large book and requires concentration and study for integration of the information. Of the books which deal with transcendental topics, my opinion is that the discourse between Krishna and Uddhava has the complete information about the realities in existence. This book is the one which removes massive existential ignorance.

Meditation Series

Meditation Pictorial

Meditation Expertise

CoreSelf Discovery

Meditation Sense Faculty

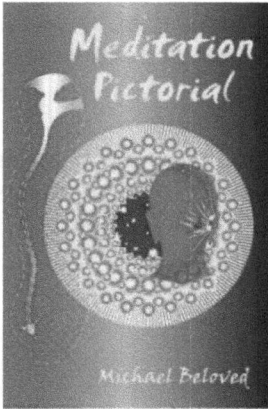

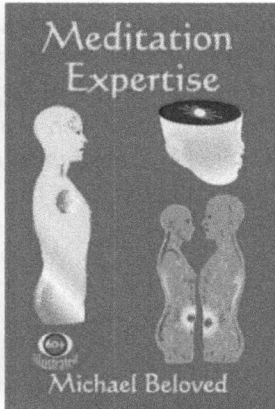

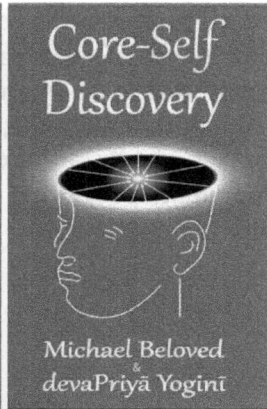

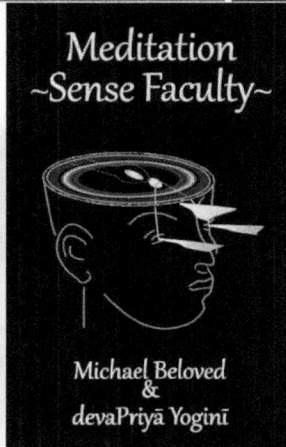

The specialty of these books is the mind diagrams which profusely illustrate what is written. This shows exactly what one has to do mentally to develop and then sustain a meditation practice.

In the **Meditation Pictorial,** one is shown how to develop psychic insight, a feature without which meditation is imagination and visualization, without any mystic experience per se.

In the **Meditation Expertise**, one is shown how to corral one's practice to bring it in line with the classic syllabus of yoga which Patañjali lays out as the ashtanga yoga eight-staged practice.

In **CoreSelf Discovery**, (co-authored with *devaPriya Yogini*) one is taken though the course of *pratyahar* sensual energy withdrawal which is the 5th stage of yoga in the Patañjali ashtanga eight-process complete system of yoga practice. These events lead to the discovery of a coreSelf which is surrounded by psychic organs in the head of the subtle body. This product has a DVD component.

Meditation ~ Sense Faculty (co-authored with *devaPriya Yogini*) is a detailed tutorial with profuse diagrams showing what actions to take in the subtle body to investigate the senses faculties. The meditator must first establish the location and function of the observing self. That self must be screened from the thoughts and ideas which usually hypnotize it.

These books are profusely illustrated with mind diagrams showing the components of psychic consciousness and the inner design of the subtle body.

Explained Series

Bhagavad Gita Explained

Uddhava Gita Explained

Anu Gita Explained

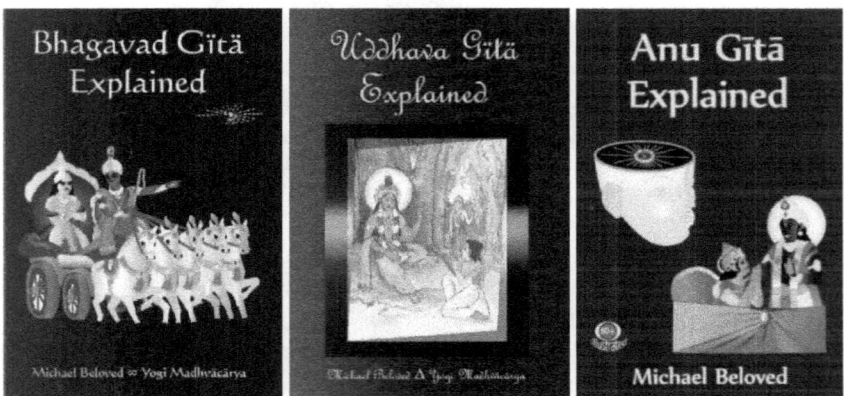

The specialty of these books is that they are free of missionary intentions, cult tactics and philosophical distortion. Instead of using these books to add credence to a philosophy, meditation process, belief or plea for followers, I spread the information out so that a reader can look through this literature and freely take or leave anything as desired.

When Krishna stressed himself as God, I stated that. When Krishna laid no claims for supremacy, I showed that. The reader is left to form an independent opinion about the validity of the information and the credibility of Krishna.

There is a difference in the discourse with Arjuna in the *Bhagavad Gita* and the one with Uddhava in the Uddhava Gita. In fact, these two books may appear to contradict each other. In the *Bhagavad Gita*, Krishna pressured Arjuna to complete social duties. In the Uddhava Gita, Krishna insisted that Uddhava should abandon the same.

The Anu Gita is not as popular as the *Bhagavad Gita* but it is the conclusion of that text. Anu means what is to follow, what proceeds. In this discourse, an anxious Arjuna request that Krishna should repeat the *Bhagavad Gita* and again show His supernatural and divine forms.

However, Krishna refuses to do so and chastises Arjuna for being a disappointment in forgetting what was revealed. Krishna then cited a celestial yogi, a near-perfected being, who explained the process of transmigration in vivid detail.

Commentaries

Yoga Sutras of Patañjali

Meditation Expertise

Krishna Cosmic Body

Anu Gita Explained

Bhagavad Gita Explained

Kriya Yoga Bhagavad Gita

Brahma Yoga Bhagavad Gita

Uddhava Gita Explained

Kundalini Hatha Yoga Pradipika

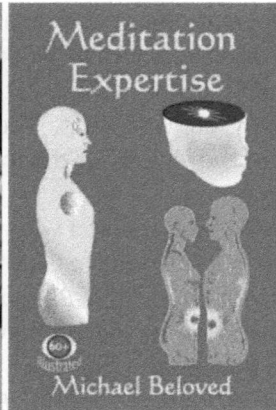

Yoga Sutras of Patañjali is the globally acclaimed text book of yoga. This has detailed expositions of yoga techniques. Many kriya techniques are vividly described in the commentary.

Meditation Expertise is an analysis and application of the *Yoga Sutras*. This book is loaded with illustrations and has detailed explanations of secretive advanced meditation techniques which are called kriyas in the Sanskrit language.

Krishna Cosmic Body is a narrative commentary on the Markandeya Samasya portion of the Aranyaka Parva of the Mahabharata. This is the detailed description of the dissolution of the world, as experienced by the great yogin Markandeya who transcended the cosmic deity, Brahma, and reached Brahma's source who is the divine infant, Krishna.

Anu Gita Explained is a detailed explanation of how we endure many material bodies in the course of transmigrating through various life-forms. This is a discourse between Krishna and Arjuna. Arjuna requested of Krishna a display of the Universal Form and a repeat narration of the *Bhagavad Gita* but Krishna declined and explained what a siddha perfected being told the Yadu family about the sequence of existences one endures and the systematic flow of those lives at the convenience of material nature.

Bhagavad Gita Explained shows what was said in the Gita without religious overtones and sectarian biases.

Kriya Yoga *Bhagavad Gita* shows the instructions for those who are doing kriya yoga.

Brahma Yoga *Bhagavad Gita* shows the instructions for those who are doing brahma yoga.

Uddhava Gita Explained shows the instructions to Uddhava which are more advanced than the ones given to Arjuna.

Bhagavad Gita is an instruction for applying the expertise of yoga in the cultural field. This is why the process taught to Arjuna is called karma yoga which means karma + yoga or cultural activities done with yogic insight.

Uddhava Gita is an instruction for apply the expertise of yoga to attaining spiritual status. This is why it explains jnana yoga and bhakti yoga in detail. Jnana yoga is using mystic skill for knowing the spiritual part of existence. Bhakti yoga is for developing affectionate relationships with divine beings.

Karma yoga is for negotiating the social concerns in the material world. It is inferior to bhakti yoga which concerns negotiating the social concerns in the spiritual world.

This world has a social environment. The spiritual world has one too.

Currently, Uddhava Gita is the most advanced and informative spiritual book on the planet. There is nothing anywhere which is superior to it or which goes into so much detail as it. It verified that historically Krishna is the most advanced human being to ever have left literary instructions on this planet. Even Patañjali *Yoga Sutras* which I translated and gave an application for in my book, **Meditation Expertise**, does not go as far as the Uddhava Gita.

Some of the information of these two books is identical but while the *Yoga Sutras* are concerned with the personal spiritual emancipation (kaivalyam) of the individual spirits, the Uddhava Gita explains that and also explains the situations in the spiritual universes.

Bhagavad Gita is from the *Mahabharata* which is the history of the Pandavas. Arjuna, the student of the Gita, is one of the Pandavas brothers. He was in a social hassle and did not know how to apply yoga expertise to solve it. On the battlefield, Krishna gave him a crash-course on yogic social interactions.

Uddhava Gita is from the *Srimad Bhagavatam (Bhagavata Purana),* which is a history of the incarnations of Krishna. Uddhava was a relative of Krishna. He was concerned about the situation of the deaths of many of his relatives but Krishna diverted Uddhava's attention to the practice of yoga for the purpose of successfully migrating to the spiritual environment.

Kundalini Hatha Yoga Pradipika is the commentary for the Hatha Yoga Pradipika of Swatmarama Mahayogin. This is the detailed process about asana posture, pranayama breath-infusion, complex compressions of energy, naad sound resonance intonement and advanced meditation practice.

This is the singular book with all the techniques of how to reform and redesign the subtle body so that it does not have the tendency for physical life forms and for it to attain the status of a siddha.

These books are based on the author's experiences in meditation, yoga practice and participation in spiritual groups:

Specialty

Spiritual Master

sex you!

Sleep Paralysis

Astral Projection

Masturbation Psychic Details

Spiritual Master — Michael Beloved

sex you! — michael beloved

Sleep Paralysis — Michael Beloved

Astral Projection — Michael Beloved

Masturbation Psychic Details — Michael Beloved

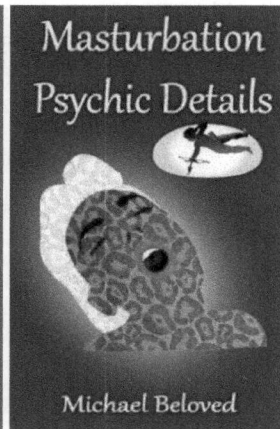

In **Spiritual Master**, Michael draws from experience with gurus or with their senior students. His contact with astral gurus is rated. He walks you through the avenue of gurus showing what you should do and what you should not do, so as to gain proficiency in whatever area of spirituality the guru has proficiency.

sex you! is a masterpiece about the adventures of an individual spirit's passage through the parents' psyches. The conversion of a departed soul into a sexual urge is described. The transit from the afterlife to residency in the emotions of the parents is detailed. This is about sex and you. Learn about how much of you comprises the romantic energy of one's would-be parents!

Sleep Paralysis clears misconceptions so that one can see what sleep paralysis is and what frightening astral experience occurs while the paralysis is being experienced. This disempowerment has great value in giving you confidence that you can and do exist even if one is unable to operate the physical body. The implication is that one can exist apart from and will survive the loss of the material form.

Astral Projection details experiences Michael had even in childhood, where he assumed incorrectly that everyone was astrally conversant. He discusses the lifeForce psychic mechanism which operates the sleep-wake cycle of the physical form, and which budgets energy into the separated astral form which determines if the individual will have dream recall or no objective awareness during the projections. Astral travel happens on every occasion when the physical body sleeps. What is missing in awareness is the observer status while the astral body is separated.

Masturbation Psychic Details is a surprise presentation which relates what happens on the psychic plane during a masturbation event. This does not tackle moral issues or even addictions but shows the involvement of memory and the sure but hidden subconscious mind which operates many features of the psyche irrespective of the desire or approval of the self-conscious personality.

inVision Series

Yoga inVision 1

Yoga inVision 2

Yoga inVision 3

Yoga inVision 4

Yoga inVision 5

Yoga inVision 6

Yoga inVision 7

Yoga inVision 8

Yoga inVision 9

Yoga inVision 10

Yoga inVision 11

Yoga inVision 12

Yoga inVision 13

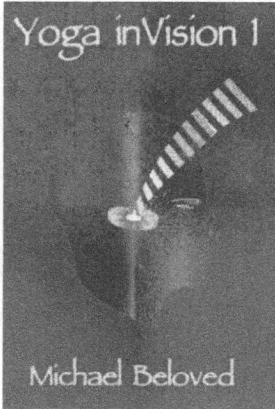

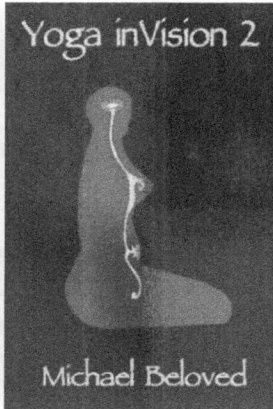

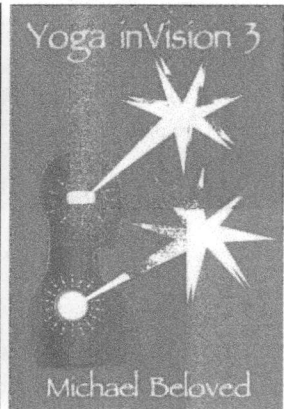

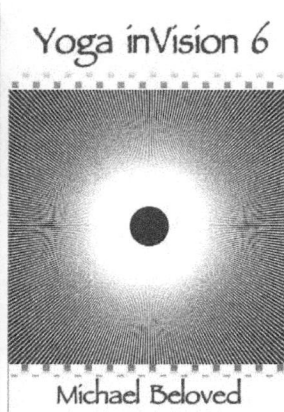

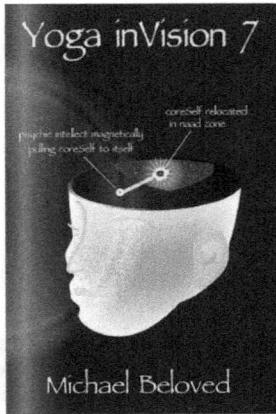

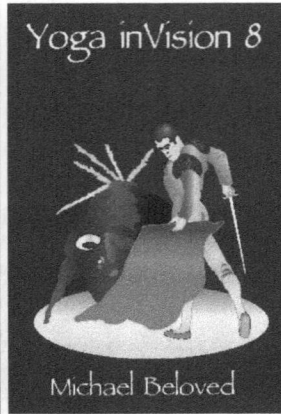

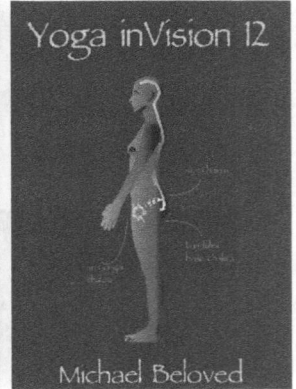

Yoga inVision 1, the first in this series, describes the breath-infusion and meditation practices during the years of 1998 and 1999. There are unique, once in a lifetime as well as recurring insights which are elaborated. inFocus during breath-infusion and the meditation which follows is an adventure for any yogi. This gives what happened to this particular ascetic.

Yoga inVision 2 reports on the author's experiences from 1999 to 2001. Each day the experience is unique, illustrating the vibrancy of practice. Many rare once-in-a-lifetime perceptions are described.

Yoga inVision 3 reports on the author's experiences from 2001 to 2003.
Yoga inVision 4 reports on the author's experiences from 2006 to 2009.
Yoga inVision 5 reports on the author's experiences from 2006 to 2008.
Yoga inVision 6 reports on the author's experiences in 2010.
Yoga inVision 7 reports on the author's experiences in 2011.
Yoga inVision 8 reports on the author's experiences in 2011.
Yoga inVision 9 reports on the author's experiences in 2012.
Yoga inVision 10 reports on the author's experiences in 2012.
Yoga inVision 11 reports on the author's experiences in 2012.
Yoga inVision 12 reports on the author's experiences in 2012-2013.
Yoga inVision 13 reports on the author's experiences in 2013-2014.

Online Resources

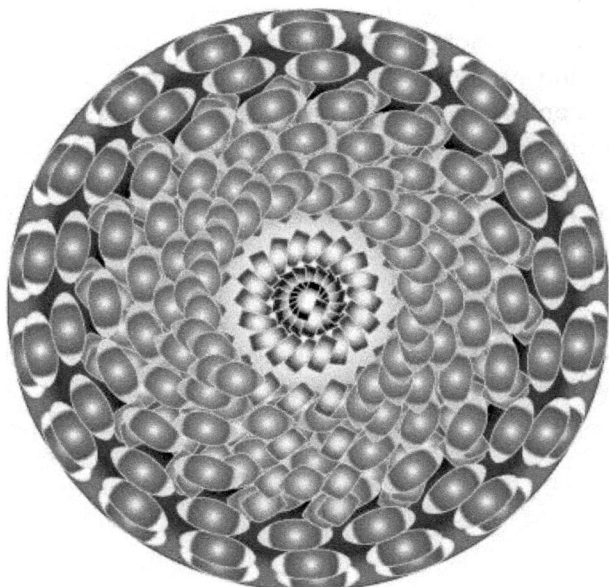

Email:	michaelbelovedbooks@gmail.com
	axisnexus@gmail.com
Website:	michaelbeloved.com
Forum:	inselfyoga.com
Posters:	zazzle.com/inself

www.ingramcontent.com/pod-product-compliance
Lightning Source LLC
Chambersburg PA
CBHW072340090426
42741CB00012B/2863